FAMILY POWER

A CELEBRA BOOK

FAMILY POWER

The True Story of How
"The First Family of Taekwondo"
Made Olympic History

Mark, Steven, Diana and Jean Lopez

CELEBRA
Published by New American Library, a division of Penguin Group (USA) Inc.,
375 Hudson Street, New York, New York 10014, USA
Penguin Group (Canada), 90 Eglinton Avenue East, Suite 700, Toronto,
Ontario M4P 2Y3, Canada (a division of Pearson Penguin Canada Inc.)
Penguin Books Ltd., 80 Strand, London WC2R 0RL, England
Penguin Ireland, 25 St. Stephen's Green, Dublin 2,
Ireland (a division of Penguin Books Ltd.)
Penguin Group (Australia), 250 Camberwell Road, Camberwell, Victoria 3124,
Australia (a division of Pearson Australia Group Pty. Ltd.)
Penguin Books India Pvt. Ltd., 11 Community Centre, Panchsheel Park,
New Delhi - 110 017, India
Penguin Group (NZ), 67 Apollo Drive, Rosedale, North Shore 0632,
New Zealand (a division of Pearson New Zealand Ltd.)
Penguin Books (South Africa) (Pty.) Ltd., 24 Sturdee Avenue,
Rosebank, Johannesburg 2196, South Africa

Penguin Books Ltd., Registered Offices:
80 Strand, London WC2R 0RL, England

First published by Celebra,
a division of Penguin Group (USA) Inc.

First Printing, November 2009
10 9 8 7 6 5 4 3 2 1

Library of Congress Cataloging-in-Publication Data:

Family power: the true story of how "the first family of taekwondo" made Olympic history/Mark, Steven,
Diana and Jean Lopez.
     p.   cm.
   ISBN 978-0-451-22851-2
   1. Tae kwon do—Anecdotes. 2. Lopez family—Biography. 3. Olympic Games (29th: 2008:
Beijing, China) I. Lopez, Jean, 1973–
   GV1113.A2F36 2009
   796.815—dc22   2009024976

Set in Adobe Garamond
Designed by Ginger Legato

Printed in the United States of America

To our wonderful parents, Julio and Ondina Lopez:
Your love and guidance have given us the courage to reach for our
dreams as you reached for yours.

CONTENTS

Preface

The Olympic ideal doesn't have one country. It doesn't play one sport or come in one size. It may not have a definition that is any clearer than the perfect sunset or perfect wave, but it is certainly shaped by courage, will, grace under pressure and, in the case of the Lopez family, even the irrepressible industry of toiling in a garage, the most humbling of venues, to thrive on the world's most glorious sporting stage, the Olympic Games.

Out of that humility came a sporting résumé that is unique in our lifetime: a family with four children assuming four places (one coach and three athletes) on one squad (the 2008 U.S. Olympic team) in a sport (taekwondo) that wasn't even on the Olympic program when they were born.

In two decades of writing about the Olympic Games, I have never seen anyone embody those traits more nobly than the Lopezes have. In 1999, a year before any of them had ever competed at an Olympics, I stared at a photo of their exclusive training megaplex—their unremarkable garage—and said simply, "And this is it? The magic happened here?"

Maybe it was magic. Their journey is nearly fantasy.

Start with the immigrant parents, Julio and Ondina, arriving in New York from Nicaragua with a hope to better their lives and pass on their dreams in spite of a new language, new culture and daunting job prospects. Move on to the eldest son, Jean, who shed an early inability to communicate to his teachers in school to become the most honored communicator and teacher in his sport and throw off a heartbreaking defeat seconds from becoming a world champion, to enable his siblings, Steven, Mark and Diana, to achieve the very honor that slipped through his hands. Theirs has been a journey of firsts: first set of four siblings, including a coach, to be represented on a U.S. Olympic team; first set of three siblings ever to win Olympic medals from the same Olympic team; first four-time world champion and three-time Olympic medalist in taekwondo from the United States (Steven).

When nobody believed and many impeded, the Lopezes drew such strength from the belief in one another that they overcame the doubters and the odds no other family ever has. As a new country reshaped the fate of a simple family, the simple family reshaped the rigid ways of a complex sport.

Perhaps it was the fantasy of an American dream to start with nearly nothing and achieve nearly everything. Yet more than what they have reached for and achieved, the Lopezes are more remarkable still for the values of family unity and dignity of purpose that they have never left behind. To meet their challenges with their uncommon grace is the essence of the Olympic ideal and a unique tale of hope fulfilled.

—Brian Cazeneuve, 2009

Introduction

by Jean Lopez

We share everything. If one member of the Lopez family starts ailing, the rest of us begin to ache. If one of us achieves a goal, the others will feel like climbing onto a podium to accept a prize. From sympathy pain to shared glory, we always seem to do it together. Sure, we quibble and fuss like everyone else, but I can't remember any significant time in our lives when we didn't look out for one another and didn't have one another's backs. On the night we made Olympic sports history, we even had one another's fingernails.

On August 22, 2008, my sister, Diana, and my brothers, Steven and Mark, walked with me into the lobby of the Hilton Hotel in Beijing where my parents, Julio and Ondina, were staying. Before Mama and Papi could take us up to a midnight dinner, we each hugged and kissed and held quick medical debriefings. Over the previous forty-eight hours, Steven, Mark, and Diana had each won medals, the first time three siblings had ever done that at any Olympic Games. I was lucky enough to be on the competition floor with all of them, as the head coach of the U.S. team. But since our sport is the Martial art of taekwondo—translated from its Korean origin, it means "the way of hand and fist"—many people simply think of it as the way of kicking and punching. Our hands and feet are uncovered, so it's pretty rare to see even the most triumphant champion of our sport who isn't hobbling around with some malady after a major competition.

At the Hilton hotel in Beijing, my sister Diana was feeling the highs and lows of her Olympic bronze medal. She was saying something about a migraine and nursing her hand, which would need surgery after we got back home to Houston. Despite that, she walked over to our mother, gave her a hug, and said, "Mama, are you okay? Did you survive?"

"Yes, baby, I'm fine," she assured Diana.

Just after that, Mark walked up to my mom with his left hand in a cast. He had suffered a broken hand in his very first bout of the tournament, and still won the contest. He won three more fights before finally losing in the final and capturing a silver medal. Like Diana, his mind was in the same place. "Mama, how do you feel?" he asked. "I was worried about you."

"Oh, I'm all right," she told him, smiling and patting his arm.

Steven was next to embrace my mom. He was on the wrong end of what we all felt was a bad judging error in Beijing. We all knew in our gut that he'd been robbed. It can happen in any sport that has judges or referees. Even when he was walking around with a bad limp from all the blocked kicks of ten hours of competition in Beijing, he probably smarted the worst of all of us. How can you not when something you worked so hard to achieve has been taken from you? Steven reached out to our mother, too. "Mama, did you make it through okay?"

See, our mother is our biggest supporter, but she gets too nervous to watch us fight. Really, when we're kicking as hard as we can at an opponent's head, when that opponent is punching as hard as possible into one of our stomachs, when fists and feet are flying at lethal speed against the most skilled fighters in the world, the most endangered person in the building is the one sitting next to my mom. She tries to maintain her composure as the kind, modest, almost shy lady friends know her to be, but when one of her babies is on the floor, well, she needs to register her fingernails with law enforcement.

In that moment at the hotel, like all the others in our lives, the wins and losses didn't matter nearly as much as our time together. The efforts are always shared and our achievements honor our entire family. There was actually one trophy in my parents' home that one of us earned at a tournament, but without a name on the trophy, we couldn't remember who won it. The prizes aren't unimportant, but they have meaning only because of what it took to get them in the first place.

We sat around a buffet table that night, our matches behind us and our appetites ravenous for both food and talk of more chances to make history as a family. We hadn't spoken often about the next Olympics, the 2012 Games in London that seemed another lifetime away, but we all felt it. My father mentioned it as he proposed a toast—okay, so maybe we toasted with bottled water and sports drinks—and we hugged and spoke of our blessings. Even as we looked ahead, we were all thankful for the remarkable journey of sacrifice and dedication, of faith and hope that brought us there together.

CHAPTER 1

A Land of Hope

by Diana Lopez

When people talk about the American dream, they could easily be talking about our parents. It's a success story of hard work, faith, determination, and long odds that never seemed to stop them. If people look at me and certainly my brothers and they see strength and guts, they'd have to know my parents. If they wanted to know why we're so close as a family, that closeness comes from my mother and father. They set such a solid foundation for my brothers and me that I can't imagine us not succeeding at something. When people wonder how we learned to work hard at taekwondo, they need only look at the sacrifices our parents made to make a new life for themselves in the United States, a place where they didn't speak the language right away and had almost no friends.

Neither one of my parents played sports at a very high level when they grew up in Nicaragua. My dad played baseball. He was a good-hitting first baseman and his dream was always to play in the States in the major leagues. My dad needed to work off all his energy, because he grew up around food. His father ran a bakery that was below their house in Diriamba, in the western part of the country. The storefront was located at the entrance and the kitchen was in the back, and the entire place smelled like fresh-baked bread. By the time my father would wake up in the morning, my grandfather had already been up for hours working. Most of the family helped him, too. My dad especially loved the empanadas with sugar, beef, or gooey cheese seeping out of the sides. Since my father was the youngest brother in a family of four boys and four girls, he had to maneuver for his food, kind of like me sometimes. Because I have three older hungry brothers, my stomach can sympathize.

My grandparents imposed very strict rules on their kids, and if anyone in the family, including my father, chose to disobey them, they would usually feel my grandfather's belt. That was how things were done then. Of course, my grandfather also set a good example. He always talked to my father about being honest. Even if people steal your material things, or if you don't have many to begin with, he told his kids, they can never take away your word. My grandparents were also very spiritual. My grandmother's room was filled with carvings and drawings of saints, almost like a room in church. Anytime someone in the family had a problem or a goal, she would go into the room, look at the saints, and pray. Every first Friday, my father would go to confession, and he took very seriously the faith he would someday transmit to us.

When my father was eleven, he almost lost two fingers on his left hand when it got caught in the two steel rollers that my grandfather used to prepare the dough. The doctor wanted to remove the fingers because of the complications from the wounds and the injury. My dad kept the fingers, even though today one of them is missing tendons and the other one is missing bones. To my dad, the worst part of the accident was that he had to stop playing baseball. He was right-handed, and if he tried to catch a hard-hit ball in the glove on his left hand, the force of the throw might rip open the stitches that were still holding the fingers in place.

He was still able to play some basketball in high school, but when he was fourteen, he found an athletic passion that sort of led to ours. He and eleven other guys started a weight-lifting and bodybuilding club they called Los Gladiadores (the Gladiators). They created a set of rules for the club that included a regular exercise routine that featured track and field, cycling, swimming, and, of course, weight training that kept them in shape and, you know, could impress the girls. They also imposed some rules on themselves about keeping a healthy lifestyle, like no smoking and no lawlessness. All the men are in their sixties today and they're all still alive and healthy. Los Gladiadores set a strong foundation for the physical and social ambitions of the Lopezes to come. Still, my father had only read about Martial arts like judo, karate and jujitsu. It would be a while before he ever heard of taekwondo.

Everybody in my father's family had to finish high school, and the four girls all went to college. Still, my grandfather saw my dad as the logical person to take over the family business. He certainly enjoyed enough of the fringe benefits of sniffing around the bakery, so someday he could be the one to run it. But my dad had other ideas. He likes to say he was just kind of a restless animal with a different vision of life, one that went not only beyond his kitchen, but beyond his borders.

When he was eighteen, my dad went off to college to become an architect. My grandfather's strict rules and those days as a Gladiador had given him great discipline. He studied architecture and was fascinated by buildings, shapes, and structures, especially the ones he'd read about in New York. In 1965, he began working for a small company as an architectural engineer. Building of almost any kind was under government control, and in 1968 he took a job with the government as an inspector for his region, making sure that builders paid their taxes and had the proper permits, since the industry was not always well regulated. People who had permission to build a small shack would take their permit to break ground and start erecting three forts and a convention center. It was overkill, kind of like somebody going into a taekwondo bout with an armored tank. Everyone had to respect my dad, because he was the one to enforce the rules.

When his plant opened a cartography department, he spent a year in Panama studying maps. When he came back, he was put in charge of thirty people who traveled to the jungles each week and created maps so the government would know where it was safe to build and where it just didn't make sense. He was twenty-six years old in 1969, and his base was located in the Banco Central, the Central Bank in Managua.

One day, my dad went to a party nearby and spotted an eighteen-year-old student from across the room and found he couldn't take his eyes off her. I can picture my dad being the charmer as he introduced himself. It was a bold move, especially since at the time, my mom was talking to another guy. "Is that your boyfriend?" my dad asked. "No, he's just a friend," my mom told him. They started to talk about their families. My mother was the oldest of nine children, five boys and four girls, so she had experience sharing responsibility for a large, sometimes loud group of kids. She was born forty-five minutes outside Managua, and her parents moved her to the big city when she was five. At the time, that was a big move. Her school was right next to my dad's office. Ah, fate. He walked her home that day, taking the first steps in a lifelong romance that is still thriving forty years later.

My parents shared great moments together. They enjoyed long walks in the park, strolling by the lake, traveling to his aunt's farm, eating out when they could save up enough money, and going to movies that usually came to Managua some months, even years, after they appeared in the States. *Ben Hur* was one of their favorites, and I'm sure that when it replays on one of those classic-movie stations these days it makes them think back to one of those simple first dates they had together. Even though my dad wouldn't say it, I bet he saw a little of Charlton Heston in himself back in the day. He used to say, "When you are in love, it doesn't matter where you are; the city is perfect. It doesn't matter if it rains; the day looks clear. It doesn't matter if you are sick; you feel like the healthiest, happiest man alive." People in Managua didn't have a lot of money, and most of them, including my parents, didn't have a car. Large families, like my mother's and father's, were the norm, and children usually lived with their parents until marriage and sometimes even after marriage. Instead of weekend getaways during the warm summer months, couples often brought folding chairs onto their porches or sidewalks and simply sat around and talked. My father remembers the day he and my mother saw an older couple lounging together, and saying, "Do you think we're going to grow old together like them?"

My parents saw good and bad aspects to their lives in Nicaragua. My mother had always felt comfortable growing up in an area where everyone knew everyone's name, neighbor looked after neighbor, and people who left their doors unlocked at night didn't have to worry that somebody would try to break in and rob them. But the country was getting overpopulated and starting to lose the benefits of its simplicity. Jobs were becoming scarce. My dad saw a lot of educated people with impressive degrees driving taxis. At the same time, the rebellious group known as the Sandinistas was launching violent raids against various branches of government. Even people who were just making maps or overseeing buildings had reasons to worry for their safety. Somewhere in the back of his mind, he thought of making a life with my mom in a land of greater opportunity.

My parents married in 1972. It wasn't part of their culture for a man to propose formally to his sweetheart, so my dad never got down on one knee with a ring tucked away in his pocket. It was just sort of accepted and expected by their parents that after a couple spent a certain amount of time together, marriage was the next logical step. I think he wishes he'd had the chance to do something special, even something silly, to show her how much he loved her and wanted to spend the rest of his life with her.

The wedding was pretty small compared to some of the ones they have in the States. But their dreams were getting bigger. Soon after they married, my dad talked to my mom about moving to the United States. It was an exciting idea. To my mom, America was a land of abundance where everybody had a huge apartment or a big house with a white picket fence. If your car broke down in the States, well, you could just leave it on the side of the road and get another one. If the United States was the most powerful nation in the world, surely the people living there had an easy life with few worries about putting food on the table, finding good schools and medical care, and getting jobs in their thriving economy. Like many people who had second- and thirdhand impressions of what life could be like in this fantasy-land called America, she couldn't see that in return for opportunity, you had no guarantees, and the road to a happy life could be paved with challenges you never imagined. That's my mom, the dreamer, but even my dad, who was older and had fewer stars in his eyes, figured he'd be able to find work pretty quickly because of his background. He budgeted some time into the process to learn English, but he was a quick study. The decision was made. My father sold his TV, his music collection, anything he could to finance the trip and turn this fantasy into reality. When he had enough money, he would send it to my mother so she could come join him, which she did six months later. Just like that. Welcome to a new world and a new life.

In retrospect, my parents picked a great time to leave. Two days before Christmas that year, a major earthquake struck Managua. Roughly two hundred and fifty thousand of the city's four hundred thousand residents lost their homes, including many of my parents' friends, and ten thousand people were killed. Four out of every five commercial buildings were destroyed. So much of what my father had played a small role in helping to build was now ruined. People around the world donated money and other resources to help those affected by the disaster, but many of the funds never reached their intended recipients. Some of the food aid went bad by accident, but most of all, there was corruption and chaos at various levels.

Two years later guerrillas started attacking government buildings, and by 1979 they had taken over the country. It was not a great time to be in Nicaragua, and yet the hard realities they soon faced in their new lives almost sent my parents back.

My dad knew that companies in the States were looking for architects, so he applied as a draftsman, someone who is skilled in drawing up architectural and engineering plans. He received a temporary visa and set out for New York City. My mom stayed behind and would follow him to New York later, after Dad had time to establish himself and get settled. It was a great plan, but it was nothing like what they expected.

When Papi arrived, because of his poor English he started going to a private college for architecture, mostly to learn the technical vocabulary. Since he couldn't get a job yet in his chosen field, he found work at a place called the Felco factory making New York Yankees baseball hats. It almost broke him, and he thought about giving up and going back. Why, he asked himself, did I give up my position to work like a slave in the States? What was more, New York is a huge city with five boroughs, and my dad was spending his days in three of them, commuting on long subway rides to get to school and work. He and my mom found an apartment uptown in the Bronx. He'd take two subways for nearly an hour to get to the factory on Twelfth Street in the lower half of Manhattan to start his workday at eight. At five, he'd get on two more subways to head for his college courses in Queens. By the time he got back home it was usually around midnight, because the subways didn't run as often at night. In the early seventies, New York subways were rife with crime, drugs and graffiti. My dad was lucky he never had any incidents. But as much as he loved looking at the architecture of some of New York's classic churches and older buildings, he also walked past homeless people sleeping on the front steps of many of those churches. Coming from a Latin culture in which there was always someone to look after you, he was really shocked. Who were these people living in poverty next to such wealth? Were they once people of hope who abandoned their dreams? My dad was determined never to lose sight of his. If you don't have a goal in life, anything can break you, he thought. For three years, he made hats in the factory, delayed his promises to my mother of a better life and kept dreaming.

The neighborhood where my parents lived in the Bronx was basically bilingual, with many residents who spoke Spanish. That made the transition easier for them. In the meantime, they started our family. My brother Jean was born in August of 1973. My mom would take him to Central Park, and she remembers his eyes following everything in front of him: people, dogs, birds—almost as if he were getting a head start on studying movement. I can picture it: Hey, pigeon, your wing's a little low. Time to get flapping, buddy. If you don't do it, there's probably some other pigeon in Korea flapping twice as hard.

People in the factory liked my dad because he worked so hard, so they promoted him to foreman. He made five hundred dollars a week, which was a healthy salary for the seventies. But it wasn't his calling. He gave it up to take a job in his chosen field, earning a hundred and eighty dollars a week as an architect. He moved to Little Falls, New Jersey, where the cost of living wasn't as high, and he felt great because he was in his professional environment. Then, six months after he started, he was laid off and the company went into bankruptcy. A month went by, then another. There were no jobs for him. He told my mom it might be best to go back to Nicaragua.

In 1978, he heard from a friend and fellow architect named Augustine Bosseo, who had moved to Houston from his native Colombia and called to ask what my dad was doing. When my father told him he was looking for work, Augustine said he could find him a job in Houston. What did they know about Texas? Did people speak Spanish there? Would this new life be a tougher transition than the first one? My parents agreed to a three-month trial. My dad went down to Houston to see what work he could find, while my mom stayed in New York with Jean. If nothing happened, they agreed, they might have to go back to Managua.

His friend was right. It took my dad all of one day to find a job in the city, and after Augustine helped him find an apartment, he settled in almost immediately. Construction in Houston was booming in the late seventies. My father began work as a draftsman, making ten dollars an hour working for a boss who came over from Lebanon and started his own business. Dad found it pretty easy, but he also wanted to make some calculations as an engineer. Even though he knew what he was doing, he still didn't have an official license, because he didn't have an engineering degree from a U.S. institution. Why do I need a title? he wondered. I've been doing this for most of my professional life. Still, he went to the local community college to take the necessary courses and get the degree he needed to be a certified engineer.

My mom was pregnant with Steven while my dad was still in Texas. Leave it to Jean, the team leader at age five, to take the reins as coach. When it was time to deliver, he got her downstairs and called the cab to get her to the hospital. Then he made sure to get in touch with my mother's friend so she could call my father. Papa got on the first plane he could and stayed in New York for eight days before he had to return to work in Houston. Forget Jean's age. You could have thrown him in the middle of anywhere, big city or small town, with people speaking English or Spanish, in busy streets or open fields, and he would have known exactly what to do. Some people are naturally born with a coach's hat. Jean's was already starting to fit.

CHAPTER 2

Follow the Leader

by Jean Lopez

L ife in the Houston suburb of Sugar Land was different from what I had known in New York. Now that I had a baby brother, I had to make new friends, and I absolutely *had* to learn English. I already knew a few words, but in our bilingual neighborhood in New York City, I could easily sneak by with little-kid gestures, giggles and my mixed vocabulary of Spanish and English words I sort of knew how to pronounce. Life in Sugar Land was indeed very different. I was older and I felt very isolated in school. I remember not understanding my elementary school teacher and having a huge level of anxiety that I couldn't communicate. Vowels? How could I recite them if I didn't know what they were?

During my first few days at the Townewest Elementary School, I was looking around, scanning the class for kids in similar distress, trying to identify with other kids in the room who might have been in my position. There weren't any. I was the only one who was thinking my thoughts in Spanish, hearing words in English and trying to translate their meaning to myself before I could answer the teacher or even start a conversation with classmates. It wasn't just a matter of memorizing new vocabulary. I was on par with the other kids when it came to word definitions, but the sentence structure in English is different. In Spanish, for instance, the noun usually precedes the adjective. The opposite is true in English. For the description I knew as *el coche rojo*, I would say "the car red" instead of "the red car." I'd be wearing a hat blue, carrying a book heavy and looking at the building tall. I always had to study a little bit harder just to keep up, because I had learned different habits from Spanish and instinctively tried to apply them to English. It's ironic that when I speak Spanish these days, I think in English first and then translate in my head.

Not until fourth grade did I really start to get a good grasp of the language. At that point I'd study vocabulary a little extra on my own so I could get ahead. My parents always made flash cards for me to help me learn my vocabulary and multiplication tables. They made it such a routine that it was something I just did. They didn't have to remind me. I have very good memories of my father sitting down and explaining anything to do with math, since he was very good at it because of his engineering background. Still, his way of doing division was different from the technique I was learning in school. If he divided eighty-one by nine, he would have the divisor and quotient in the reverse order. He would say, "This is the real way to do it," and I would say, "Well, it isn't real to me, because we do it differently over here."

My father was always reading. He liked poems and Spanish novels, but he also picked up the newspaper to stay current with world events. By observation I thought reading should be important to me, too. I enjoyed Dr. Seuss books that could make the language seem fun by playing around with the words in ways I understood. I also loved the Encyclopedia Brown detective stories. Even though I never solved the crimes, like the really serious offenses about stealing backpacks or spraying graffiti, the unsolved mysteries always made me read to the end. I was always excited about the school book fairs, and I took real pride in being able to figure out the puzzles and games in the *Highlights* magazines.

My first athletic events I can remember were the field games we had in kindergarten. We jumped, threw things and ran potato-sack races. To get me psyched for the big day, my dad bought me a brand-new blue-and-yellow shirt. I felt I was decked out. I really felt special that my parents bought something just for me for that day. Even today, when I see the blue and yellow colors for a Swedish national team or the blue and gold colors of the Michigan football team, I smile and think about me and my new shirt hopping along in the potato sacks.

It wasn't long before I also started to pick up an after-school hobby. I suppose it really began when I started watching kung fu theater movies with my father every Saturday. My dad always liked to watch films with Chuck Norris. I preferred Bruce Lee. My dad would concentrate when he watched, almost like a film critic. I'd be like a cowboy, copying some of the swagger and the moves. I thought the whole subculture was so cool. The grand master or master knew it all. There was always a pupil who was trying to learn and had to go through so much adversity. Sometimes the actors would fight in an octagon, similar to the ones you'd see today in mixed Martial-arts battles; another time, they fought in the Roman Colosseum. Of course, the dialogue was cheesy and predictable. I didn't pay a lot of attention to the plot. I went around for weeks repeating my memory of one actor's line: "Don't focus on my little finger, young one; focus on the heavenly glory. No, don't look at the finger; look at the moon and the heavenly glory." Okay, so there were no Academy Awards, but there was a kind of action I loved. The good guys could kick, punch, or fight their way out of danger and somehow always overcame the bad guys. They did those things in such acrobatic ways, too: screaming, bouncing off walls, breaking boards. They were acrobats and crime fighters. To me, they were the coolest guys around.

When I was eight, my dad saw an ad for a karate school one day and asked if I wanted to go and see what it was like. Wow, imagine me kicking and screaming just like Bruce Lee. Imagine Jean Lopez chasing the heavenly glory for real. Sure, I told him, sign me up. In the days leading up to that first class, that introduction to karate was all I could think about. But right before I went into the school, I started getting cold feet. Maybe I was in over my head. I didn't want my dad to know that I felt that way, so I just went with it. Of course, it was nothing like either of us expected. For one, the Martial art they practiced wasn't really karate at all. Most people had heard about karate, so that was the word the instructor used in the ad to encourage new students to enroll. The actual activity was a different form of Martial art known as tae-kwondo.

It is a Korean-based art form practiced by more than seventy million people around the world. It allows punching to the body, but emphasizes kicking to both the head and the body. Students start with white belts and work their way up to black belts, with the dans (wearers of the black belt) able to advance to nine levels once they reach black belt. Because the sport originated in Korea, most of the commands we had to learn were in Korean, like *charyeot* (attention), *junbi* (ready), *sijak* (begin) and *gomman* (stop). It's the same for boxers, who always learn the commands in English, like "box" and "stop," even if they're fighting in a place where the first language is different.

I remember seeing this one Korean man in his uniform with his black belt around his waist. I looked up to him and that melted my apprehension away. I still didn't feel completely comfortable communicating with people in English, but here I'd be able to communicate with my body, to express my emotions through action. Yes, this was new, but I knew right away that it was where I belonged.

Those first few days were still pretty overwhelming. Everyone was yelling. Everyone was in uniform. Everyone was in straight lines. The class was so structured. The master instructor was Mr. Pak. With his voice and his gestures, he seemed straight out of one of those kung fu movies. I remember the carpet. The whole room looked really big to me. When I got older I realized fifteen hundred square feet wasn't as large as I thought, but at the time it seemed like a football field because of my perspective. The master told us we would have to break boards, be proficient in certain self-defense moves and know our forms. I remember doing those things in front of hundreds of people. I went up and down in line formation executing different blocks, kicks and punches. As competitive as kids in the class could be, we actually collaborated pretty well, because we all wanted to make sure we lived up to our instructor's expectations of us. As his expectations rose, so did ours, and we got better because as students we started to hold ourselves to higher standards. In such a passionate and structured environment, nobody had to force that feeling of accountability down our throats. We felt it so strongly ourselves.

It was a few months into my classes when I first started light sparring and when I first had to kick another person. Even if it was only in controlled practice session, it was a daunting thing to do. I was nervous about doing it. I didn't want to get hit, but I was also concerned about hurting the other kid. It didn't feel natural, because I'm not a naturally combative person. It took a while for me to feel comfortable knowing that we could kick and punch into one another's padded equipment without getting hurt. I'd watch seasoned fighters put on the protectors for their hands, feet, chest and head, but the idea of sparring was still foreign to me. The instructor gave us periodic challenges, testing who among us could execute a skill most proficiently and consistently. He would regularly announce which students from each age group performed best. By the end of the first year, he was announcing my name more and more often. It made me a little embarrassed, but also quietly very proud. His feedback fueled my confidence. Maybe I had worried about my struggles in school because I didn't yet have the language skills that my classmates had, but in the taekwondo classroom, I was thriving. I could feel one improvement mount on top of another, and I couldn't wait to go to practice.

It was a good thing for my parents that I had this positive outlet in my life, because their attention was about to be pulled in two other directions. In April 1982, my youngest brother, Mark, was born, strutting his way into the family and never looking back. Diana would follow in January 1984. As the eldest brother, I took my responsibilities as the exemplary sibling pretty seriously, cleaning up and making sure to do my fair share of chores. But one topic turned me into a wide-eyed dreamer: this thing called the Olympic Games. I had never seen them in person, but I heard about what they represented: a chance to bring the whole world together in one place for healthy sporting competitions among young people. Imagine the strongest, fastest and sleekest people you've ever seen from every country on the planet doing what they do best. Wow!

In fourth grade, several students from our district took part in an art contest to win tickets to the Olympics, which were being held in Los Angeles the following summer. The theme was actually rodeo, which isn't an event at the Games, but whatever the connection was, the winner would receive two tickets to the opening ceremonies and two tickets to two different events. I wasn't a natural artist, but I put pen to paper and did my best. I drew a field, a pasture, one horse and a barnyard in the farm. No, I didn't win, but the experience whetted my appetite to check out the events on TV the next year.

I watched the opening ceremonies from the Los Angeles Coliseum and couldn't take my eyes off the television screen. They had cowboys, balloons, a hundred grand pianos. Rafer Johnson, the great decathlon champion, ran up a very steep, moving staircase to light the torch. He had spent his post-Olympic life running the California Special Olympics, using his fame not for himself, but for the greater good of people around him. How cool was that? Around the length of the Coliseum, fans held up colored placards that dotted the stadium and formed each of the flags represented at the Olympics. Ours was one of them. My parents talked to me about the importance of what the United States flag meant to them: that it represented an opportunity for a better life not only for them but also for my siblings and me. More than sixty-eight hundred athletes marched around the track that day behind their flags, representing their families, their opportunities and their dreams. Even though I had always liked watching professional sports, I realized that the Olympics were somehow bigger than the NFL, NBA and MLB sports events I'd watched before. It wasn't just Jean against Joe; it was the United States against some other country. It felt like more people had a vested interest than just the guys out there on the floor or on the field. For two weeks I watched Carl Lewis run faster than any man alive; I saw Mary Lou Retton flip and twist the way the human body is not supposed to move. I saw boxers like Mark Breland and Evander Holyfield fight the good fight. I watched Michael Jordan lead Team USA before there even was a Dream Team. I identified with anything that seemed like superhuman feats that regular people couldn't do. It was an honor to be a part of the Olympics, and somewhere in the back of my head, I wanted to know what that honor was like.

As I started to get better in my own sporting world, my parents would take me to local and regional tournaments in places like San Antonio and Louisiana. Some were just recreational tournaments, but I started winning them and bringing home trophies. The first one was made of spiral wood with a kicking fighter perched on top. It said, FIRST PLACE, TAEKWONDO. It was cool. The next week I'd come home with another one and then another. Some of them were taller than me. I was also pitching and playing the outfield for a Little League baseball team at the time and it took a whole season just to win one trophy. My father used to set up the trophies on a giant table, then in a corner of the living room, then in a second corner. Steven was starting to win them, too. I would wake up and see my father slowly buffing them with his wood furniture polish. He looked so at peace and so proud. It motivated both of us to want to win more. It wasn't really about the trophies themselves—that first trophy is missing now. It must have been thrown out, even though none of us can recall getting rid of it— but what mattered was the look of satisfaction on my father's face. Whenever Mama and Papi would give me that job-well-done look, I might as well have been on top of the Olympic podium.

Forget Carl Lewis and Michael Jordan for a minute. Even kids in grade school have their sporting standard-bearers to look up to. Mine was Zach Trusdale. I was reasonably strong, fast and athletic. But I'd watch Zach throw a football and I felt I was back in kindergarten. He played everything. He aced everything. We were both in fifth grade, but Zach had an eighth-grade game. He'd be the guy who'd tell you to "back up, back more, back up way more" before heaving the ball over your head just to show you he could. If I had those trophies, Zach must have had his own warehouse. At least Zach wasn't a jerk about it.

We got along okay. These days he owns a couple of bars in the Houston area. I run into him by accident sometimes and I always tell him he was my early standard for athletic talent.

That isn't to say jerks didn't exist. In seventh grade, I was pretty unassuming, skinny and small. I never flaunted my taekwondo skills and I wasn't one of those brats who tried to beef up his school status by giving other kids a hard time. No, that was Dax. He thought he was the baddest dude around, with bad hair and bad hygiene to match. He probably failed a grade only once, but my impression at the time was that he had failed about six times. He was the stereotypical bully. He had a Metallica jean jacket and he was the only one who wouldn't dress out. The teachers always made an exception for him and never made him do anything he didn't want to do. In the long run, that was probably a bad thing for him. He was an eighth grader, but looked like a recycled senior who had walked into the wrong building. I'm not sure why guys like that have seek-and-destroy radar out for the quiet kids, but at some point he began harassing me and harassing me. He used names, insults and shoves that I always tried to ignore. My parents had always told me to avoid trouble, and that was also a tenet of taekwondo. True, knowledge in Martial arts can help you defend yourself, but you are not supposed to show off your skills in an offensive way. It is always preferable to avoid danger, even as you are training to be able to confront it. One day, Dax started shoving me against a wall. My first reaction was to ignore it and walk away, but he shoved me again and then a third time. Finally I turned around and kicked him pretty hard in the face and he went back against the lockers. People started shouting, "Fight, fight, fight." It took a while for the adults to get in there and break us up. At that time, the coaches had the authority to "give us pops," which entailed hitting us with a paddle. I expected to get popped, but I never did. I think the coaches were sympathetic, maybe a little confused that the polite, scrawny kid stood up to the bully. From that point on, the other students started to call me the Karate Kid, which was okay. It was an important moment— not because I got the better of it, but because I stood up for myself in a way that was fair. I didn't start trouble. It wasn't what I did, and my parents wouldn't have accepted that behavior from me. But I was taking a stand, a defensive stand, because I felt I had a right to do it on principle. It was one of those moments that shaped me.

Of course, we were also starting to shape one another. Each of my siblings began taekwondo at age five, and we all loved it. But we didn't have a large arena or a full stadium. Instead we had our garage. We would go down there and shadowbox, kick paddles, pound the heavy bag, work on technique and try not to damage the garage. Don't be fooled by the fact that we were from Texas, either. We had winter and it could get cold. We would be in school during the warmest times of the day, so we would practice between five thirty and six thirty a.m. Then I'd come back after playing baseball and practice with Steven between six and seven in the evening, before I trained by myself for an hour. We would sometimes mimic the scenes from the kung fu theater movies. Being the older brother, I would nominate him to be one of the bad guys. He was always game and brave during our practices, but the eight-year-old didn't experience too much heavenly glory against his thirteen-year-old brother. My mom would make sure her laundry schedule coincided with the times her kids wanted to kick one another. That way, she could run the dryer and keep us from freezing as we worked out. At one point a tube that led outside was either loose or off, so the entire garage was steamed up. We trained on unpadded concrete made slick from oil stains, and left telltale holes in the wall where kicks went astray. We'd wear these kung fu shoes that were black with brown bottoms. They didn't have taekwondo shoes for us then. Instead of paint and plaster, we would cover up the holes with posters. One said, CARPE DIEM (Seize the Day). Another said simply, BE THE BEST.

In the summer we used to leave the garage door half-open to let in some air. It also let in some curious eyes. Kids would pass by, hear the screaming and want to check us out. They would spread the word to other kids in the neighborhood, and before long we were a travel destination for anyone on a bike. We knew most of the visitors, but sometimes a random kid we had never met would stop by. Some guys would watch and leave; others would ask to come in so they could watch. Some even took up the sport. I started to create structure for my siblings and any other kids who came over. I guess it was my first period of informal coaching. Steven had a friend named Angelo Decamps whose cousin Javier Bolivar came over to see what we were up to. Years later, Javier made the national team.

I had a friend from my classes named George Weissfisch who was curious to see where we trained. He couldn't process the idea that we trained in an actual garage, and he could barely speak when I lifted up the door to show him our training multiplex for the first time. "Where's the carpet?" he wanted to know. "I thought it was a gym you called the Garage as a nickname or something. You don't even have mirrors in here. There's no heater. There's no air conditioner. How did you guys get to be so good training in a place like this?"

I played along for a while, asking George if he had ever signed up for a sports class in a garage.

He was in a daze. "Yup, it's a garage, all right. You really train in your garage."

George became a great friend and teammate. He was a guy who challenged my methodology and tried to poke holes in everything I did. He disciplined me and forced me to have the answers because he was so inquisitive about everything I did. I started working with George between 1990 and 1993. These days, he works as an assistant district attorney and he has a taekwondo school. That's quite a step up from the garage.

That dedication we showed by training there was about to become singular dedication. I was fifteen and getting better at baseball. I loved to play the game, just as my father had, but that summer we watched another Olympics on television, the 1988 Summer Games in Seoul, Korea. Because Korea was the traditional birthplace of taekwondo, our sport was included as a demonstration sport at the Games. During the opening ceremonies, the hosts put on an amazing display that featured hundreds of taekwondo artists all moving in unison. Our sport was hitting the big time. This was a huge deal. At the time, judo was the only Martial art on the Olympic program. Judo had its origins in Japan, and it made its Olympic debut at the 1964 Olympics in Tokyo. That sport had been on the program ever since. So maybe, just maybe, taekwondo would become an official medal sport someday. It was a distant dream, but somewhere in the back of my mind, I could always fantasize that there would come a day when a Lopez would march in an opening ceremony at an Olympics.

"Jean, you have to make a choice," my father told me, snapping me back to reality. "You have achieved a lot in taekwondo, but if you are going to go any farther, you'll have to give up baseball. If you'd rather play baseball and maybe aim for a college scholarship someday, you have to give up taekwondo. You need to focus as you move up in levels. It's going to be more challenging to improve as you get more advanced. And with everything you're doing, you're not even starting your homework until nine. Sorry, but you have to choose pretty soon."

In retrospect I probably could have stayed with both sports, except that I was still a student first. My favorite courses were biology and history. Miss Graves, my tenth-grade teacher in world geography, really helped me value education and make school relevant. Up until that point, there were many days when I did it because it was something I had to do. She made me feel in my gut how important formal education really was. It wasn't only to get the best jobs or the most money from those jobs; it was about gaining knowledge in areas you were really interested in and understanding those you didn't know so you wouldn't be caught off guard someday. I was starting to travel to more places at that time, so her subject really struck a chord with me. My eleventh-grade teacher, Mr. Bean, had us read Teddy Roosevelt's book *TR*. We had to dissect it inside and out. I went through that book painstakingly, especially the parts about the way he emphasized a vigorous life of exercise and physical exertion in an era when many people didn't think it was a big deal. He traveled, hunted, went on safari and was built like a linebacker. He epitomized what the United States achieved in its heyday: growth in industry and turning personal risk into success. I also remember reading about the stock market collapse of 1929 shortly before the market tumbled again in 1987. We dedicated a whole semester to the factors that led to that first collapse. I remember a quote about how you needed to know your history in order to understand your future, how history sometimes repeats itself. It was a good mantra for a future coach to learn.

When I wasn't in the garage, I was leading some of the other students through their taekwondo forms at the gym. I was fourteen when I looked across the floor and caught the eye of a girl in the class. Man, did she have the most beautiful emerald green eyes, the most enchanting smile and the sweetest way about her. I didn't usually get butterflies in my stomach when I went up to talk to girls, especially in the intensity of a taekwondo class, but Tabetha Rubio made my stomach rumble. I just felt different around her. I'd go home and think about her, daydream about her in class and growl at the thought that she always seemed to have a boyfriend around. I never really told her what I felt. What the heck, it was only puppy love, right? Right? I'd forget about her, right?

On many Sundays, we went to Saint Theresa Catholic Church in Sugar Land, but our parents didn't want us to think that sitting in a pew fulfilled our obligations as people of faith. They wanted us to be mindful of those beliefs, of how fortunate we were, of how we treated other people and how we made the most of our privileges. How did we conduct ourselves in the eyes of God and Jesus? I would read the Bible every night, and I gained the most strength and inspiration from the section where Jesus was put on the cross. He was going through such sacrifice, but He knew He was doing the right thing for mankind. He was persecuted for His beliefs, but He stuck to them. If I ever felt weak or if I ever questioned the standards I was trying to uphold, I tried to think about the strength He showed, and I would tell myself, "C'mon, Jean, if He did that, you can do something as simple as this," whatever it was.

With that perspective, I understood that my sacrifice of giving up baseball was not really a big deal. I had to think about the choice, but

I felt pretty solid about the decision. The travel was a big factor. It was one of the benefits I looked forward to, because I'd hear stories of national-team members traveling to exotic lands. I thought to myself, I can win a state tournament in baseball and maybe get to another state, but with taekwondo I can go to another country and see another culture. My mom would tell me what a great opportunity it would be to see the whole world and learn about different people and how they live. It's ironic that she had always talked about China, because she gravitated to the culture. She collected Confucian figurines, and she and I would watch how the Chinese celebrated their New Year, with the lions dancing down the streets of major cities. Who knew we would all be there together one day?

For now, I was about to make my first big overseas trip. I was sixteen when I made my first junior national team, and I was headed to Venezuela, Germany and Greece as a representative of the U.S. team. What an honor. When those first national-team warm-ups arrived at the house, I was so excited, I could hardly wait to rip open the box. Seeing the USA letters on the back of my jacket gave me goose bumps the size of small islands. I showed them to my parents and we shared another moment of appreciation. They always raised me to be grateful for the chance I had to grow up here, especially because of everything they went through and gave up to be able to bring up their kids here. It's something my parents always made me aware of. They would never really talk to me about that right before I fought, but it's something that was really ingrained in all of us from a very young age. It wasn't one defining moment that made me appreciative of or patriotic about my country; it's a cornerstone of our family's values to take pride in the country where we live. People in other countries are very patriotic about their countries, and sometimes they see that missing in the United States, maybe just because we have it so good over here, it's easy to be complacent about what we have.

As I started to travel for competitions, I began a personal tradition of taking photos of myself striking a taekwondo pose, usually kicking, in front of major international landmarks. Over the years I've smiled, kicked and confused onlookers in front of the Hermitage in St. Petersburg, the Christ statue in Rio, the pyramids in Egypt, the Eiffel Tower in Paris and the seawall in Cuba.

In 1990, I fought one of the most important bouts of my career against a guy named Clay Barber in Colorado Springs in the semifinals of the Elite Open, a precursor to our current U.S. Open. Clay was a great barometer for my progress in the sport. Pound for pound, he was the most talented U.S. fighter of that era. He was always in my featherweight division, and even though I always wanted to fight him, it always made me nervous. I knew how good he was. Clay kind of commanded the mat. His friends gave him the nickname Hollywood, because he seemed like he was straight out of the movies. Ironically enough, that's where he ended up. He later became an actor and stunt man, appearing in films such as *Alias*, *American Pie 2* and *Batman & Robin*. Clay had a lot of people cheering for him.

I really didn't have a full-time coach with me, so I just had my dad in my corner. While I really appreciated having him on the floor with me, he didn't have any formal training as a coach. He was long on encouragement, but short on tactical advice. He had heard that glucose tablets, or sugar pills, could help give you energy during a fight. But he was so nervous, he stuffed about eight of them into my mouth in between rounds. I started choking on the pills because I didn't have enough water. It was too much sugar at one time, and I started to get dehydrated. He was such a wreck, and I was calming him down, telling him, "Papi, you've got to relax for me. I'm getting overwhelmed and dehydrated here." I ended up pushing the match, being aggressive, leading with my front leg, a strategy that Steven is known for these days. The strategy paid off. Twice I cut down Clay's attacks with the front leg and scored points. I was elated that I had beaten the guy I looked up to, but I also felt sort of bad that I had beaten my hero. Whom did I measure up to now? At the same time, I felt good because I knew I was moving up. I was on my way. It was a defining moment for my career.

The way I beat Clay validated what I'd been working up to. In

1988 and 1989, I had been making a transition into what we know now as Olympic-style taekwondo, which consisted then of three three-minute rounds (now three two-minute rounds). Fighters score one point for each kick or punch to the scoring target, designated by a body guard. A kick to the head scores two points, and a blow that knocks an opponent down scores an extra point. Points are awarded by four corner judges who use electronic devices to mark points. A center referee controls the match and can give half-point warnings called kyong-gos. Two kyong-gos lead to a full point deduction, or gam-jeon. Punches to the head are forbidden, but judges rarely award points even for legal punches to the torso. Fighters often use spin kicks, back kicks, double kicks and fancy 360-degree kicks known as nadabongs. Fighters can defend by lifting up their legs or jamming, which means getting close or into a clinch to prevent opponents from being able to strike. With so much to learn and improve upon, a fighter certainly relies on solid instruction from a seasoned pro.

I didn't know what I was doing without a full-time coach, so I would go back to the drawing board and say, "Okay, that didn't work. Let me try something else." A year earlier I had fought my first domestic men's division match against Dong Lee. I thought I was getting the best of him in the first round, and then in the second round he sort of lured me in with what I know now was a trap. Once I got to within striking range, exactly where he wanted me, he dropped me with a spinning hook kick and almost knocked me out. He dropped me to the floor and I remember shaking my head and thinking, Man I was really suckered into that. It was another step in my development, because I had never seen that before. A culmination of all those experiences got me to the point of fighting Clay. I was learning and improving with each match, and I was starving for more knowledge. I guess I needed to be careful what I wished for. Somewhere in my future, there was an international trip I would never forget.

CHAPTER 3

Looking Good

by Steven Lopez

I was always a shy kid and I was pretty worried about the unknown. I distinctly remember walking to the first day of kindergarten with my mom. As we got closer and closer to the school, I started holding on to my mom's arm tighter and tighter. Before she even opened the door, I told her, "Mom, I want to go back home. I don't want to go in there." She was pretty understanding about my worry, but also pretty firm. "No, baby, you have to go to school," she said. "All the other kids are going to school today for the first time. You have to go, too." I started crying before she opened the door, but I really fought back the tears so the other kids wouldn't see me cry. That would have been a bad introduction to my new peer group. I told her that the only way I would walk in there was if she agreed to go in with me and stay in the room. The teacher introduced me to the rest of the students, as she did with all of us. I didn't say much at the beginning of the day, but eventually I started to open up. The teacher gave us some posters to color. I started drawing with a few of the other kids. Once we all started talking, I remember the teacher signaling my mom as if to tell her, *Hey, he's okay now*. Instead of ignoring the signal, I looked over at my mom; I walked over and told her, "Yeah, I'm okay now. I'm with these kids. I'm having fun." My mom left once we both knew I wouldn't cry.

I was fine after that. Once I broke the ice, my competitive nature started to emerge. We used to play a game in school called Around the World, in which we'd have to solve a problem from the multiplication tables. If we answered correctly, the next student would have to solve a problem, then the next and the next. The fact that the teacher turned this into a game, into a kind of contest, was enough to make me study my multiplication tables on my own at home.

I was a little perfectionist. My parents would have me draw a picture, which didn't always come out too well. I would get upset because I knew I had messed up somehow. Maybe I had gone outside the boundaries of whatever I was trying to draw or I had used the wrong color, but since I hadn't drawn in pencil, this masterpiece-to-be was beyond hope. When I would ask my parents how it looked, my mom would tell me it was beautiful, because she felt the effort was more important than the result. It didn't fly with me. I was almost setting my parents up. I wanted them to be real and point out where I messed up.

I was also competitive with sports. I was kind of a popular kid, but I'm not really sure why. I used to look out for the underdog. If one of the bigger, more aggressive kids wanted to pick on one of the weaker kids, I liked jumping in and standing up to the bully, kind of the way a superhero would defend the common citizen. I was usually pretty tall for my age, so I could get away with it.

When Jean first started taekwondo, I used to watch him dress up and put on his uniform. My parents used to get excited to take my brother to taekwondo lessons, so I'd get caught up in their excitement. I'd sit on the side with my dad watching, slowly getting comfortable with the idea that this was something I could do, too. It was fun for me to see Jean do so well, because I looked up to him and wanted to be like him. My parents knew I wanted to join Jean in his classes, but they made me wait until I was five. They had sort of looked the other way when I started taking baby steps onto the mat in regular clothes when I didn't think the instructors were looking. I was seeing how the mat felt, looking at the lines of kids doing their forms from up close. It was great. What kid doesn't like to kick and punch like Power Rangers?

My first day was a big deal. I was pretty nervous initially because there were all these other people around. It was really cool to wear the same kind of uniform as Jean, wrapping the white belt around my waist, but actually getting out there took a little nerve. I knew Jean was training at a pretty advanced level, so I wasn't ready to keep up with him. But I saw this one girl out on the floor who seemed to be doing fine. She was really small, but she didn't have any fear of running into people's paths or following instructions. I thought that if she could do it, there was no reason I couldn't. So I pretty much followed her lead the entire afternoon. At the end of the day I was just really excited to be doing something with Jean.

Once I was in it, I was really excited to put on all the equipment and start sparring. At first you learn the commands, and counting to ten in Korean. It was fun for me to memorize my first form at home. I made sure to go into class prepared so I could impress the instructor. The first day I put on my equipment at home, I stared at myself in the mirror for the longest time. Yeah, I thought, this is me. This is Steven, who's going to be just like Jean. I was ready to go. I had seen other kids crying and falling over and I thought to myself, Why the heck are they crying? It doesn't hurt that much. It's fun. I didn't understand the idea of crying because of embarrassment. I didn't understand doing anything badly enough to get embarrassed. To begin with I was eager to fight.

I was kind of mean, because I took some sort of pride in making the other kids cry. I didn't want to hurt other kids; I just wanted to win, and since we were still not competing with points and clocks, that was a way of proving superiority. I wasn't breaking any rules, and it just felt natural to want to win by kicking the other guy. Hey, it isn't ballet. You're going to get clipped once in a while.

There was a kid in the class named Sam Yu who was my fiercest rival. We wore shin pads and instep pads, but we didn't have to wear chest protectors or helmets when we sparred. We should have. We would punch each other as hard as we could. It wasn't until we were nine or ten that the instructors made it mandatory for everyone to wear helmets when we sparred, mainly because they watched Sam and me kick the heck out of each other.

I had my first competition when I was only six. I don't remember much about those first matches, except that the other kids always fell down. At that age, we weren't really too coordinated. We looked like Teletubbies. Our awkward chest protectors were so big, it was hard to get out of your own way when you kicked. We fought under different rules then, so each time we scored, we'd get a red ribbon on the back of our belts. The first person to reach four points would win, and since kicks to the head counted for two points, I usually tried to end each bout with two quick kicks. Sometimes I fought so hard, I'd get disqualified for being too rough. I was seven when I started winning my own trophies. I never liked showing them off. It was good to have them, but mostly I just wanted to fight.

I didn't really notice how many trophies I had accumulated, but one day, after a few years' worth of tournaments, I did an inventory check and I had thirty-three of them. My parents would drive us to about two tournaments per month. Most of them were within the state—in Houston and other places, like Brownsville, Dallas, Corpus Christi, San Antonio and Fort Worth. I can't even imagine what my mom did with all of those trophies, since Jean and I had over a hundred of them. My dad was always proud of them, but I think my mom might have given some away just so we could have room for other things in the house, like, you know, a kitchen and some beds. When I was starting out, the people running the meets used to put me in the heaviest weight classes based on my height and my reputation rather than my actual weight. Since I was tall, skinny and weighed only about sixty pounds when I was nine years old, I usually ended up fighting heavier guys. We had a Grand Championships tournament, pitting the winners of the two heaviest weight classes against each other. I prevailed and brought home a trophy that was six feet tall, making it the tallest member of the house.

I was always a good student, usually a well-behaved kid. I was afraid of getting in trouble with the teachers, having them write in my folders that I had been talking in class or anything like that. Ultimately, I never wanted to have to answer to my parents, because my dad wasn't shy about taking out his belt if he felt I needed a spanking. From elementary school through high school, my teachers almost always loved me, because I didn't give them trouble. They cut me a lot of slack if, for instance, I had to miss an exam or some classes because I had to go away to a tournament. As long as I kept my grades up, they would usually make sure I didn't get penalized for being away. I remember having a very demanding third-grade teacher named Miss Ball. She was very difficult. I hated how hard she was on us, but I remember thinking, I'm going to be a lot smarter because of this woman.

I learned a good lesson at junior nationals in 1989, when I lost in the quarterfinals at age eleven. Honestly, the kid I was fighting scared me. I had watched his earlier matches and I saw him take people out very quickly. I was pretty nervous, and I lost because I was too scared to engage him during the match. I remember going back into the restroom, crying out of disappointment at myself. Before I left the room I made a vow to myself that I would never punk out on a match like that again, no matter how good the other guy was. I wasn't vowing to win every match, but I was vowing never to be scared to try my best.

I got my black belt when I was twelve, after I had proven my sparring ability, mastered my forms and nailed some of the drills the instructor had for us, including breaking boards. If he wanted us to do a jumping side kick, I could break four or five boards. I would break three if I were using a back kick. We had another drill that required us to do both a side kick in the air and a punch at the same time. That one hurt, but it was also a really cool technique. The black belts could always do the coolest jumps. We also had to jump over people, eight or nine at a time. The younger students would line up and assume a prone position, the same way you would get under a table to shield yourself during an earthquake. At the end of the row would be two guys holding a board, and I'd have to jump over everyone and execute a flying side kick. Or there would be two guys bowing back-to-back with each other and I'd jump over them. I really enjoyed the technical side of being a Martial artist. A lot of kids today graduate right to Olympic-style fighting without having the proper technique to perform a flying side kick. I always loved learning the proper, crisp way to do something. It took time to perfect an element, and it was sometimes more exciting just to go on to the next battle, but the technique training I learned from my instructors at the school and then from Jean really made me more aware of my body, my limitations, my reach and what I could and could not do once I did get into competition.

If the competitions were in Dallas or San Antonio we often drove in on the morning of the meet. We'd be up at five o'clock and on the road at five thirty. We'd start our day with a big breakfast at McDonald's, something we did only on meet days. After each tournament that I won, my dad would buy me a new Nintendo game. It was so much fun to go to Toys "R" Us on the way back from a meet. Not only would I have a new trophy, but I'd have the newest and coolest video game.

When I was in third grade, the area was hit by a big oil crash and my father's employer went into bankruptcy. My dad lost his job and we had to move into an apartment in the Houston suburb of Alief. We were without our garage for a year, and without the comforts of a homey backyard. The kids from the area were the ones who hardened me and turned me into a tougher fighter. A lot of them were children of immigrant parents, too, and they fought for everything they had. I got into five fights that year, because kids found out about my Martial arts, so they wanted to take me on. Given the relative stage of my progress, those were some of the meanest, toughest matches I ever fought.

One year, I saw a lot of kids getting involved in gangs. Our teachers talked about them, too, during our drug-awareness programs. There was a kid in school named Kerry whom I didn't like. He belonged to a gang, so I talked to some of my friends and tried to form my own gang. We had our own rules and initiations. It came to a close one day after a kid was giving me a hard time in class. I later chased him home on his bike, but didn't actually put a hand on him. I guess I wanted to scare him for saying bad things about me, but his mother complained to the principal and the police about her son being chased by a kid in a gang. The next day, I started hearing announcements over the school's loudspeaker for my friends in our so-called gang to visit the principal's office. One by one they were called until I heard my name. I knew then that there was trouble. I was embarrassed, because I was usually well behaved in front of the teachers. Instead, I had to explain myself. I tried to point out that even Diana was a member of this "club," as I called it, hoping that the principal would ease up on us. Instead, that made it even worse because of the idea that I had gotten my little sister involved. Well, maybe the whole gang thing wasn't such a great idea. My dad had to come pick me up that afternoon. That's never good. I tried to make out as if it were no big deal. "Dad, c'mon," I said. "Me? A gang? We have a club and we just call ourselves a gang."

Right from the time I started school classes, I always wanted to sit next to the girls, especially the one in my kindergarten class with beautiful blonde hair. Girls always get you in trouble. The one time I got into a really bad fight in school back in fourth grade was because of . . . girls. In fifth grade I walked around with a girl named Maria, then Carolina. I remember they would write me these little notes and cards. Hey, it was an ego boost even then. But it was a sign of just how much I was into taekwondo that in high school I didn't go to one homecoming or to my prom. I never had a serious girlfriend in high school.

My dad was trying to keep food on the table, so he jumped at the chance when his friend Mark called and told him he had a job for him, even if it paid twelve thousand dollars less per year. Mark was very kind to my dad. Yes, Papi's job paid less money, but as we started to improve and travel for competitions Mark gave my dad time off to see us compete. He said, "Don't worry." After one year, Mark started paying for plane fare and hotels. That was big for my dad to be able to see us and, in many cases, coach us. When my dad tried to do something for Mark, he wouldn't want him to do anything. You see one person on the victory stand, but there are so many people behind him or her who belong on the stand too.

My father was able to move us back into a house a year later. I was nine when I joined Jean for training in the garage around the time I competed at my first junior nationals. As I got better at some of the drills the instructor gave us, I could tell my technique was really improving. I always had markers with my peers. I was always lucky to have older students like Jean around to set a standard for me.

I always wanted to hang out with Jean. I wanted to go where he went and play what he played. If my older brother did it, I wanted to do it. Then I started to win local competitions. It took me a while to understand I was good at it. My dad started to take us to nationals and Junior Olympics—figuring out where the sport could take us. When Jean made the junior team, I vowed to make the team at a younger age. I wanted to be better. Jean trained harder than anyone. He did twelve three-minute rounds on a heavy bag in the garage at five a.m. I would hear the bag-pounding sounds. I'd lie in bed and think how amazing it was. That's what it takes. Jean never had all the technique because he wasn't taught by advanced coaches, but he had the belief to catapult him over people with better technique.

He was a great older brother, because he was always willing to include me in whatever he did. Maybe it was a pain in the neck to have this little kid tagging along with him, but he never made me feel that way. When he went to go to his friends' houses to play things like board games, Nintendo, basketball or baseball, I always wanted to tag along. I remember playing Dungeons & Dragons with a large group of kids who were all older than me. It seemed like a nerdy game after a few years, but back then we all sat around and played for hours. One guy would be a sorcerer. Another would be a wizard. They nominated me to be a person who could communicate with animals. Sometimes one of the kids would say, "Okay, Steven's on my team, but he doesn't really count." I didn't care. I was playing. I was included. I was learning how much fun it could be to compete at something.

I wasn't limited to one sport or even one position on the diamond. I played first base, pitcher and shortstop. I would go from baseball straight to taekwondo, and I'm pretty sure that if Jean had stayed with baseball, I would have followed him. The double duty was exhausting. I was usually up by five thirty, and I wasn't happy about it. "Papi, I don't want to get up," I would say. "Some kids want to be an astronaut or a fireman. They don't have to get up at five thirty, do they?" Why did I want so badly to be an athlete in taekwondo? In between afternoon practices, I would change in the car from one uniform to the other. The first team I played on was called the Padres, which, of course, made me a fan of the San Diego Padres for a while. I was seven years old, had no front teeth and took the biggest swings you ever saw in my shiny blue uniform, even if I didn't hit anything. Over the next few years I got pretty good. We had tryouts before the season started when I was ten years old. I muscled up for the first pitch of the tryout, thinking home run all the way, and I hit it out. Then I hit the next one out. I hit the third one near the fence, and I knew after that I'd be on a good team. As a little kid, I used to like the Pittsburgh Pirates for two reasons. First, the day after I hit those home runs, the people who ran the league and divided up the players put me on a team called the Pirates. Second, when I started to watch some of the major-league games with the Pittsburgh Pirates, I really took to this guy who used to play second base for them named Phil Garner. They used to call him Scrap Iron, and he had these huge forearms that made him look like Popeye.

Like Jean, I eventually had to choose between baseball and taekwondo. As I got older, the small, informal matches gave way to bigger tournaments, and the kids and coaches at the baseball games began to take them more seriously. It was pretty hard to keep a full schedule of games and practices in both sports. Instead I made taekwondo the priority, and my baseball coach wasn't happy about it. He told me that if I missed one particular practice he wouldn't play me in the next game. I didn't think he was serious. First of all, the practice conflicted with another one I had for taekwondo right before a big tournament.

And besides, I was one of the best players on the team. Didn't he want our team to win? He wouldn't really bench one of his best players, would he? Sure enough, I showed up for the next game and the coach made me sit out. I was so upset. Of course I cheered openly for my team, but I didn't know whether I really meant it. Silently I didn't think it bothered me that our team lost. That would show him to make an example of me. See what he got. The next year I played for the same coach on a different team. The other players weren't as good, we didn't win as much and I started to get impatient whenever I thought my teammates didn't try hard enough. That was it for me and baseball. Maybe I was just making excuses, but I was starting to think that team sports weren't worth my time. After playing two years of football in junior high, I gave them up for good.

I was in GT (gifted and talented) classes. In high school, I really liked math and science classes. I was lucky that whenever I had big projects, I could always rely on my older brother for help. I could say, "Jean, I need to come up with a hypothesis. These are the variables. This is the conclusion I want to reach." Jean never did homework for me, but he was very patient, and he made a lot of things easy to understand, kind of like a translator. More than once I thought, Man, I'm lucky to have Jean by my side on this one. Sometimes older brothers liked to pick on their younger siblings. Okay, that might have been me once in a while, but Jean never did that. He was an easy person to lean on.

I still wanted to be like Jean when I was in seventh grade and he was already a senior. He started going clubbing and I thought that was cool: One day I was going to get to go out to clubs as well.

In eighth grade I started to have my own sense of fashion without having to look at what my brother was wearing. As a little kid, I also took care of my presentation of how I looked. My mother used to tell me, "How they see you is how they treat you." Whenever I wanted to go out with Jean, I always took a shower and made myself look as neat as possible, so there was no way my mom wouldn't want me to go because I wasn't properly dressed. I'd be waiting at the door for Jean.

Before I became more interested in how I looked—now I teach my older brother how to dress up. Right, Jean?—I used to follow Jean's style. He used to roll his pants up at the very bottom. Over his Chucks or Converses, he'd make a tight roll like the other cool kids in school. I used to wake up early so Jean could help me roll up my jeans, and I thought it made me the coolest kid in my class.

My parents would always buy the same thing for Jean and me. It was pretty embarrassing at first for Jean, because we would always walk around wearing the same stuff. I thought it was so cool. He didn't. By the time I came of age, my friend Jason Torres and I would attack Jean's closet and take all his shirts, even those that would be two sizes too big for us. I would leave them at friends' houses. Friends of mine would show up wearing his clothes and he would say, "Where'd you get that shirt?" Now it's ironic, because I'm the guy telling him how to dress. I think of myself as the trendsetter of the family. Jean will admit that there are times he copies my style.

I always thought I had an easy job being the second. Jean would help me with big projects, especially in math and science. I always fell back on him. My brother sacrificed so much. There were nights in his teenage years when he'd tell friends he couldn't go to a club because he'd be looking after me. Sometimes we would go to the movies. Even today, I still look to him for motivation and inspiration, and I have complete trust in him when he's in my corner.

Even people who weren't part of our family wanted in. During my senior year, I had a teacher for my anatomy class named Mr. Henry. I admit I was kind of his pet. We didn't look much alike—he was a tall, bald black man—but he would go around telling people, "This is my son." There was another girl in my class who, for some reason, always assumed she was in competition with me. She'd compare scores with me and try to ask smarter questions than I did in class. I didn't understand her motivation. Mr. Henry would tell me, "No, Steven, you don't have to do that assignment until next week. I know you'll be off conquering the world at some tournament this week."

It used to make her furious. "Why doesn't he have to?" she'd ask.

He'd just look at her and say, "Oh, because he's my son." I guess he was giving me preferential treatment once in a while.

My classmates did the same. In my senior year at Kempner, they voted me most likely to succeed. I hope it wasn't for being a teacher's pet.

Even during my school years, I had a very strong faith, one I always felt inside of me. I don't know how it first happened. We didn't go to church as a whole family. Jean and I were part of a church group for kids. During Christmas the church would take us to great neighborhoods with lights. My father printed out the Lord's Prayer and put it up above my bed, so I would read it each night before I went to sleep. Jean taught me how to pray and we would pray together before we went to sleep. I started making the sign of the cross before my fights when I was about thirteen years old. My dad bought a kids' book for me that had Bible stories about Samson, Adam and Eve, and David and Goliath. I enjoyed it. I remember the saying, If you have faith the size of a mustard seed, you can move a mountain. It stuck to me and it gave me a real purpose. God and our faith have been foundations for our family since I can remember. Before each bout, I ask God to be with me—not to help me win, but to help me do my best, fight with honor and stay safe. It gave me a sense of peace and purpose that my parents always reinforced. Taekwondo was the chosen vehicle for me to achieve my goals, and my father was adamant that the goals never left us. "Whatever you do," he told me, "you have to do something more to be better for your culture and your family."

CHAPTER 4

Behold the Conqueror

by Mark Lopez

'm Mark "the Great" Lopez. I can climb mountains, lift boulders, dodge bullets and, most of all, kick your butt in taekwondo. Then I'm going to dance.

Okay, now that we have that out of the way, you can blame Jean. As the youngest brother, the runt of the family, the kid who was naturally small and clingy, I was his science experiment. Jean was going to make me believe I was the best. I was Napoleon in a white robe, with an in-your-face flair and a strut that could make you want to step on me. The experiment was for my own good. Jean had made Steven into such a smart scientist of the game; I was going to need a lot of attitude just to keep up with my brothers. Jean wanted that for me. He wanted me to be the best, to be better than him, to be at least as good as Steven, and to set the competitive table for Diana. I don't go around today thinking about how great I am—whatever good I've done or can do is only because of the shoulders I stand on in my family—but when I was growing up, when I was paving my path out on the mat (and maybe a few times away from the mat), I was a product of my brother's infusion of will to be the very best and to uphold the name Lopez.

That took some doing, because long before I became the family showman, I was more of a no-show. I was really small, maybe no more than three, and I was at home while Jean and Steven were at school when my mom had this lady come over to the house to talk with her about the Bible. I was really shy and afraid of being around certain people, so whenever the doorbell rang and I knew she was coming, I'd instantly run to my room. I don't quite know the physics of how I did this, but I would jump into my crib and try to make myself go to sleep. It was hard, because I loved to jump around more than anything else. When our family would go to a hotel, the first thing I'd do was jump on the bed, then go from bed to bed, even if there was a large gap in between. My mom would tell me to relax, and it would work for a good twenty seconds. Then I'd torpedo to the other bed again.

In kindergarten I was really shy, and my parents put me into an English as a Second Language class. I really didn't belong, because there were other kids in that class who didn't speak English at all. I did, but I didn't complain much about the class, and it probably didn't help my cause that I was quiet.

I remember going to local tournaments with my mom, dad, Jean and Steven. They'd take place at high school gyms. The gyms didn't have air-conditioning, so I'd be pretty hot. I would take naps in my mom's arms for most of the day, and she'd wake me to watch Jean and Steven fight.

Like my brothers, I really enjoyed watching Bruce Lee films. In one of his films, *Enter the Dragon*, he walks into a room of mirrors and runs into a guy who takes off his hand and puts on a black bear claw. That scene was pretty impactful for me. I remember always wanting to wear the kind of kung fu shoes Bruce Lee would wear, even in the garage. It wasn't a good idea, because they don't have any grip at all, especially on cement, but I just thought it was cool to wear kung fu shoes.

I just remember Jean jumping rope for such a long time. I always wondered what he was doing in the garage making that sound for so long. Then my dad would go down there, holding the bag while Jean kicked it. They could go for twelve rounds, three minutes each, and I would just hear this banging downstairs. I was so curious about it that

I looked forward to my day of going in there. When I was in the tae-kwondo school just watching, I would take time on my own to kick and punch. This wasn't like being at home when that woman would come over to talk to my mom; this was a place where I wanted to start doing what my brothers were doing, making my own noise just like them. I don't recall asking my parents to put me in; they just did it once I was five years old.

Once I started, I felt I was important. I was finally part of it. It felt comfortable, because Jean was leading a lot of the classes there. It was easy being with my brothers. I wanted to do everything perfectly, to impress everybody and gain their approval.

I had my first competition later that year. I fought only two matches, and I won both of them. I came back with a trophy that was taller than me. The garage was already packed with trophies and med-als, and it was getting out of hand. We didn't need decorations, but my dad had to start throwing things out because we had so many trophies. The matches were easy. I would just kick and kick and keep on going. For some reason, I remember wondering why the kids across from me wouldn't fight. The matches never seemed to last long, and the other kids wanted them to be over. I thought that was all there was to fight-ing. As a boy I visualized only winning, never the alternative. I never feared losing or getting hurt. I just went out and did what I was told.

It wasn't so much the trophies; I just wanted to do something my brothers did. I never really admired their medals; I just thought it looked cool to be able to punch, kick, be in a uniform and do some-thing like Bruce Lee. Imagine being able to kick and punch people without getting into trouble. I was too young to understand that my brothers were successful at what they did.

At a very young age, I discovered a talent for walking on my hands and doing backflips. I was very energetic, but also very gymnastic. But like most kids, I had two speeds: full-throttle and out cold. After a few flips and some creative dismounts off furniture, it wouldn't be long before I was searching for my mother's arms again so I could take a nap. Jean actually helped me to tumble before he helped me to fight.

I used to love watching gymnastics all the time. I would gape at figure skaters on TV performing triple axels and wonder how they could keep the kind of balance they needed to land on their feet.

I would practice push-up handstands, which were cool once I got the hang of them. Steven and I would put our hands behind us while lying on our backs and try to pop ourselves up. I realized everything I wanted to do, I had to try over and over to get it right. Steven and I would walk around the living room with me standing on his shoulders. Jean would be on his back with his feet up and he would do a quick leg press and catapult us into the air. It was fun until the time I landed on my head.

I took some lessons at a small gymnastics school near where Jean and Steven did taekwondo. I loved doing rolls and flips. When I was nine, my parents put me in a more advanced class. It lasted for three months, because it was too expensive for me to do both gymnastics and taekwondo.

That year, I went to my first junior nationals in Rochester, Minnesota, and I actually suffered my first loss. Losing? I wasn't supposed to lose. I had no idea what it felt like to lose. I was in the finals as a green belt. The fight wasn't going as it usually did. I was used to the feeling of the referee grabbing both of our hands and then raising mine. Each time I'd feel his grip on my wrist, I just assumed it meant my hand was going up. I got used to it and how good it felt. This time, he didn't grab my wrist quite so tightly. I felt odd. Then he lifted the other guy's hand in the air, and I didn't understand it. What was this? The referee raises my hand. That's how it works, right? I was crying. I was devastated. What had I done wrong? That was the last time I ever lost the junior nationals, but I never forgot it.

My alter ego, Mark "the Great," was probably hatched in second grade, when Jean and I watched a documentary on Muhammad Ali (while we were wearing large mittens and shadowboxing), and I also read a children's book about Alexander the Great. Alexander at a young age wanted to surprise everybody, impress everybody and surpass people's expectations of what he could accomplish. I connected with the ambition in the story.

Yes, I was a cocky kid growing up, but especially with my size, it helped to have confidence that other people wouldn't give me. It was a confidence that Jean always wanted me to have. He was my Aristotle. As I got older, I realized it wasn't very nice or very Christian to have a big ego and flaunt yourself in other people's faces. Teachers weren't amused. Every Tuesday, they'd file a progress report about the students and we'd have to bring the report back to our parents. One teacher said she was disturbed that I would always write "the Great" on all of my papers. My parents saw my side of that one. They still kept my feet on the ground and made sure I didn't break any rules, but they answered the teacher by asking what was wrong with their child building his self-esteem. If I didn't think big, I wasn't going to be a success. Jean would reinforce that, too, by telling me there was never anything I couldn't do. He didn't brainwash me, but he always patted my back whenever I did something well.

In elementary school, I was lucky enough to be the kid everyone wanted on their sports team. I always made people laugh and tried to be the most popular kid. I was always competing for something, even if it was just my classmates' attention. I never abused that position, though. I always felt bad for the nerds in the class. If anything, I wanted them to like me, too, so I was one of the guys who welcomed them into my circle of friends.

As early as third grade, I remember thinking that girls were really cute. I wanted to sit with them, talk to them and impress them by showing not just how cool I was, but how smart I was. Even though I never misbehaved badly because I was always scared of punishment, I would try to show off to the girls by doing silly, mischievous things like making faces and throwing paper balls, even if I always made sure not to get caught. In third grade I was a pilgrim during a pre-Thanksgiving play we put on at school. The pilgrims were supposed to be sharing a meal of corn, so we represented that with a bowl of popcorn. Well, we didn't usually get to eat popcorn at the house, and it looked pretty good to me, so I started eating it. The teacher got mad at me, but the curtain hadn't been raised yet, so she just replaced the popcorn. So I went off script. Great actors chew up scenes all the time, right?

Another day I brought a whistle to school and broke it out during recess. Teachers would blow a whistle when it was time for the kids to go inside. I hid behind a tree, started blowing my whistle and watched all the kids lining up. The teachers just looked at one another with these confused faces and never quite figured out what happened. I would sometimes get my name written on the blackboard or get a U for "unsatisfactory" on my report card for behavior. If I did get into trouble, I usually tried to charm my way out of it by making the teachers laugh. I could always make them laugh, and, well, I could usually get out of trouble. I once got written up for throwing paper on the bus, and got put on detention for getting a friend to install a video game on my computer, but those were misdemeanors.

My parents were pretty firm about our behavior. If we talked back to them or disobeyed, my mom wouldn't hesitate to pinch us and my dad wouldn't hesitate to spank us. My dad would set me straight for something I did wrong, but he always made sure I understood that there was a reason for the punishment. My dad never spanked any of us without making it clear why we were being spanked, kind of like a judge reading a list of charges before sending someone off to the slammer. He wanted to make sure we always understood that it was punishment and not something random. If we didn't misbehave, we wouldn't get spanked. A spanking was usually followed by the this-is-for-your-own-good talk, or the this-will-hurt-me-more-than-it-will-hurt-you talk. The thing is, I believed it.

Usually if one of us misbehaved, the other wasn't far behind, so these spankings often went in tandem. It may not have hurt that much, but we always cried, because we knew we had let our parents down, which we never wanted to do. One day when my dad went to his closet to get his belt because and Jean and Steven had been doing something wrong, Steven promised himself he would not cry when my dad spanked him. When his turn came, he did everything he could to hold in his tears. My dad kept going, but Steven didn't react. The lesson apparently wasn't having its desired effect. Even Jean was telling Steven to go ahead and cry. My dad didn't know what to do, so he left Steven alone in his room. It was the last spanking Steven ever remembered getting. I wish I could say that. The thing is, the last time my dad spanked me, he put his arms around me afterward and told me he loved me. There was no spite involved with his making sure we understood right and wrong.

Even at that young age I was really competitive and I wanted to be the best at whatever I did. I was very small, but very rambunctious. To make sure I wouldn't feel insecure about the fact that I was smaller than kids my age, Jean simply told me to be better than everyone else, almost like I could do it by flipping a switch. I still have the record in my elementary school for most sit-ups and fastest mile run, and my oldest brother/coach/mad scientist wouldn't have it any other way.

The teachers would separate the students into those in the average classes and those in the gifted and talented classes. To prove myself, I always looked for ways to compare myself to the other kids. Our teachers used to give us timed multiplication questions, and I studied my tables on my own so I could be able to go to the teachers and show them that I was the fastest. I told my parents; I told Jean; I told the teachers—I wanted to be in that class. Finally the teachers agreed to give me a standardized test. It was like the LSAT test, with logic and analogies. There were patterns of numbers I had to complete. I never saw my score, but it was good enough that they agreed to move me to the GT class. It was the first step in my being recognized by the National Honor Society years later, but then again, you don't get a black belt on your first day either.

Ever since my parents stuck me in that ESL class, I had been determined to be a pretty avid reader in school. I liked *1984* by George Orwell, *Brave New World* by Aldous Huxley, *The Old Man and the Sea* by Ernest Hemingway and *Of Mice and Men* by John Steinbeck. I was pretty naive about politics and social issues until I started reading books like *Animal Farm* by George Orwell and *The Jungle* by Upton Sinclair, the latter of which described the crazy process of meatpacking during the industrial revolution at the turn of the century.

Of course, I still liked video war games like *Street Fighter* and *Mortal Kombat*. There is a debate going on now about video games. Parents won't like this, but I actually think the games helped me with strategy and figuring out patterns. When I fight, I always look for patterns of my opponents just the way I would when I play a video game. Not buying it, huh?

My parents didn't mind the video games, so long as I didn't take my creature comforts for granted. My mom had us pray before each meal, thanking God for the food we had in front of us and for the roof over our heads. I watched *Ben Hur* and *The Ten Commandments* with my parents, so Charlton Heston was a big part of our lives. I would cry when the scene came on when they put Jesus on the cross. We were baptized as Catholic and we went to church sometimes, but our parents never required us to go. They were more interested in making sure we were thankful and humbled by the sacrifices that were made for us. That was another thing I picked up by watching Jean and Steven. They took their spiritual sides to heart, and I wanted to follow them.

Growing up, I couldn't really fit into Steven's clothes the way Steven fit into Jean's, because I was just too short. I liked hanging out with Steven's friends, and I always tried to go with them to play sports or games whenever I could. Steven didn't want to have to take me along, but I didn't really care. I'd try to comb my hair like Steven and listen to his kind of music. If I could be like him, I was pretty cool. He used to make a high wave in the middle of his hair, so I did the same. He wore Looney Tunes shirts, so I wanted the same kind of shirts. He listened to Beastie Boys and hip-hop music, so I liked those things, too.

Of course, we all loved Christmas. Even when Jean stopped believing in Santa Claus, he'd keep the fantasy going for the rest of us. We'd have a big tree with all the lights. My mom put Christmas carols on in the background. It was just like you'd see in the movies. Under our tree, we might find Atari games, board games like Monopoly, remote-control games or He-Man figures. I used to like the electronic cars that would talk to you. Even if all they said was, "Get in the car," I thought they were really cool.

Mostly, my parents always wanted us to be together at holidays. We didn't place the emphasis on presents, especially since some years it was hard for my parents to buy many of them. It was more about being together when we did either open presents or enjoy Christmas dinner together. It was a good respite from the day-to-day stresses of finances and chores and work. A lot of friends from the neighborhood might stop by because they always knew it was a welcoming home. We could have as many as twenty or thirty people over. We'd play music, have great food, great conversation. I can't think of a better place to be than our home at holiday time. I know it sounds corny, but I didn't really think that much about what I'd be getting, but about how glad I knew my parents were to have us around, and how no matter what else happened on a given day, that rock of stability was always something we could count on. We had balloons; we had cake; we'd take the same picture every year of my brother Jean with the knife cutting the cake. That was the big joke every year. I could always count on Steven to say, "Hey, Mama, are we going to take the picture of Jean with the knife?"

If Steven wanted to venture out on his own when it wasn't holiday time, Jean always worked hard to make up games we could all play. He never wanted anyone to feel left out. If we played baseball, Jean always wanted to make sure I had a chance to play, even going back to the days when my turn didn't count because I was so small. I used to love it when Jean would bring a girl over. He always had great taste, and I'd keep it to myself that I'd have a crush on his girlfriends.

I had a lot of fun playing Little League football, even though I was always so much smaller than everyone else. That never stopped me from loving the contact, even if I was the one getting hit. I played quarterback and linebacker and never hesitated to dive into the pile. My coach, Jack Bennett, says he put me at quarterback because I was the only guy on the team who could remember all the plays. I was ten when I got my dad's approval to give up taekwondo and stick with football instead. That lasted for about a week, before I got frustrated and went back. I never understood why some kids would be afraid of the bigger guys on better teams. Why couldn't those guys just be brave and try to make themselves better? C'mon, guys, compete, compete, compete. If I wanted my side to stare down the next big challenge, I had to do it myself. My days weren't long for football. I did play for another year or two. In junior high we had A and B teams. Given my size, roughly five feet and a hundred pounds, I was stuck on the B team. Our scrimmages weren't really much fun, because the A guys would just stomp on us. I didn't care, because I just wanted us to show up. There was a great athlete on the A squad named Julius Preston, who seemed destined for a career in the NFL. At around five-nine, a hundred and sixty pounds, he was big, fast and mean. One day he received the ball on a kickoff, and everybody sort of moved out of the way because they didn't want to get run over by him. I knew he was bigger and faster than me, but I wasn't going to punk out and let him get by me. I was the last man back, so I threw my arms out to tackle him and just got nailed. I heard church bells ringing in my head as if it were twelve o'clock for the next hour. But I stopped him. See, guys, compete, compete, compete.

We had a sort of initiation place called the bullring where everyone faced one another and two guys would face each other and try to bring each other down. The coach called me out, and everyone wanted to get in the bullring with me, because I was small and cocky. One of the bigger guys named Mike jumped in there with me and ran at me full speed, wanting to separate my head from my neck. All I did was take a sidestep and take him down with an improvised judo move.

Even with those moments of glory, I didn't have a serious future in football, and with the opportunities that were available in taekwondo, I had to give up my second sport. I could make the junior national team and travel around the world, facing the best and learning about the world with taekwondo, or I could sit on the bench and travel across the city to play another team in football. Easy call.

Travel always appealed to me. In ninth grade I had world geography with Mr. Bockington. He was the first one who made me think about different cultures, places, religions and all the complex problems in the world. It was an advanced class and he was very demanding. I really respected the way he taught the class and brought his own travel experiences into it. At the time, the crisis in Rwanda was in full swing, so he used to tell us about the Tutsis and the Hutus. He made me realize how big and diverse the world was, but he also made me grateful to be where I was, just as my mom and dad did all the time. My problems seemed pretty small when I'd be learning about what other people around the world were going through. I always liked to read about Greek mythology. Being an architect, my dad used to talk about how advanced their culture was, and how so many of our buildings were influenced by the Greeks. I'd learn about how their theorems in math and art still impact the way we see things today. It was a place I really wanted to visit someday for myself. Heck, I wanted see the world. And I wanted to conquer it.

CHAPTER 5

As I Was Saying

by Diana Lopez

I am Diana Lopez, vocal family spokeswoman, coming to an arena near you. Anyone who has anything bad to say about my family or doesn't do right by them will hear from me. It could be loud. Be sure you make the distinction between cheering respectfully for one of my brothers' opponents (acceptable) and insulting one of my brothers when he fights (punishable by audible assault and sensory retribution). I'm told I'm a nice person, but sometimes my feet and my mouth act without thinking.

I was always Marky's speaker, even though he was a year and half older than I was. If we were at a restaurant, he was too shy to order what he wanted from the menu, so he would whisper his choices to me and I would tell the waitress. Even Steven would do that sometimes. If a wrong order came, my family was so nice and shy, so I would be the one to speak up and say, "No, you got this wrong. You need to fix it." When we have to give interviews at competitions these days, things are reversed. My brothers often speak for me. I never want to talk during our group interviews. Maybe it's because I don't like taking credit for things. I've grown up always being aware of how much I owe my parents and my brothers for good things that have happened in my life, so I'm embarrassed to take too much credit. Of course, I didn't want to get lost in the mix, so I figured I had to speak up for myself.

I talked a lot in school. I was a good student, but I would crack jokes. I knew when to speak and when not to. I was a tomboy as a child. I'd play football with the boys. I was usually picked first for sports teams. I wanted to be able to hang out with my older brothers, and I wanted to be involved with what they did. I never wanted to be left out. Mark helped me learn how to line up for kickball, and to throw a football with a spiral. No girl in the Lopez household was going to throw like a girl. Just being in the mix with all of them, I had to be active—and maybe a little rough—as a child.

My mom wanted me to play sports, but she also wanted me to be supergirlie. I didn't understand that. She'd put rolls in my hair and I'd say, "This hurts me. What are you doing? I don't care if my hair is neat." She'd dress me up anyway or take me to a party. By the end of the day, I'd get involved in some sort of sport and my hair would be a mess again. She used to call me *Bruta* in Spanish, or Brute in English, mostly because I was really clumsy.

When I was two, I followed Mark's footsteps when he tried to jump off a bookcase in the little library we had. He jumped, so I jumped. All was well until I broke my arm. My family had this beautiful grandfather clock. I was in charge of making sure the bells in the clock worked. All was well again, until the whole grandfather clock fell on top of me and I started screaming. "*Bruta*," my mom would say. "Oh, *Bruta*."

My mom was very insistent on making me up to look like a girl when we had family outings, but I was just as insistent on saying, "Mom, I'm playing sports." I didn't care about the danger involved, even if I was the one causing the danger. I tried to dive into a swimming pool once and landed just a little bit short. I don't recommend hitting your head on the side of the pool deck before you go into the water— not because it gives you a red welt on your forehead, but because if you have an older brother like Steven, you have to listen to him tell you that you look like a *Star Trek* character for the rest of the day. To this day, when he gets into one of those have-fun-with-little-sister moods, he puts his pinkie and ring fingers together and starts making the *Star Trek* sign.

Maybe it was my experience as a school drill-team member, but I was always our family cheerleader, and I didn't mince words. Some people let out a "yea, team" at the local soccer game, but when my brothers fought, I was the one yelling, "Knock his head off. Destroy him." Victory is so much nicer when you can behead the loser. I didn't really *say* those words, either. They just came out of my mouth when I wasn't looking.

When Jean was there, I could always return the trash talk to Steven and Mark, because I had Jean to protect me from the insults and ear flicking that were usually waiting for me. He called me his little princess, and I really missed Jean when he went away. I'd write him notes telling him he was the best, or get out the coloring book and make a nice picture for him. I even left a note for Santa one year to bring him some cologne for his next trip.

Jean always looked after me and used to take me skating at the Galleria. Jean always bought my school supplies, and he made sure to spoil me. He wouldn't spoil himself as much, but he'd always buy me the nice folders and the best-looking backpacks. I'd pay him back by reading to him and driving him nuts. Do you know the Elmo book with the theme "Are we there yet?" Well, I read it to Jean all the time. I'd see the way he handles his kids today and remember how nurturing he was with me, and I'd always think, Man, I hope I find a guy like Jean someday.

I looked forward to the days when Jean would call up from another country to tell me about his adventures, and I would say, "Oh, I want to go. When do I get to go?" I could hear him laugh on the other end as he said, "Well, you need to take up a sport like taekwondo first, and then you need to train really hard and get really good at it." I'm not sure anyone thought I'd take him up on it.

I don't think I really wanted to be a movie hero like Jean, or take on the impossible challenges like Steven, or fight like a samurai the way Marky did; I just wanted to see the world and share the travel experiences with my family. Even when one of us competed regionally, we would drive somewhere, laugh along the way, stop at a McDonald's and just have fun as a family. I always loved getting attention and approval from my brothers. They always knew they could get under my skin by telling me I couldn't do something. Whatever that was, they would make me want to do it more. If I had to do that through sports, then *Bruta* was going to be the best she could be in spite of her tangled feet. It wasn't something I ever felt forced to do; if my family put on robes and belts, then that was what I wanted to wear. Putting on a belt and training was like going to elementary school to me. The Kennedys did their thing. The Bushes did their thing. My family did taekwondo, and I wanted to be an important part of the family.

I began my contributions by serving iced tea and lemonade to my brothers during workouts. I was very subtle about telling my parents I wanted to practice taekwondo with my brothers, and I don't think I badgered them more than every five minutes. I remember doing frog hops and bear crawls in training when it was over a hundred degrees outside. I couldn't do that now, but I never really had an exercise I didn't want to do.

I may not have been coordinated in everything, but I was flexible and I could kick as high as anyone in the class. I don't think I would have stayed with it if I hadn't started to win. My parents entered me in my first junior nationals when I was seven, and each year, for ten straight years, I'd come back with a gold medal. It didn't seem like a big deal; it was what I did. Sometimes I would have to fight guys when we went to local tournaments. It would have been a psychological blow for them to lose to a girl, but I understood that guys were sometimes stronger, so it didn't hurt my ego. That doesn't mean it didn't hurt. We went to one tournament where I faced a guy who was, like, a whole head taller and twenty or thirty pounds heavier than I was. I didn't question it out loud, but what was I doing in there against him? He landed a big kick to my stomach and took the wind right out of me. I cried, but I went back in there to compete. It was a character builder. Taekwondo is a contact sport, and I was either going to quit or keep going, just like the guys. Jean would also remind me that the pain would go away soon, but the feeling of doing my best would last much longer. If I wanted to be the best, I had to wake up when I wanted to sleep, train longer when I wanted to go home, and get back up and fight when I wanted to sit down and lick my wounds. I don't know why I kept coming back. I would hurt at practice. I would cry at practice. But I would punch and kick and cry and jump back in like I couldn't wait for more.

When you're a little kid, bringing home six-foot trophies really boosts your confidence. I'd bring the ones I could carry to show-and-tell in school, and the other kids would admire them. I didn't like to wake up early for practice, but once I got into it, I would really take pride in the fact that I was working when other kids were sleeping. My PE teachers were good about letting me skip the basic PE classes a lot of the students had to take, because they'd see me running past the school before they walked in the front door. I would go out with the boys at five a.m. As the siren at the nearby prison would go off to wake up the inmates, my brothers and other teammates and I would be outside trying to burn up the track or the road. They would make up military-style chants and they would inevitably sprint off ahead of me. As long as I could stay within shouting range of the chanting, I'd feel good about my run, and it didn't matter if we were in the dog days of August.

Even in summertime, my parents always insisted I spend at least an hour doing some kind of learning that exercised my brain. Unlike my brothers, I was pretty lazy when it came to academics. They were in advanced classes and honors societies. I thought more about training than studying. My teachers had to tell me to think before I spoke. My mouth was usually going too fast for my brain to filter what I was trying to say. My dad always hoped I'd be more interested in science. It broke his heart that I really didn't like math. "Diana, why don't you like geometry?" he'd say. "It's so beautiful." Beauty was in the eyes of the beholder.

I've been lucky enough to have the same best friend since I was nine. Maria Figueroa (now Morales) is pretty much my adopted sister. She was my classmate and frequent companion on a lot of my trips. We'd play games like Girl Talk and Ask Zandar. Maria and I loved to make sticker books. We used glitter, paste-on hearts and photos of the *90210* characters. Some boys traded baseball cards; we traded stickers. She's two years older, so if I had questions about boys, she was usually my sounding board. My family liked the idea of my having another girl to hang out with, so they would invite her along on a number of our trips.

One day, Maria and I went to AstroWorld at Six Flags in Houston. I wasn't into boys at that age, but Maria always caught the boys' attention. We were taking a ride in a cart when she started chatting up a few of the boys who were waiting for a ride. It was the type of cart that would keep moving, so you had to get out or it would spin you around again. Maria got out, but I was stuck. In front of the boys, she had to free me from the ride before I spun myself out of control.

Taekwondo doesn't usually have day-to-day practical applications, unless you happen to leave your keys in the car. One night I was out pretty late with some of my girlfriends when we realized that one of them had left the keys behind before locking up. I found the right spot in the side of the window and did what they would do in the movies. I kicked in the window. A clumsy *Bruta* would have gotten glass stuck in her leg, but as long as I was using taekwondo, my technique was pretty good. We got the keys back and I still have my leg.

Cars occupied a lot of family time, because we traveled long hours to get to tournaments. It was always exciting to wake up in the mornings, pack up the Buick Regal and go. My mom would make sandwiches and my dad would brew a hot pot of coffee for the long haul. We would often ride caravan with our teammates and their families. When our group expanded, certain people would be in charge of different aspects of the trip. David Montalvo's dad, Oscar, was in charge of finding hotel accommodations. One of our mothers really liked to cook, so Oscar would try to find hotel rooms with kitchenettes. Organizing like this helped us save money. We drove sixteen hours from Houston to Colorado Springs one time. We drove through Arizona on our way to Los Angeles to see Steven and Mark compete. It was really hot when we went through the desert. It seemed like we were always stopping to eat and get water. But we were also learning a lot. Some kids would take out their maps and atlases to learn about each of the different states; we'd drive through each of them. It was a fun adventure. If we weren't looking out the window, enjoying the scenes, Mom would get upset because we weren't appreciating the opportunity to travel: "Look outside. This is a chance to see something you'll never see again." My mom always wanted us to soak in our surroundings, and she would point out every landmark, each building and every tree. If we tried to go to sleep, she'd wake us to point out another one-in-a-million sight that looked a lot like the one we just saw five miles earlier. "Okay, Mom, same trees," we'd tell her. As we got older, we'd tease her: "Mom, how come you're not looking at the trees?"

Jean was in charge of what to do to keep us all entertained. The good brother he was, he would keep playing no matter how much we tired him out. We played Sorry, Uno, Geography, I Spy, tic-tac-toe and Connect Four. We played a game called I Went to the Moon. It was a memory game that required each person to add a sentence to a long story. The first player might say: "I went to the moon and I brought my bike." The second would say: "I went to the moon and I brought my bike and the bike was red." The third person would add another detail. The first person who missed a detail would be out, and we kept going until only one person could complete the story in order without leaving out any of the previous details.

We played a game called Mad Libs in which you would fill in blanks with certain figures of speech. If the sentence called for a noun, we would make one up, and we'd do the same with the adverbs and adjectives. Then we would have fun reading our made-up sentences that didn't make much sense ("I went to the short store to buy a red elephant"), but at least they taught us figures of speech. We had drawing contests in which we would start drawing a subject, then pass the drawing along to a sibling and have that person finish it. Sometimes we'd make a masterpiece, if you call squiggly lines masterpieces. If there was a big eighteen-wheeler going by, we'd pump our fists, trying to get the driver to honk his horn. We had a violent version of slug bug—if you saw a Volkswagen Bug with a certain number on the license plate, you could punch the person next to you that many times. We played a game involving states on license plates ("Ooh, I found Alaska!"). Yes, I made the most noise, but my siblings weren't exactly logs in the forest. We had made-up games and acting scenarios. We would pretend to cry or be surprised by something or express rage. It was usually just make-believe. These days, people still have to tell us to calm down, even when we're playing poker, basketball or Nintendo.

Mark and I were like Bart and Lisa Simpson, always getting into small fights over silly things. Mark was a hyperactive brother, jumping around all the time. My parents always told us to be quiet, and it would work for a good thirty seconds. If you've ever seen the Chevy Chase movie about the family road trip, that was what our long rides were like. If one or two of us fell asleep, the others would draw on their faces. Take a nap, wake up with a new unibrow and freckles. Pepper was always fun, especially when you could put a handful of it in front of someone else's nose. Time the pepper with the right inhalation and watch the person's head pop up like a bobblehead doll. I'm thinking that if we had DVDs, that would have calmed us down a lot more.

Of course, on our long cross-country trips, my dad was in control of the radio, so we listened to oldies like the Platters, Paul Anka and the Drifters. Steven always loved Elvis, and he probably thinks he was Elvis in another life. My mother always thought Elvis was really good-looking, and she signed off on Steven's Elvis-like hairdo he had, with the big wavy thing in the front. We still listen to Elvis sometimes when we're on the road because it reminds us of our dad. Mark probably liked music less than any of us. These days, he never runs or walks to music. When he drives, he sometimes puts on talk radio or just listens to himself think.

I'm like the deejay of the family. In my next life, I'll be a photographer or a deejay. I like everything: hip-hop, rap, R & B, oldies. I like what's hot today, but I also listen to Foreigner, Buddy Holly, the Beatles and, yes, Elvis. Jean used to love Sam Cooke. It's funny, but if I'm working, and even if I'm reading a book, I'm better off with music in the background.

Mark and I used to play a whole lot together. He loved making me laugh. At home, we used to sing into a tape recorder and listen to ourselves afterward. I would sing "I Will Always Love You," the Whitney Houston song from *The Bodyguard*. Of course, as I was belting out this emotional ballad, Mark would sing "I'm Too Sexy" by Right Said Fred. That always cracked me up. Around the house, Maria and I would compete against Mark in hide-and-seek. We liked to play jacks against him because we knew we could beat him.

When we weren't on the road, my mom would make us spend an hour a day reading the encyclopedia, one page at a time. She wanted to make sure we were putting our minds to use over the summer, so we'd read each page from the top, and she had us write reports on each entry. Then we'd start from the top the next summer. Steven used to say, "Trust me, if there's anything you want to know about aardvarks, I'm your guy." We may have thought it was a little silly, especially because the other kids in the neighborhood didn't have to do it, but we turned the study periods into contests: "Jean, do you know this?" "Diana, what's the meaning of that?" We'd even throw some back at our mom just to make a point. She didn't mind. She knew we were learning, and that was the whole point. Soon the encyclopedias gave way to workbooks from the teacher-supply store, which were a little more manageable. Still, the rule was always the same: If we wanted to go out and play with our friends, we had to do a couple of hours of summer study work first. My dad bought tapes with reading assignments, and we would have to take tests afterward. Our summer reading assignments might include stories about anything from the origins of McDonald's to the Bermuda Triangle.

My dad calls my mom "the grandiose dreamer" and "the most courageous woman I know." She believed in aiming for perfection. We did whatever my mom thought needed to be done that day. We'd clean the garage after we worked out. We made sure our rooms were clean, made our beds, all the typical stuff kids were taught to do. We had to mow the lawn. We all did yard work and pulled up weeds. We sometimes did it reluctantly, but my mom would remind us that we had to do our best no matter what it was we were doing, even if the activity didn't excite us. We had to come with a good attitude, not just go half at it. Jean remembers not wanting to clean the garage, and his sweeping skills were pretty lazy. She'd say, "You know, Jean, everything in life that's worth doing is worth doing right." It wasn't an abstract philosophy to her; it really meant something even as simple as making vigorous long strokes of the broom to make sure we were cleaning the ground, not the dirt on top of it. She would take the broom and really give hard strokes, and Jean would see that there was a big difference in what she perceived as doing his best and what he was doing. When the rest of us got older, we got the same treatment.

My mom was fierce in that garage, so much so that she once stared down one of her worst fears in there. My mom hates snakes. She doesn't like to talk about them or even watch them on TV, and certainly she doesn't like to find them in her garage. One day, she caught a snake slithering along the garage floor. My mom was obviously frightened, but what did she do? She literally took matters into her own hands and killed it. Do not mess with one Ondina Lopez.

My dad was usually very soft with us compared to my mom. She would really push us. If one of us said, "Mom, I'm tired," she'd say, "You will feel happy after doing this because you did it." My parents played different roles. My mom would wake us, dress us, get us ready for school, feed us, put our vitamins out and do our laundry. On days we'd leave for our trips, she was always up at four a.m., either getting something ready or worrying about what she might have forgotten. In the winter, my mom would make sure to start the dryer in the garage fifteen minutes before we were set to work out. On trips, she packed clothes for six people, while my dad figured out how to get there. My dad would do homework with us. He'd drive us around to sports and practice with us. He'd barbecue for us on the weekends. The guys loved the smell of charcoal when my dad prepared the pit. I always liked looking at the fire as it went up high. To this day we're spoiled. It doesn't matter if I'm at home or on the road, I always think, "Oh, my mom will do my bed."

She also had us copy pages out of books, so we could work on our handwriting. At the time, handwriting was like training in that if we didn't practice it over the summer, our writing looked worse once school started up again. It was another example for us of how extra preparation when other people are resting can make you better. Even when I was in kindergarten, my mother would buy grammar workbooks and alphabet videos to help me learn.

She was especially picky about what her kids ate. She would often make our favorite dish, arroz con pollo (chicken with rice) and salad. She never served anything fried. In our lunch boxes she'd put a banana and a turkey sandwich. She'd give us our food at eight a.m., but by noon, the banana was dark. "Mama," we'd tell her, "everybody's bringing chips and Doritos, but my banana is dark." We were always a little jealous when we'd peek into other kids' lunch boxes and see cupcakes, Twinkies, Doritos, things we weren't supposed to have. For health reasons and also expense reasons, my parents never bought soda or junk food like cookies or chips. We always had fruit juices rather than sodas. That was another reason I liked going to my friends' houses. They had kitchens full of ice cream, chips, cookies and bad calories. The kitchens would empty pretty quickly.

The only thing she spoiled us with was cereal, letting us choose our favorites: Mark—Cinnamon Toast Crunch; Steven and me—Fruity Pebbles. It was a sort of concession to our being able to start the day and get going in the morning. But when it came time for lunch, she always kept it healthy. We almost always ate at home. If we ate out, it was usually a celebration or special day. These days, I bake cookies and buy Rice Krispies Treats, but I still eat pretty well, and my mom's lessons haven't been lost.

Like my brothers, I had another sport that briefly divided my attention. I had a friend named Natalie Torres who got me interested in playing volleyball. I never had any prior experience with the game before I went to volleyball tryouts in seventh grade. I made the A team, and we won our district championship. Volleyball was more of a fun diversion for me, kind of like playing Monopoly. I made the varsity team as a sophomore, but I was traveling a lot for taekwondo, and my coach wouldn't play me if I didn't go to practice. I worked really hard in practice and I beat all the girls in the mile run. Coaches looked at me as someone with potential to play in college. I told Steven and Jean about the dilemma as I was getting ready to start my junior year, and they both asked if I really wanted to stay with taekwondo when I could also play a sport like volleyball that offered me the chance at scholarships. How could they say that sort of thing? Were they serious? The next day I solved the problem: I quit volleyball for good. Taekwondo was my calling, and I listened long enough to hear it.

CHAPTER 6

A Long, Strange Trip

by Jean Lopez

In 1990, a few months before I graduated from Kempner High School, I was craving information and knowledge about my sport. If I wanted to get better at taekwondo, there was really only one place where I could really learn and grow within my sport that stood out above all the others. George Weissfisch and I had talked about going to Korea for a while. It was an intimidating place. The language was different from ours. The culture was so different from ours. Yet it was also the place we had to go if we wanted to put ourselves in a position to be competitive on the world stage. It wasn't just an essential part of the learning process; it was a dream to go to the mecca of taekwondo, the place where the sport was created. George would say, "Jean, you and I both know we have to go to Korea."

"George, I'm down. That's exactly what I want to do."

"Jean, they have the coaching we need. We can get only so much by just staying over here."

I said, "I'm down. That's exactly what I want to do. I've always wanted to go to Korea."

"I have a contact who could probably get us into a university over there. That's if you're really serious."

"George, buddy, I'm down. That's exactly what I want to do."

To be honest, we were both a little bit hesitant, as if we were trying to convince each other that we really wanted to take the plunge for this kind of adventure. At the last moment, I remember saying, "Wow, I'm really doing this." But then I thought, Yeah, this is really something I have to do. I was excited, but nervous about the unknown at the same time. George's instructor in Houston was a Korean guy named Jun K. Choi. He set up the connection for the two of us to train at Yong In University. He was able to get discounts for us on airfare and lodging at the university. I got some help from my parents to finance some of it. We wanted to immerse ourselves in the culture. We wanted to submerge ourselves in the way Koreans perceived taekwondo, how important it was to them. We booked a monthlong trip to Korea that would take place in December. This meant I'd be missing Christmas with my family for the first time in my life. This was a huge commitment. I had a feeling I would know how much I really loved (or didn't love) taekwondo after this journey was over.

George's instructor set us up with a guy who arranged our connection when our plane arrived in Seoul. He dropped us off at the right train station, pointed, waved and sent us off. Time to fend for ourselves. Once we got off the train, we were met by another guy from the university. We tried to speak to him in English, but he knew only a few words, so he got frustrated and stopped communicating altogether.

These days, it's more and more common for young students to start learning English as a second language in school and for student exchange programs to expose people there to different worlds. But at the time, they just didn't get many visitors from foreigners at that school. George and I just looked at each other and said, "This is going to be interesting." I was thinking to myself, What have I done? I hope I did the right thing.

We spent the first day navigating ourselves to the dorm, finding out where the kitchen was and where the bathrooms were. It was a whole discovery. "George, this isn't the Hilton," I told him. The biggest surprise was the cold. They had no heaters in the entire dorm. We followed our breath as it floated across the room. Our fingers stuck to the inside windows. Granted, I lived in Texas and I was pretty warm-blooded, but even if I had grown up in Alaska, I'd have been looking for an extra sweater.

When we got to the gym, people were training in coats, warm-ups, scarves, beanies and wrapped-up towels. The Koreans were also pretty frigid toward us and didn't seem interested in exchanging gestures or simple words with us. I felt really shunned as the outsider going into their land, and as a non-Korean trying to learn the sport that gave them so much pride. George is a heavyweight, about six-five, so they would give him looks that said, Whoa, hey, these guys are huge.

Right away we noticed their biomechanics and how fluid they were. They could kick to the face so easily, without much effort. They were so athletic, flexible and agile. Those are all things that really impressed me. Not only could one or two students do that, but the whole college of a hundred athletes per session could execute their forms on command. Because nobody there spoke English, we learned everything by observation: situational drills, concentration drills, the way they kicked with paddles and heavy shields. It was so organized and methodical. They had little cliques and a clear hierarchy that included the way they would sit with their peers. The captain was the boss, and everyone respected what he said. If he told people they had to be there ten minutes early, then everyone would be there ten minutes early. The professors would have workouts for themselves before leading the students in their workouts, but all the students understood their roles. The dynamic of that was an eye-opener. Their talent pool seemed endless. They had an amazing pipeline that began when kids from one elementary school would fight those from rival elementary schools—all the way up to high school and university levels and the professional leagues that were like our pro circuits in tennis or golf. Yet as much as I was learning from training at the school, I still felt I could make adaptations to the style they were teaching in order to become a better fighter. Maybe it was the stubborn coach-to-be inside of me, but I really liked the strategy of kicking out the front leg the way a boxer would lead with his jab. It was the ultimate preventive measure, a way of keeping your opponent from starting any sort of offensive action, because you were blocking his path without overcommitting yourself. I understood people had a difficult time dealing with it, because it's such a sound defensive technique. The instructors there didn't like it. They would motion to me to use more traditional stances and approaches to fighting. Maybe I was wrong, but I wasn't about to fold up the technique and throw it away.

This was actually the first of several trips to Korea, and they were all memorable for different reasons. When I went back in 2003 for my fourth trip, for instance, the attitude was completely different. In 2003, the kids were more westernized. When they saw Americans, it wasn't such a novelty to them anymore. They tried to speak English on the street.

In 1999, I was putting all my theories to the test. We had an English class for about seven or eight Koreans. They wanted to converse, trade words and cook with us. They wanted to hear the vernacular, and not just what you would find in a dictionary. They wanted us to teach them how to say, "Hi, wassup?" rather than just, "Hello, how are you?" They wanted to understand the words people said on MTV. I could have been a comedian over there because of the way I said things, and because we are so much more expressive with our mannerisms than they are. By 1999, they were happy to engage us, but on this first trip, I had a real sense that they didn't want the stranger in the homeland.

Even as I was embracing some of the Korean techniques of taekwondo, I really couldn't embrace the food. Each day we'd go to a cafeteria and try to survive the spicy cuisine that was probably supposed to be hot enough to make up for our cold rooms. Maybe your burning mouth was supposed to warm up the rest of you. There were tin trays full of what seemed like slop: rice, fish heads, kimchi (fermented cabbage) and a mystery soup that they served for breakfast, lunch and dinner. It was so spicy I thought I was going to explode. Take three firecrackers, four jalapeños and six habaneros. Then sprinkle them with TNT, douse them with Tabasco, detonate them and wash them down with kerosene. Never mind that my eyeballs practically popped out of my head from my taking sips of that soup, but I really needed to eat. After the intensity of the workouts, I had dropped from a hundred and forty pounds to a hundred and twenty-five, and George was staring to worry about me. He was always the heavyweight, thinking about food. The sports nutrient bars you see in a lot of stores today weren't that common then, so he brought over cans of Spam, Fig Newtons, chips, pretzels and other snacks he figured he could eat in case the food we were eating didn't agree with us.

I was making fun of him the whole time at the beginning: "George, what an American you are. That's crazy. You think they won't have food in Korea."

But he knew exactly what he was doing. "Well, Jean," he'd say, "their food might be pretty different from our food. It might be very traditional, very nutritious and so foreign to us that we won't be able to eat it. I'm just being safe."

He ended up being such a genius to do that. I'm not going to lie: I went from enviously staring at his suitcase full of food to swiping some of his rations. How desperate are you when you start swiping Spam? It was survival. I felt as if I were going to die. We had Spam and rice for our Christmas dinner. Everything was shut down in the college, so we were there for four or five days on our own. I wrote home a lot and read my Bible. It was labor-intensive to get to the phone, too, because of the long walk around several cold corridors. I never knew whether I really wanted to take a shower, because the water was so icy. Sometimes it was better just to go around smelling like kimchi and mystery soup. It was miserable. In hindsight, the trip built a lot of character and I was grateful—once I got under a warm blanket back in Texas.

We had some other food options in Korea, but it took a while to reach them, and sometimes we really didn't know what we were getting. If we rode the train back to Seoul, which we could do over the holiday break, there was a Kentucky Fried Chicken in a district of the city known as Itaewon. Many U.S. military personnel went there to eat and shop. The place was known for bargain hunters in search of knockoffs. I just enjoyed the familiar food. A number of judo students trained at the university. They were friendlier to us than those with the taekwondo group, and they pointed out a little store near our gym that sold milk and small pastries. One day they invited us over for a meal they called bulgogi. It was a delicious dish that consisted of sirloin and a marinade made of soy sauce, ginger, garlic and sesame oil. Throw in some mushrooms and cellophane noodles and serve them to a starving American and you have a friend for life. "You're an angel," I told one of them in between bites. I don't think even a native English speaker would have understood me with all that food in my mouth, but the look of contentment on my face probably didn't need translation.

One time they invited us over and served something that didn't seem quite so familiar. I was shoving the food into my mouth, as usual, trusting in my newfound culinary friends. "You like?" our cook asked. I told him I did, but I noticed it had an unusual taste and texture and I asked what kind of meat it was. He put his hand on his head to represent ears and he said, "Doggy." I froze. No, oh, no, please, no. Don't say that to me. Tell me you're kidding. I mean, I completely lost it. I didn't want to embarrass him or be disrespectful to the culture, but if I hadn't rushed outside I would have soiled his carpet right at his feet. George tried to console me by telling me that the cook was trying to say it was rabbit, which might have made me feel only a little bit better. I looked at George and wanted to make myself believe him, but we both knew what we'd heard. "George, you heard exactly what I did," I said. "George, what can I do? I just ate Benji." Every time I saw a dog on the street in Korea, my heart sank as I wondered if that was the breed of dog I ate. I had chewed up just enough of the culture and certainly the food. It was time to go home.

Even though I couldn't stomach everything that happened in Korea, I was certainly better off for the experience. I came back to the States fired up to have a really good year. By then, there were a number of us who were winning most of the domestic featherweight competitions, including Kevin Padilla, Clay and me. Clay was the guy I really looked up to. Kevin was a smart fighter. He had a way of setting me up for traps and making me expose myself exactly as he wanted so he could strike for the decisive point. I was finally getting to the point where I wasn't just using my aggression; I was also using the strategy I had learned from all those other matches and the month in Korea.

That summer, I won nationals and competed at the U.S. Olympic Festival, both for the first time. The festival was a sort of multisport competition for all the Olympic sports, held in one U.S. city for American athletes. Instead of competing for different countries, we were divided up into East, West, North and South. The festival was being held in Los Angeles that year, and I reached the featherweight finals before losing to Clay, 3–1. That summer, I barely lost out to Kevin at the trials to see who would go to the Pan Am Games in Cuba. The match went back and forth, and I was trying to be careful not to get trapped for a two-point blow to the head. I understood when Kevin was trying to trap me, but he always had a good back kick, and he beat me off the mark with that when I was trying to attack him with a roundhouse kick. He countered and scored with his back kick. I was unable to make him commit to it prematurely, and he knew exactly when I was coming.

At that time, the guy in my corner was my first coach, Larry Rodgers. He didn't know much about Olympic-style taekwondo, except that he had won a bronze medal at the national level back in the eighties. I worked with Larry for three years. He had a lot of passion and really believed in me. I made the eighty-minute drive each way from home outside Houston to be able to train with him on the weekends. When I was fourteen, a man named Mark Giambi and I would get together on Sundays and battle it out with adults. My dad would bring me in to see Mark. He was twelve years older than me, but he took me under his wing and kicked my ass every Sunday. He was the first one who took me seriously enough to rock and roll with me. I loved the fact that I was going to get better just by being in the ring with those guys, but I also feared for my life. I knew I'd get out with some lumps and bruises, but also with some knowledge. I knew that was what it took, and I really appreciated the fact that those guys took the time to work with me and make me better and challenge me in every aspect possible.

In 1992, I moved up in weight class and nearly got knocked out in one of my first meets. I had a concussion and I remember eating Chinese food afterward and not having all my marbles. Maybe I wasn't saying, "Moo goo gai pan" because of the food in front of me. I fought the same guy again and ended up breaking his arm. It was a war. I felt vindicated, because he gave me my first lessons in Olympic-style taekwondo.

Our junior team traveled to Brazil for a meet that year. I remember staying in a neighborhood that scared the pants off me. The building felt as if it were about to come down, and the neighborhood was known to run somewhere between violent and deadly. It was interesting, of course, that our officials from the United States Taekwondo Union, our nationally recognized governing body, all stayed in fancier hotels. They were on the water. They rested in relative luxury. Things that make you say "Hmmm . . ."

If there was one thing people knew me for at the time, it was how physically strong I was and how hard I kicked. Technically I wasn't the most beautiful fighter, but I was always ready for a war. I definitely wasn't meeting my full potential. I didn't have a professional who could dedicate him- or herself to training the way I could do it for my siblings and my other athletes. The stars would have been the limit. I had all the passion, all the drive, all the determination. I didn't have the refined skill. I'm a lot better now as a coach than I was as an athlete. I really needed someone with formal knowledge who believed in my abilities.

I realize now that I was taking the wrong approach to some things. First of all, I wouldn't have been so barbaric in my training and early coaching approach. I had a Rocky-style mentality. I thought more was better, that working harder was the same as working smarter. Looking back on it, I realize many of the demands I put on my body and then passed on to my siblings were completely unnecessary. The training drills may not have been the best things physically, but in a way, mentally those things made my siblings the athletes they are now. I understand so much about sports science now, so I see that a lot of the things I did to myself were counterproductive. I'd work out five days a week for seven hours a day and run anywhere between five and eight miles a day or every other day. I'd hit the heavy bags often in the workouts I used to do. I'd do that for twelve rounds, three minutes each round, once a day. I'd jump rope for an hour at a time as fast as I could, as hard as I could. I really overtrained and drove myself into the ground, but at the time I figured I could add up the miles, the kicks and the stretches and count on that to get me through matches. I knew nothing about moderation, pacing and the benefits of rest, especially before big competitions.

I overemphasized quantity instead of quality. I would do what were called squat jumps, bending at the knees and leaping to strengthen the legs. Like anything else, a few can be beneficial. A few zillion of them can turn your legs into ground beef. I would do those squat jumps for minutes at a time. At this point I'm really glad I can walk and run and do everything functional. If I didn't learn what I've learned now, I'm not sure I'd have a normal life. I'm amazed I never had stress fractures. I think genetically our family is just physically very resilient. All of us, especially Steven, have a higher pain threshold than most, and our capacity to recover quickly is very good. Those elements made us survive those barbaric training days.

In 1992, taekwondo was still a demonstration sport at the Olympics. I still hadn't reached my peak, and since my featherweight division wasn't included, I still had to wait for my chance at the Games. Instead, I made the national team for the first time and won the Pan American Championships in Colorado. I was the only American who won. I fought Milton Awama from Brazil. He was the top guy at the tournament. We were tied in the final round of the final match. At a decisive point in the match I heard a voice in my mind screaming at me to do something. At that moment I attacked with what we call a nadabong, a spinning roundhouse kick, which is difficult to pull off. I blasted him with it for the deciding point. I was completely jubilant and validated. I knew I was getting better and better. I felt very patriotic about the result, and happy I could win for the United States. I celebrated with my father and called my mother. That was the biggest event I could have won for the year outside of the Olympics.

The next year, I made a very significant decision to move to the U.S. Olympic Committee's Olympic Training Center in Colorado Springs. I always wanted to be part of the OTC, because that was the apex of training for a lot of Olympic sports in the United States, especially for taekwondo at the time. Athletes in more than a dozen Olympic sports lived there year-round with free room and board, and those from other sports would go there for periodic training camps. Colorado Springs is located 6,035 feet above sea level, so athletes who could survive training in the thin air of high altitude could also build their endurance by increasing their capacity to use oxygen. I had already been there for camps, and it was one of the few places where I could really learn more about my craft. They had recently switched taekwondo coaches to a guy named Han Won Lee. I kind of identified with him, because he was a bit of a rebel and someone who wasn't afraid to employ new techniques. I put the word out that I really wanted to train there, and I was just ecstatic once I got the invitation. At the same time I was torn, because I knew I'd be leaving Steven, Mark and Diana to fend for themselves. I wanted to devote some of my time to them, but I had no idea if or when I might do that exclusively.

My time at the OTC made me feel like a professional athlete rather than just a weekend warrior. We stayed in college-style dorms, and each morning I'd walk past the large Olympic rings that had been a powerful symbol to me since fourth grade. I'd see those rings and be instantly energized, knowing I'd arrived.

The coach-to-be inside me would observe not only how the staff treated the athletes, but also how they talked to the athletes about injury recovery and injury prevention. They had extensive departments in areas like sports medicine, sports science, biomechanics and sports psychology. Our team had a psychologist who used to give us a particular exercise: She had me place an orange sticker on my shin pads. The sticker was a visual cue. Each time I looked at them, the stickers would remind me to do away with anything in the past and focus on the present. It helped me get into the habit of understanding that the important challenge was the one in front of me at that moment rather than one I could no longer do anything about. It helped me to eliminate any thoughts about what might have happened in the past and to measure future expectations. It's something I preach to all my athletes. Every day you go out, there is a new beginning. It's a chance for you to go out there and prove that you're the best, regardless of what you've done before. These days I use verbal cues rather than stickers, but the idea of incorporating cues into training started for me at the OTC.

We athletes had our own cafeteria, with a menu that was especially geared to feeding people who needed healthy fuel: useful carbs, high protein, high energy and fresh ingredients. My mom had been my original nutritionist without having any formal training or education in that area. She understood that fresh foods were always better for you, that fried foods were bad. She was really keen on avoiding empty calories. She built a food base that the training center reinforced. I became even more conscious of calories I took in. I had to be aware of how to cut weight and manage portions. Every dish at every food station in the cafeteria was broken down for us by its nutritional content, because having the proper fuel in the tank could have a significant impact on our training and performance. I understood that I couldn't eat a Double Whopper with cheese after I cut weight but felt like cramming calories. As much as I might crave something like that, the best thing to do was get my fluids, make sure I rehydrated myself with healthy things like fruit and make sure I stayed away from fattening or oily foods that could upset my stomach. There were a couple of times when I cheated and indulged in bad fuel. Each time I cheated I paid the price somehow. Those were lessons learned in stomachaches.

Colorado was a great place to live and train. I went to school at the University of Colorado–Colorado Springs. I loved the Rocky Mountain weather and the clean, dry air. Growing up, I sometimes had trouble with asthma, but the air in the Springs, while thin, was still easy on my lungs. In the summer, I played sports like volleyball and basketball outdoors with my teammates. I loved walking around the relaxing nature preserve there called the Garden of the Gods. I read a lot in my room: anything from inspirational books to athlete biographies to *Sports Illustrated* to my Bible. There were usually thirty rooms on each floor, including both singles and some doubles, so there would be forty to forty-five people on a floor. I'd be on the phone a lot to my friends and family. That was before the Internet, and we didn't have cell phones back then. So my parents would call the hall phone in our dorms. If we were expecting a call, we'd be kind of trapped in our rooms. When we'd hear a ring in the hall, everyone would get out of their rooms and run to the phone, because we didn't want to miss the call. Every hour you'd hear, "Who's it for? Who's it for?" We were pretty isolated, and those calls were nice prizes at the end of a long training day.

The following year I moved up to lightweight, made the national team again, and went to Costa Rica to win my second straight Pan American Championships. Against my Dominican opponent in the finals, I really felt as if I were taking ownership of what I was doing. I was the only U.S. athlete who won a gold medal there, and I was really feeling like a team leader on and off the mat. That was the good news. The bad news took place in an Olympic committee boardroom somewhere. With the 1996 Atlanta Olympics approaching on home soil, the International Olympic Committee (IOC) decided to drop taekwondo from the Olympic program altogether. Those of us in the sport had hoped it would evolve from a demonstration sport into a full medal sport, with the same official status as sports like track and field, gymnastics and swimming. Now we would have to wait until at least 2000 before taekwondo athletes could compete for Olympic medals.

With the multisport Pan American Games in Mar del Plata, Argentina, and the world championships in Manila, Philippines, on the horizon, I was still ready for a big year in 1995. Then I would finish my degree in psychology at UCCS and train through 2000, when we all hoped our sport would be on the Olympic program for good. It seemed like a sound plan, but I never anticipated the obstacles.

I wasn't prepared for the humidity in Argentina. I felt it from the time I arrived, but it had been years since my last asthma attack, and I didn't think this was anything I couldn't handle. I advanced to the quarterfinals against Cuba's Roberto Abreu and fully expected to reach the semis. I was the aggressor for most of the match, but could feel myself losing energy before giving up a point in the final round. That was the least of it. Not only did I lose, I was also hyperventilating, choking up and having trouble breathing. In one burst, energy just flowed away from me and nerves took over. This couldn't be happening to me, could it? I never lost consciousness, but American and Argentine doctors helped me to an auxiliary gym at the Club Once Unidos and put me on an inhaler until I recovered. They told me later that I might have had a respiratory infection. So much for that meet.

My main goal for the year was to win worlds. No American male had ever achieved that, and I was determined to be the first. I flew through the team trials and was having some very strong training sessions three weeks before the championships when I started sparring one day with my training partner, David Kong. David and I are both lefties, and in one exchange we went for the same move at the same time and banged each other's knees. At that moment, a loud snap echoed throughout the gym like a gunshot. We were both on the ground and we were both in so much pain, I wasn't sure who got the worst of it. I just didn't know who the gunshot victim actually was. As it turned out, David was the one with the torn ACL. My knee swelled up right away. I just thought, Oh, my gosh, here I had my opportunity to go to the world championships and it's up in smoke.

Fortunately I ended up with just a really bad sprain and bruise, but I was told not to train for the three weeks leading up to worlds. Instead I relied on a lot of visualization, sports psychology and virtual preparation, turning phantom movements into positive associations in order to offset some of the actual physical training I was unable to do. I did a lot of swimming exercises during my recovery, mimicking some of my training motions against the forgiving resistance of the water. The sports medicine guys at the OTC told me I had to rely on the visualization and avoid contact until the first match I fought. They would turn a switch to generate currents that they aimed against my body, in essence generating strength-building resistance without impact that could aggravate my injury. I would kick, bring my knee up, try to block and improve my range of motion. That helped me build up some strength in my injured leg without worrying about reinjuring the sprain or making it any worse. I would be in the water visualizing the opponents I would be fighting and the techniques I'd be using to try to beat them. I would do whatever I could to copy my workouts and matches, anything I could do to fuel my confidence. I'd spend three to four hours a day in there, and in the one week leading up to the competition, I started getting a little of my mobility back.

Once I finished my water training and left for the Philippines, I had convinced myself I actually had a chance to win as long as I didn't reaggravate the injury. Just be smart, I told myself. Don't take chances, and make the most of your openings. I had to rely on my prematch strategy, since the guy assigned to be our coach, So-moon Lee, didn't speak a great deal of English. I couldn't really talk to him once the matches started, so if I wanted to make adjustments during the bouts, I had to figure them out on my own.

The first three matches against fighters from Ireland, Japan and Italy went pretty smoothly. I felt strong and explosive, and had good stability in my knee. By the time I reached my semifinal match against Liu Tsu-Len of Chinese Taipei, the knee started swelling up. I remember thinking, Oh, no, here we go again. I had to grind those last matches out. I was trying to slow the game down, turn them into games of numbers rather than using raw aggression on every exchange. The tempo worked really well. I would jam up a lot, frustrate my opponents and kick with my right leg, which wasn't as hurt as the left one. I advanced to the finals and was one match away from making history. But this would be a tougher challenge. Now I was up against

José Marquez of Spain, the guy who would go on to win worlds in 1997 and the European Taekwondo Championship in 1998.

For two rounds everything was working perfectly, just as I envisioned. I figured out his timing, scored without taking risks and had my defense working. As I took a one-point lead in the third round, I also had the clock on my side. Time was ticking and my heart was racing. Tick-tock. Sixty seconds. I tried not to take victory for granted, but I remember thinking, Man, this is way too easy. I was in control. I had a good rhythm. Tick-tock. Thirty seconds. I didn't need to go forward, didn't have to engage him, shouldn't have attacked and given myself a chance to run into a kick. But I did. I was just fifteen seconds away from a world title, match in the bag and history in the making, when I went on one final attack. It was a fatal mistake, a tactical and psychological error. I can say now with some certainty that the physical limitations I felt because of my knee weren't nearly as significant as the strategic limitations I had. I wish I'd had a coach to help me set the parameters of what to do under those circumstances, but I still should have known better. In those final fifteen seconds, Marquez let go of an ax kick, grazed my helmet and scored two points. I went from one point up to one down on the last attack of the match. I had won a silver medal at worlds, equal to the best result ever for an American male, but I had fallen short of my goal when it was practically in my hands. Several years later I saw Marquez at a seminar I was giving. "Jean, you really deserved to win that match," he told me. "You did everything you needed to do to win, but unfortunately you just got outcoached. A good coach can make the difference between winning and losing."

Of course, at the time, I just felt the disappointment of the whole thing. I thought about what I could have done differently. I tried to temper that by thinking to myself how far I had come on my own, but the thought of being fifteen seconds away from becoming the first U.S. world champ overcame me. I took a shower and went to sleep. I was dreaming about everything. When I woke up, I wondered if it had all been a bad dream. Then, after a little time went by, I started to feel all the aches and pains that had accumulated all over my body during the competition. That was my confirmation that yes, I had competed and no, I didn't win my last match. The reality of disappointment was still blasting through me.

I started to snap out of it when I got back to Colorado. I took some days to heal from everything, but the first light postchampionship workout really helped. I knew it was my first worlds, and I felt I had a couple of others left in me. Instead of beating myself up about what I didn't do right, I started reflecting on all the things I had done well under the circumstances, and I reminded myself about my lack of experience. There would be other world championships in 1997 and 1999. If all went well, our sport would be in the Olympics in 2000. I had my best years ahead of me. Okay, Jean, man up and move on. It's time to get excited again.

A few days after I arrived in the Springs, Coach Lee sat me down to speak with me. I told him I was disappointed with missing out on a gold medal, but still really excited for the future. I expected him to say, "Wow, it's amazing we've been able to do this. Now let's build on that success and take it up to 2000." Instead he turned my world upside down. "You know, Jean," he said, "I'm really not focused on the existing elite athletes now; I'm really looking at the young guys who are going to peak in 2000. I'm not convinced that you're one of them."

Huh? What? Come again? Do you even have another athlete who has brought you to within an eyelash of a world title? Do you have anyone else who could do that at the next worlds? The worlds after that? What are you saying? What are you thinking? This was devastating. I felt there was no place for me. I wanted Coach Lee to tell me he wasn't serious.

"What you can do is help me with all these other athletes who are coming in," he said.

Why? What was the point in that? I had already neglected Steven, Mark and Diana in order to pursue my career. If I was going to be a coach, what was the point of staying at the OTC when I could go back and help them? Was I getting too much credit for my success? Was my

success showing up his success? Was my independent thinking somehow a threat to the way taekwondo was run in this country? I was
confused. I was devastated.

I told my family I was coming back home. They weren't sure that
I was sure, and they were right. I needed to know for certain that my
competitive career was really about to disappear before I actually believed it myself. I was still going to compete, but the focus on my own
career would start to dwindle as I turned to my brothers and my sister
to give them the technical knowledge and the coaching I wished I'd
had myself.

Coach Lee was pretty offended when I told him I was moving
back to Houston at the end of 1995. So were the people in the United
States Taekwondo Union (USTU) office, which was located in Colorado Springs. "If your siblings are going to be any good," they said,
"you'll have to bring them here. Your future is here. Theirs will have
to be here. The people who know what's best for U.S. taekwondo are
here in Colorado Springs."

I couldn't help but think they knew what was best for them, but
not for the athletes, especially the ones who were left to fend for themselves at matches with coaches who couldn't communicate with them.
I tried to explain that I wasn't trying to overhaul their insular world
out of spite, as they suspected; I wanted what was best for Steven,
Mark and Diana, and I had seen enough of the USTU and gained
enough knowledge about the sport to believe strongly that they were
better off with me.

I was planning to go back to Texas to fulfill another dream: of
opening my own gym, a place where the family could train together
and have control over how we prepared. On March 1, 1996, I opened
the Elite Taekwondo Center. The gym brought with it a lot of hope
and expectations. I know my dad was proud of his son opening his first
business. It wasn't going to be a fancy building—we didn't even have
mats—but it was going to be the place where I honestly believed we
were going to build the best team in the country and then the best in
the world. I felt I could poke some holes in the Korean style with an

American style that was more strategic and less confrontational, more like boxing. I guessed that the decision wouldn't be popular in some circles, but I had no idea the repercussions would be so extensive.

Even though the sport was not going to be in the Olympics in 1996, we were still competing for spots on the national team. One day during nationals, my former coach Han Won Lee took me into the bleachers before the competition and told me in no uncertain terms that if I opened the school, I would be blackballed. If I opened the school, he said, I'd be competing with another school that had opened five miles away and was owned by a Korean; I would be disrespectful.

It's hard for me to understand the complexity of this culture. The people in charge were threatened by the fact that I was going to open a gym and potentially compete with them for athletes, business and prestige within the sport. It was tough enough for me to be away from home, but on top of that, it was the last thing I wanted to hear after winning a world championships silver medal. I expected to hear that I was the country's best prospect for 2000 and that they were going to support my Olympic dream in every way possible, because it would also benefit taekwondo in the United States.

I think he really thought I was a threat because I was an independent-minded athlete who was coming into my own, and I was a threat to them. I wasn't one of theirs. I wasn't part of the clique. I wasn't Korean American. I had trained away from the gym (and the Korean masters) in a garage. I had an unusual style of fighting with my left leg out. I fought like an Americanized fighter. I didn't follow accepted traditions. I had different philosophies and styles on the sport. After I opened the gym, they hated the fact that I never had a Korean flag put up in my school. That caused such a stir. Every taekwondo school in the States had a Korean flag hanging from its walls. Sometimes it wouldn't even have an American flag hanging there. I remember Lee's words so clearly: "I hear that you don't even have a Korean flag up. That's being disrespectful to the history of the sport." They considered that a sacrilege, almost as if I were spitting on the pew in church.

Okay, yes, we owe a great debt to the Korean heritage of the sport and the discipline that the sport's grand masters instilled in their students, who passed those attributes down. But I felt strongly that embracing that tradition is one thing and bowing to the Korean flag is another. Coach Lee said specifically that I wasn't being a real Martial artist if I didn't want to display and bow to the Korean flag. I listened to him, but I was getting a little red-faced at his insinuations. I certainly was a Martial artist and a very respectful human being, especially when it came to parents and elders. But, I told him, I was an American, and my loyalty was not to the Korean flag. I revere my flag. The issue also conflicted with my philosophy. If I bowed to the Korean flag, how was I supposed to compete against Korean fighters? How was I supposed to beat them if I were being reverent to them?

In 1997, the referee chairman at nationals told me my students were being disrespectful because they weren't bowing to the officials—both referees and people running the USTU—when they passed in front of them. Well, maybe. I certainly respected certain aspects of what the tradition was intended to represent, but there were some things about the clique that I didn't respect based on the way they treated people. More on this later, but I think what they wanted from people were gestures of submissiveness rather than gestures of respect. I made sure to speak to my parents about that, because I have always had the highest respect for them and I have always conducted myself that way. They understood that I wasn't expressing an act of blind defiance that they wouldn't approve of, but of principle.

In those years, you could be eating in the cafeteria and if one of the officials walked by, you were expected to stand, get into an attention stance and bow. If you didn't, the officials would make a mental note of your actions and might hold it against you when they judged the competition. My athletes today don't do that with me and I certainly don't expect them to. I don't expect them to say, "Hey, bro," and throw spitballs at me, but I don't expect them to stop what they're doing and pay tribute to me. Just work hard for me—and for yourselves—in the gym. Respect your sport by conducting yourselves with honor, but don't worry about stroking my ego.

The referee chairman wasn't finished. He told me I would never win another domestic tournament as long as I was still competing. Really? You mean I went from the best in the country who was just hitting his stride to someone who could never make another national team just because he didn't bow or wave a flag? Yes, he said. I had that right.

Sure enough, I finished second at the national team trials in 1998 and 1999. The writing was on the wall at that point. There was no opportunity for me to represent the team any longer. If I'd had any doubts about my fate as an athlete, I now knew for sure I was going to have stick to coaching. I would have fought that harder, but now I had my siblings' futures to think about.

Steven was my perfectionist. I had to be on my toes with him, because he was that way with me. Marky was my accepting soldier who had total faith in what I was telling him. Diana was just plain fierce. If I told her that eating nails for breakfast would make her tougher, she'd buy up the hardware store.

I used to watch all the highlights on ESPN and notice the way athletes in other sports would handle themselves after defeat and victory, the comments athletes would make that sounded good and the ones that didn't sound good, how the way they handled themselves in those public situations would change my perception of them for better or worse. Sometimes they made me cringe. When Charles Barkley tried to tell people he was not a role model, his words really disappointed me. I always looked at that obligation as part of an athlete's job description. Yes, you're training and toiling in private, but once you get into the arena or you're in front of a camera, you become more than just an athlete to the public at large. You're also an entertainer and someone who affects the way other people, especially impressionable kids, try to conduct themselves. If you tell them that their behavior doesn't matter, they're going to be indifferent about it and disrespectful to their sports and their fans. Anytime you're referred to as an athlete, there's a responsibility with that. I'm not suggesting we, as athletes, don't make mistakes, because we do just as much as anyone else, but just to go out there and not try, to say you're not a role model, struck me as very wrong. I thought to myself that if I ever got to a platform where I would be an inspiration to other people, I would accept it with grace and see it as a privilege rather than a burden.

Without an Olympic platform, I had only limited opportunities to speak in front of a camera, microphone or just a large group of kids. I was going to make sure that if Steven ever had that experience, he would be fully prepared.

"Steven, good workout," I'd say. "Now I want to interview you."

"You want to what?"

"Interview you. It's part of your training."

Steven rolled his eyes so far into the back of his head, he almost lost them somewhere in his skull. He laughed, he giggled, he complained, but he did it. I would ask Steven, "So, that competition didn't go as well as possible. How do you feel?" Or I would say, "Congratulations, you won. How does it feel to be a champion?" I wanted to hear from him a sense of dignity in his answer about losing and humility in his answer about winning. I would also ask how it made him feel to be an American, because that was such an honor, or how it felt to beat his opponent, because it was always important to respect the man he had just beaten.

I also tried to do that with some of the other athletes on the team from my school. In 1996, a lot of the kids I was working with were Hispanic. Some of them were like I had been, trying to learn English as their adopted language rather than their native tongue. They were very good kids and I wanted them to be able to represent that. Not all of them were going to need to know how to speak in front of a camera, but I would tell them, "You never know." If they were working on their public speaking, it was another positive aspect of working toward becoming a champion. You never want to come across as cocky. You want to be humble. You don't want to be a brat or look for scapegoats.

You want to accept responsibility for the times when you fall short. I also made them aware that reporters can direct you to a certain place you don't want to go by the way they phrase a question, but you can always redirect them. Or if you can't think of a graceful way to do that, just be honest and say you don't feel comfortable answering the question. Just take ownership of the interview. That would come into play for Steven years later.

I think that came from my dad telling me that anytime I traveled, I was, in effect, being an ambassador for my country—not in a political sense, but in a human sense. I tried to win the hearts and minds of people we met, some of whom were meeting Americans for the first time. I always took great satisfaction in hearing people say, "You know, I had these preconceived notions about Americans. Maybe they were cold or conceited or ungrateful, but then I met you." Whenever I turned around any kind of negative perception about our country by the end of a conversation, the thought would stay with me and make me feel good for a long time.

When Steven and I were in Cuba for a competition, we met a wrestler who was walking along the beach. We started to talk and he was instantly curious about our lives. I could almost see his impressions of us change as we walked and talked. "I see how open you guys can be and how much more you and I have in common as athletes and as people," he said. He talked very softly about the great things about his country that brought pride to him, but also the injustices that he felt, because he couldn't buy basic goods for his family and he couldn't speak about it openly. When I mentioned Castro to him, the guy practically wrestled me to the sand. "Are you crazy?" he said. "Don't you know they can throw you in jail for that? They can throw me in jail for that just because I'm talking to you." It was an eye-opener to realize that some of the simple, basic liberties we have in our country don't exist in some other places.

Here we were, so close geographically, but we were so many worlds apart. We were told not to bring a Bible to Cuba, and I remember seeing Che Guevara's face plastered everywhere. Anytime the Cubans spoke to us, they whispered. When we talked, we just spoke our minds without having to be calculating. We feel we can express ourselves without restraints or fear that there will be people listening to our conversations and reporting us to officials so that it might get us into trouble. I felt sorry for him. His conversations were very monitored when he traveled, because officials didn't want him to defect or speak ill of Castro's Cuba. With us, he asked if it was really true that we had such great opportunities and could try to be anything we wanted. He wondered what I made in a month as an athlete, what kind of car I drove. The cars in Cuba were especially fascinating to me. So many of them came from the pre-Castro fifties, because Cuba didn't produce much of anything besides cigars, sugar and some citrus. They couldn't export those things to us because of the embargo against their regime. Really, everything was stuck in the 1950s. Nothing had changed and nothing new had been built since their revolution. So old men would stick rusty wires under the hoods of these Lincoln Continentals and slowly . . . *vrr, vrr, vrrmm.* The ingenuity came from a basic need, a strong desire to make the most of difficult circumstances and still look after those around them. Besides giving me another reason for pride in our own country, that desire I witnessed on the trip was a good lesson.

CHAPTER 7

Heavy Medal

by Mark Lopez

I was having a lot of success at the junior level. Each year, I went to nationals with a feeling of indestructibility. At one of our junior nationals in Dallas, the referees would laugh and snicker on the side, because I would do the Ali shuffle, switch stances and have fun. It may sound like an ego trip, but I felt like I would play with the kids and entertain the crowd so I wouldn't get bored. Some refs would tell me to ease off the intensity and not hurt the other kids. I would wonder why, because we were fighting. At one junior nationals, a couple of parents protested because they thought I was older than I said. No, I wasn't. I always fought in the lightest class. When I was ten, one parent brought out a weight scale and had the officials weigh me, because he thought I was too strong to be at that weight. Nope, wrong again. It took me until 1998 before I fought at anything other than the lightest weight.

I was twelve when I went to a junior camp at the OTC in Colorado Springs one year. Man, I felt like royalty, because Jean made sure his friends took care of me. I was so proud of Jean. You know how some people say they don't like to be known as so-and-so's brother because they want their own identity? Feel free to refer to me as Jean's kid brother anytime.

At the 1997 junior nationals in Louisville, I fought one kid named Steven Martinez who was tall for the division. He was knocking kids out and he looked like he could fight like a man. If I were ever going to get intimidated, that was the time. I learned to stay close, jam in and frustrate him so he couldn't use his length and power. I scored points off little openings he gave up, and won the fight. I had never fought anyone who was that much bigger and stronger.

For some reason, I never felt I was faster than the other kids, but I was often stronger and I could usually outthink them and be more scientific about fighting.

These days I play a lot of chess on my iPhone. It keeps me thinking a lot about strategy. Back then, my dad and I used to watch a lot of boxing, and he always taught me the importance of timing and distance and how that could make up for a lack of speed. If I wasn't faster, I could still know when to move out of the way and counterattack. I could still close in or stay back to take away an opponent's ideal striking position. We watched Hector "Macho" Camacho, the boxer who used to do backflips when he came into the ring. When I played video games, I would kick and get out of the way. When they expected me to jam in, I'd move back. When they thought I'd move back, I'd jam in.

When Jean went to the OTC, I worked with Jesse Torres, Jason's dad. He was very good to us. He was a military man, very strict and very organized. He gave me the nickname of Pit Bull because of the way I fought. I liked it. If I had to retire the name Mark "the Great" Lopez because it wasn't so tolerable once I became a teenager, Pit Bull sounded pretty good. How about Jean's kid brother, Pit Bull?

My first overseas trip was to Barcelona for the Spanish Open in early 1998. It was my first time competing at the senior division. I didn't know if I was physically ready. It was fun. I got to hang out with Jean and Steven. We went with David Montalvo, George and Jason. I was very happy to get second place there. I felt like one of the guys because I was able to go out with them to one of the clubs. Yes, I was only sixteen, but, hey, this was Europe, and I think the age requirement for clubs was about five.

We also went to Korea in 1998 and trained with Jean and Steven at the university there. By then things were more westernized. So I ate mostly rice and beef and they had fried chicken. The showers were so cold, because they didn't have warm water.

The trip opened up Jean's eyes to the fact that we were using techniques they had never really seen. It made him see that his goal of making the U.S. taekwondo team the number one squad in the world was realistic. Jean actually demonstrated the use of a certain step and spin kick to the Korean captain. Afterward, the man had his team trying to learn it, and it took them a while to figure it out. We went to the professional team that represented Samsung. They took us to the dorm of Moon Dae-sung the great Korean heavyweight. I couldn't resist jumping on his bed. I felt as if I were swinging one of Tiger Woods's clubs. Their gym was in the penthouse of the Samsung building. The floors were matted. They had high ceilings, ten kicking bags, and mirrors all over. Their practices lasted for three hours. The drills included carrying teammates around the gym and sprints up stairs and mountains. We went running up a mountain and one of the Koreans who spoke English asked Steven to slow down because they would all be punished if he came in first.

Diana and I went to junior worlds in Istanbul in 1998 and had a great time. Jean and Steven weren't there, so that made me feel like a veteran because I was looking after my sister. We have different personalities and traits, but because we're so close in age, we really get each other. It wasn't always true that I would carry myself with a strut and she would get her feet tangled up, but consider the time we were walking along when I spit out a piece of gym . . . and my sister promptly stepped on it.

Diana had never heard of Turkey and didn't even have a valid passport, but once she did, it was about to fill up quickly. On the way in from the airport in Istanbul, she started taking picture after picture of every building she passed. Our family photo whiz was like a sprinter in the marathon, the way she kept snapping furiously. I told her she should pace herself and at least wait until we got to some tourist sites so she could actually get in some of the photos, and so the pictures wouldn't all look the same.

I love hotels. The first thing I would do was see if they had a swimming pool or Jacuzzi. In Turkey, Diana and I visited an old castle. I had just learned about Constantine and the Ottoman Empire in my world geography class. We ate chicken schnitzel, went to a black market, saw the Black Sea and gazed across the strait, where we could see the European boundary.

I think most people expected that I would win the meet and Diana was going there for the experience. Wrong on both counts. Diana and I were competing and then going back and forth to pump each other up. Each time we went into the holding area, there would be fewer and fewer people milling around, stretching and kicking, because more and more would be eliminated.

I beat fighters from Canada, Argentina and Greece before I fought a Korean in the semis. We were tied with a couple of seconds left. I got myself into a bad position and fell rather than getting hit. The ref gave me a second kyong-go and the deduction cost me the match. That was my fault. I shouldn't have let myself get into that position. I was actually pretty lucky to have Diana there, because she saw how upset I was in the holding area and she started to focus her energy on me when she still had to fight. That's the kind of sister Diana is. It made me perk up and fight my emotions to get over the disappointment— not for me, but for her. I wanted her to be able to think positively.

As a junior who was still a red belt, Diana just fought. She didn't think about strategy or who she was fighting. She fought athletes from Croatia, Germany, Mexico and Greece. All of her fights were close. She was aggressive, but she would also fall down a lot. We called her the Terminator because of just how fierce she was. At five-eight, one hundred and fourteen pounds, she'd be this tall, skinny fourteen-year old string bean fighting seventeen-year-old women who were developed and had real muscles. She survived, because she just never stopped kicking. She was like the Energizer Bunny who never got tired. She would use double and triple kicks. She doesn't even kick that much now. The other girls would look for an opening, but there wasn't one. If anything, she wore down the judges, too. They really didn't give her points for specific kicks; they just couldn't watch all those kicks and not score one by the end of the match. Even without Jean on the trip, Diana was starting to study technique very closely. If there was another girl who was fighting well, she'd be able to copy what she was doing. If that girl switched stances, she'd do the same thing.

I teared up after the matches in a mix of joy and disappointment. Diana called home and simply said, "Collect AT&T call from junior world champion."

Jean was surprised. "Wait," he said, "you won and Mark got bronze? That's amazing."

"Yes, I won," she said, laughing. "How come nobody has confidence in me the way they do with my brothers? You see, Jean, I'm a part of this legacy now, too, and you have to believe in me."

"No, it's not that I don't believe in you," Jean told her. "It's just that you're way ahead of the expectations I have for you."

"Well, then it's time to reassess your goals for me."

It was the first international victory for the junior Lopez, and it made her want to work even harder to keep up with us.

It was a great trip, but not quite perfect. Our team received a bomb threat during the competition. We had to go back to our hotel and watch on TV as our teammate Heidi Gilbert climbed onto the podium without us there to cheer for her. Home, home.

In 1999, I moved up to the senior division to try to make the national team and get to my first senior world championships. In the finals I beat Jin Suh, who was twenty-five at the time, so there was just a little disparity in experience. His son is competing now. It was only my second time in the senior division. I threw my first triple kick in competition—three roundhouse kicks in a row—to score a key point in the match. It seemed he had cut a lot of weight for that bantamweight division. He looked fatigued near the end of the fight, so I kept the pressure on and tried not to let him catch a breath. In the last thirty seconds, I was up by a couple of points and I knew he didn't have enough to catch up. I was really proud that I made the team at the same age as Jean. Of course, Steven made it at fifteen, so I was still a couple of years behind.

Steven couldn't compete in worlds in Edmonton that year, because he had a broken hand, so it was up to me to win a medal for Team Lopez.

Jean still wasn't selected to be the coach in my corner. That assignment was in the hands of Kim Dodson-Peck, a former fighter who did a good job with me in Edmonton. She understood my comfort level with Jean and she knew to tell me to look at him on the side for my instructions.

I looked at worlds as an experience. It was the most difficult competition in taekwondo, and I didn't necessarily think I'd win the whole thing. Jean wanted to build my confidence. He reminded me I trained with the best and had beaten some good people. "Don't give anyone too much respect," he told me. Steven came along to watch, even though he was injured and unable to compete.

The competition draw came out the day before the competition, and I remember people looking at the brackets that listed who would fight whom and telling me how tough they looked. I beat a guy from Sweden in my first match. I had a tough fight next with Mehdi Asl Bibak, the defending World Cup champion from Iran. He was as tall as Steven and he came from a powerhouse team. I got off to a slow start and fell behind, 2–0, in the first round. In the second round, I noticed that he was getting tired. Maybe he had trouble making weight before the match, but his aggressiveness completely vanished once he had his early lead. I kept after him, as he kept moving back and not fighting. He started building up deductions for not fighting and was two half-point deductions away from being disqualified for having six half-point deductions. My strategy in the third round was simple: Make him fight or get him disqualified. I rushed him as soon as the third round started. He caught me with a good roundhouse kick to the face, but I kept the heat on. The ref gave him another kyong-go, so now he figured he had to fight back. It may not have showed, but I was getting exhausted, too. I kept kicking and trying to cut off his escapes. If he didn't quit soon, I was going to drop, myself. Finally, he backed away one too many times. The ref gave him his final kyong-go and he dropped to his knees in disappointment. I put my finger up in the air and barely enough energy for my trademark post-victory back-flip after the match. I had just beaten my toughest opponent yet. Even today it remains one of the proudest moments of my career, because I did whatever it took to win.

I lost the semifinal against Ko Dae-kyu from Korea. He really outclassed me, the way he played with the distance between us and timed every kick just right. Each time I tried to counter, he was just out of reach. I knew pretty early on in the fight that I really didn't have an answer for him. I broke my left thumb blocking a kick at the end of the fight, and I lost 4–0. The doctors there reset my thumb and put a splint on it after I picked up my bronze medal in person. Wow, a world medal felt heavier than I expected. This wasn't a six-foot-tall trophy, but it was certainly an impressive ornament, and nothing was going to keep me from picking up my first world medal in person. I still see the after-effects of that injury today. If I give people a sort of go-get-'em signal, my left thumb goes back way too far.

The first qualifier for the Olympic trials took place the following January. I won that one once I cut some pounds from my national team class at bantamweight (a hundred and thirty-six pounds), down to a hundred and twenty-seven. That year, I beat Juan Moreno, the two-time Olympic silver medalist. He had beaten Dae Sung Lee at seventeen, and now I beat him at the same age. Unfortunately, I let my seventeen-year-old mouth get a little ahead of me. I was talking to a reporter from the *Colorado Springs Gazette* and trying to express my excitement. I told the reporter that Juan had been the man, but now I had beaten the man, so I must be the man. I shouldn't have said it, but I did. The next day, they posted the article at the entrance to the competition. I heard Juan saw it and was very upset about it. I can't blame him for feeling that, and I know he was just waiting for a chance to get even.

After each competition, I usually ask a member of the medical staff to help me look after any aches and pains I have from the competition. They gave me ice to put under my left knee, because I had a bruise there. Usually you keep the ice on for fifteen minutes or so. Since nobody had told me when to remove the ice pack, I just kept it on for an hour or so, before I finally asked when I could take it off. "Oh," the trainer said, "you were supposed to take that off a long time ago." Once I did, I felt like my foot couldn't move. I went back to the hotel to take a shower, and I still couldn't move my foot up and down. I had frozen part of my leg and caused damage to a nerve. I needed surgery a week later to release the pressure on the nerve.

Once I got back into training, I had to be careful about how I lifted up my leg. If I tried to run on it, I would end up tripping on my own feet. I went to rehab in the time leading up to team trials and didn't feel a hundred percent prepared.

In May four or five months later, I grew a lot and I had to cut even more pounds to make a hundred and twenty-seven. That was a lot for me, because at that age I didn't have much fat at all. By May I was up to a hundred and fifty-two, so it was really a steep cut to make one twenty-seven. I didn't fight nearly as well as I did in January. I fought Juan again at the Olympic team trials that year and—careful what you wish for—I lost. It was the first time I can remember being really nervous at a competition to the point that it affected me. It was the very first match of the whole Olympic trials and it felt overwhelming. For some reason, it was even bigger than the world championships. I didn't fight as I usually do. I felt slow and heavy. Juan scored early on with a spinning hook kick and then kept beating me off the clinch a few times. He won easily, and he made a lot of noise afterward because he beat me. Juan then beat Jason Torres and made the Olympic team. It was a double blow. Because of the stress I had put on my left ankle in compensating for the nerve damage under my knee, I developed bone spurs there and had to get another surgery after the team trials.

I handled the personal post-Olympic letdown pretty well, partly because I still knew I had my best years in front of me. That fall, I started going to college. I was always interested in business and the concept of money. Every semester I took twelve hours or four classes, so I would be able to graduate in five years, while still training full-time. I had to keep a full load, because I was on academic scholarship at the University of St. Thomas in Houston. They have an excellent business school with small classes. I had thought about Rice, but it seemed too big. I thought about doing information management systems, but I've never been into computers. I liked my accounting classes, because the information in them was completely objective. There are no referees standing on the side to tell you that five actually equals four. I also enjoyed my history classes and seeing how civilizations have started and ended. I did an internship at a firm that had me make cold calls to prospective clients. I was used to saying, "Hello, sir, might I be able to interest you in . . . Sir? Sir, are you still there?" I also took a theater course that got the better of Mark the Great and Mark the Showman. I always liked acting and admired the work it takes to be an actor. I had to do a monologue for one assignment and I picked a very challenging one. I stayed up late trying to memorize it. The next day the lights came on and I was like a deer in headlights. I got through the first line. Then I froze. I asked the teacher if I could look at my script, but it didn't help. I whiffed. If it had only been a scene from a kung fu film with Chuck Norris.

CHAPTER 8

From Garage to Penthouse

by Steven Lopez

When I was thirteen, I won the U.S. Open Taekwondo Championships, my first experience fighting people from other countries. I went from local to regional to national and international fights. The U.S. Open convinced me that I was pretty good. Instead of just beating a guy from down the block or even Brownsville, now I was beating a guy from Mexico. Hmm, I thought, that covers a lot of people, and I was still able to win. Maybe I have a future in this, like my brother.

In 1993, I went to Korea for my first overseas trip. I thought it was really cool to go to the place where the sport originated. I was only fourteen, traveling to another country and culture. The fact that I was winning these smaller local and regional meets still didn't give me a perspective on how good I could become. But if I was going to the other side of the world with the U.S. team, I knew I had to be good. I wasn't just comparing myself to the kid down the block; I was putting my skills on the line with the rest of the world. This was what I was talking about. I missed a lot of dances, movies, hangout nights with my friends, and I never regretted it, but the chance to go on this trip just confirmed that decision and gave me the feeling I had arrived.

I also loved the team aspect: comparing apparel, standing tall with your friend as you put on the USA T-shirts. I won my competition there. My friend Jason Torres and I both won our bouts and we were fired up about it. Heck, yeah, these guys were the best, and we surprised them. I remember looking over at the Korean coaches yelling at their fighters because they expected their guys to destroy us. It was a great feeling of victory, even if I did come back with a broken left arm from punching one of the guys too hard. It was also a challenge for our guys, because we really didn't have a coach in our corner. The U.S. team assigned us some Korean American coaches who didn't necessarily speak great English or know much about our individual strengths and weaknesses. That meant that we were really on our own. With Jean away at the Olympic training center, I spent a lot of time training on my own. My dad helped with training and so did Jesse Torres, Jason's dad. They were both enthusiastic and supportive, but it wasn't the same as having a coach who had been trained in the specifics of the sport.

In 1994, our team went to George Town in the Cayman Islands. On one gorgeous day, Jean and I went to Stingray City to go for a swim. Jean has a fear of everything, so he wore two life jackets. I swear he has a fear of dangerous things like oxygen and grass. Well, not really, but he didn't want to go scuba diving. I said, "Jean you can snorkel; you just float on top of the water." I didn't wear any preservers. I actually swam among the stingrays. Looking back now at what happened with Steve Irwin, the Australian guy who died from bites in the ocean a few years ago, I probably wasn't being too smart. At one point I felt a huge shadow. I looked up and it was a huge stingray, and it kind of freaked me out.

The trip to the World Cup at the Cayman Islands was surreal. Just a year before, I had made my first junior team, and here I was on the senior national team. I was on the trip with my brother, so of the sixteen people on the national team, two of us were from the Lopez family. Most of the rest of the guys were training along with Jean at the USOTC, and most were twenty-three or twenty-four years old. Sure,

I didn't have much in common with the older guys, but having Jean there made it pretty easy to get along with people. Jean was very popular with his teammates, who all respected him, so we were kind of a package, and any group conversations usually included me. I would have been a fish out of water without my brother. It also helped that the competition felt pretty relaxed. It was set in an outdoor pavilion surrounded by palm trees. That seemed to cut the tension for me.

In my first bout, I fought Juan Ramos, a two-time world champion at the finweight level, the lightest level. Juan is only about five-five, and I was already five-eleven at the time. I was victorious, using my extra height and length to my advantage, keeping him away from me and frustrating him for most of the bout.

Then I fought Gergely Salim, the Danish world champion from 1991 and Olympic champ from 1992. I remember everyone, including my brother, being nervous about my getting onto the mat with Gergely. Jean always used to shield me from negative thoughts. When I asked Jean how tough Gergely would be, he told me, "Aw, he's from Denmark. How good can he be?" Of course, I already knew Gergely's history and the fact that the Danes had some great fighters. When I was set to fight Gergely, I promised myself I would earn people's respect. Everyone is going to notice me today, I told myself, even if this guy beats me. I took it to Gergely in that match, made some mistakes and lost 3–1. I didn't have the arsenal to beat him. I was still happy with the performance I gave, because I knew I had more to learn. Gergely was clearly the more experienced fighter, but I kept coming after him and didn't back down. I tried to make it into a real fight. I fell on him, hit him accidentally/on purpose after one break and just tried to show him I wasn't afraid of his résumé.

As I started to get better over the next few years, whenever I would see Gergely or other members of the Danish team, they would always tell me they knew I had a great future in the sport because of that one match.

I knew I was on my way to being one of the best in the world after that meet. I could gauge that from that one championship. These were men—tiny men, but they were still stronger men. I was a Bambi out there. I didn't have the strength, technique or the strategy they did.

It was hard not having Jean around to guide me on an everyday basis. He would fly into junior nationals to coach me, but at the local tournaments, either my dad or Jesse, Jason's dad, would be in the corner. I would call Jean and he would give me details about taekwondo workouts and track workouts. He'd send me videos through the mail, showing us techniques. We'd buy Sang Lee videos that showed us the details of Olympic-style movements and kicks.

The next year, we went to the Pan Am Games in Mar del Plata, Argentina. At the time, the finweight class was a hundred and ten pounds. At sixteen, I had just gone through a growth spurt, and at six feet tall, I still had to get down to a hundred and ten pounds. I was at one thirty before the fight, and I didn't perform very well there because I had lost so much weight. At the time, we weighed in on the morning of competition, so anyone cutting a lot of weight really felt it when he competed. I made weight, competed two hours later, and I couldn't feel my legs. I lost my first match. Even cutting my natural weight, I would have been at one eighteen. The last eight pounds were all water weight. My choices of food for the three days leading up to competition were either a slice of watermelon or a cup of water and a few grapes. I was overtraining in the six weeks leading up to the meet. Besides my two daily taekwondo workouts, I was biking, running or just doing something extra. I would wear sweat suits so I could sweat more. I would eat small portions of food: a small bowl of cereal, a little yogurt, half an apple or a slice of bread with turkey. Anyone have a Dorito they can spare?

I first had to play the role of older brother and leader when I was seventeen. I had never really done that before, but when Jean left for the OTC, I got it. I started looking out for Mark and Diana much more than I ever had. I actually made a conscious decision to be more responsible and supportive as the elder brother in the house. Maybe I should have been that way all along, but even as I was following Jean's lead, I wanted to be big enough to have my own identity in the family.

When I wasn't mature enough to figure out how to do that, I would find that identity by sometimes picking on my siblings, something Jean, as the eldest, never did. Once he left and I was the eldest, something clicked. I got it. I had a chance to fulfill that really important role I watched Jean fulfill. Nobody sat me down and told me to change, but I did. I tried to help Mark and Diana out with their work, take extra time to be a sounding board. When Marky signed up for straight honors classes one year, I sat down and talked to him about taking some of the load off his shoulders and settling for one or two of them while he was also training. At the same time I encouraged him that if I could make the national team at fifteen, he could do it just as fast, if not faster. I started taking Marky with me when I went to play basketball with my friends. I had done that before, but only when my parents insisted on it. Now I was volunteering. After all, it was the eldest brother's job.

I was also in the Spanish National Honor Society and the regular National Honor Society in high school. As members, we had to do charity work, such as car washes to raise money for a certain cause, or I would go to elementary schools to read to younger kids. I wanted to get involved in other clubs, like the debate team, in high school, but I just didn't have time because of my training.

By 1996, I was six feet tall, competing at a hundred and forty pounds, so I was pretty skinny. I knew a lot of the guys I competed against would be a lot faster and usually stronger. But my advantage would be my reach. If those shorter guys tried to go off the line (i.e., to the side) against me, I would just defend by picking my knee up so they would hit my shin. It would nullify what they wanted to do and break their speed. That would force them to double up and triple up with their kicks in order to score against me, and that moment of indecision would leave them open to a counterattack. Once your competitor starts to second-guess himself, you have a huge advantage. That made the competition very simple for me. There were two goals in every match: to score and not get scored upon. If I was up by one point, I could use that defensive technique to smother the other fighters. Jean taught me I could jam up, move back, move to the side and stay out of their range with my reach advantage, or lift up my leg. Nobody is so fast that you can't see a kick coming at you. The trick is to know how to avoid it, block it or counter it before your opponent can score against you.

I took that approach with me that year to the Pan Am Championships in Havana. That meet included only taekwondo athletes from the Americas region, and was different from the Pan Am Games that included all sports and took place each time in the year before the Olympics. I fought a Cuban in the finals, but I felt as if I were fighting the entire crowd. Some people are naturally freaked out by having the crowd so set against them; I love the adversity of having all that noise raining down on you. I remember thinking how much fun it was going to be to shut all those people up. I liked the people there, but I really loved the test of quieting the roar. I beat the Cuban pretty easily, keeping my distance and making him commit his first moves when he tried to reach me. He tried to use his quickness by doubling and tripling up on his kicks, but I would crowd him, jam him up, block his kicks, alter the speed of my kicks and just generally frustrate him as much as possible. Each time I scored a point or negated one of his attacks, I could hear the steam go out of the crowd, almost as if I were walking farther and farther away from a loud stereo system. I loved it.

Later that year I went to the World Junior Championships in Barcelona. The guy I fought in the semifinals from Lesotho was one of the toughest foes I ever had. He had amazing stamina. His technique was very poor except for an ax kick. He must have been a boxer, because he really knew how to punch. He beat fighters from Mexico and Spain, rallying to overcome big deficits both times, before he fought me. The Spaniard was running around, putting his hands on his knees, and the Spanish coach finally threw in the towel.

Our fight was a war. I did enough to get my points, but the hard part was surviving the punishment he gave out with his punches. A lot of them didn't hit the target area, so he didn't catch up on the score-card. Our family generally has great stamina, but Lesotho is at high altitude, so the guy just didn't get tired.

I scored one of my first victories against a Korean fighter in the final, but I tore two or three ligaments in my right ankle early in the match. I saw one opportunity to throw a defensive roundhouse kick. I landed the kick, fell to the floor, got up and spent the rest of the match lifting up my front leg and keeping him away. When you do that defensive roundhouse kick, because of the impact with the body, instead of landing forward, you're already going backward. The force of the kick causes you to ricochet off the opponent and you land in your original stance as you're going backward instead of forward. I just landed all my weight on that leg and rolled back on it and tore the ligaments.

In 1997, I won gold at the World Cup in Cairo. No American had won that since Herb Perez in 1987. I fought another Iranian. For some reason I always seemed to fight the host athletes: I fought the Egyptian in the finals. The crowd brought out the drums. They had a loud band. It was hard for me to make weight (a hundred and forty pounds) because I had grown to six-two. The whole tournament really tired me out, so after the semifinals, I found a spot in the holding area to go take a nap. I figured I'd wake up in twenty or thirty minutes, but before I knew it, the nap turned into a long sleep.

Jean was starting to panic, because he hadn't seen me since he left me alone to sleep in the back. The Egyptian guy was already on the mat when Jean finally shook me awake. I was completely foggy when I threw on my chest protector. I felt as if I were half-asleep. You know what it feels like when you set an alarm clock to music and it wakes you up from a really deep sleep? The noise feels so much louder than it actually is because the room was so quiet seconds ago and you were just completely knocked out. That's what I felt like. The drums in the stands felt like they were beating right against my forehead.

Once I cleared my head, I really needed to think quickly. I scored with a defensive move, a backward slide step followed by a defensive roundhouse kick. It really frustrated the Egyptian, because he didn't recognize my style or know what to do against me. He was so jazzed up because of the crowd that he made some very forced and predictable attacks. It was my first victory at a major world international competition, and one of the most exotic locations I had ever seen.

As a boy, I had read about the Sphinx, the pyramids and the mummies, and I was always curious about Egypt. We stayed at the Sheraton in downtown Cairo, right in the heart of one of the world's largest Muslim cities. Each day at five in the morning I'd wake up to the locals chanting their prayers. I'd open the window, see the sun come up and just be amazed at how unified everyone was in the ceremony of their culture. Most of the men wore turbans around their necks. I had a feeling someone important was staying on our floor, because there were guys with machine guns roaming the hallways. The streets were so crowded and you crossed at your own peril. It reminded me of the game Frogger. The roads may have had room for three lanes, but it seemed like the cars ran seven or eight across. The drivers made their own lanes and they drove with two or three inches to spare between their cars and the ones beside them.

I visited the pyramids while I was there, and it was confining going through the tunnels. A teammate of mine named Steven Lee actually swiped a tiny sliver of one of them. We joked with him that he would have a curse on him, and we reminded him of that again the next year when he tore his medial collateral ligament (MCL). He threw the piece away soon after. Still, the rest of us could count our blessings rather than our curses from the trip. The week after we got back to the States, the same tour bus that had taken us around Cairo was attacked by terrorists and sprayed with bullets. Living in Sugar Land, I had been so secluded from all these war stories I'd heard about on the news. For better or worse, my travel was taking me everywhere, even into the heart of battles that were greater than just the ones on taekwondo mats.

On that trip I met the girl I'd consider my first serious girlfriend. We were sitting down in the restaurant of our hotel. Jean looked across the room and pointed out a pretty girl named Kylie who was sitting with the Australian team at another table. I remember thinking she looked like she was around my age, and Jean and some of the other guys on our team encouraged me to go talk to her. By the end of the tournament, we had talked a lot, and it was pretty clear we'd be running up a big phone bill in the next few months.

In December I went to Melbourne to visit Kylie. Over the next two or three years we both made long trips to visit each other. It might seem like an odd thing that the girlfriends I had were from other countries, and they were usually in the sport. But it made sense. For most of the year, I was kind of married to my sport and all the responsibilities that go with training and travel. Then there would be windows, like soon after competitions, when I'd have time to go out, socialize and have fun, so it wasn't unusual for me to meet somebody at the after-parties that followed our major tournaments. I never really had the time to give them what most girls would want in a relationship, because I wasn't as available when those windows closed.

I caught my first whiff of anti-Lopez sentiment at the world trials in 1997. Jason was set to fight the finals against Angel Aresamende, a student who was training with Coach Lee at the OTC. Angel was too injured to fight the match, so he stood down and gave the spot to Jason. Afterward Angel told us that Coach Lee had implored him to fight because he didn't need to do anything other than step into the ring in order to win. This was difficult for Angel to say, but he was an honest guy, and he wanted us to know what we were up against. For those few years, it was almost easier for us to win our international matches than it was for us to win in the United States. Yes, there were some anti–United States sentiments abroad, but the anti-Lopez faction at home was an even tougher opponent. In a weird way, that may have helped us out by making us stronger. We knew we were never going to win a close match, so we had to win decisively in order to get credit for it.

I earned my way to the world championship in Hong Kong at those trials, and I thought since I had won the World Cup, I could be the first U.S. male to win the world championship. People told me it was more difficult to win than the World Cup, because there were more fighters from countries you'd never heard of. You have six or seven matches and it's like a tough-man contest. Sometimes the winner is the one who is actually the least injured. I may have overtrained for worlds. I thought that more was better, and I was pretty tired at that meet. Dae Sung Lee was our coach for the competition. Two weeks before that, we were in Korea. He had us kick for two hours at a time, and my body was spent. I reached the finals there, but lost again to Jesper Roesen of Denmark. He was doing doubles and triples and he beat me pretty decisively. I felt horrible because my dad and Jesse had flown to Hong Kong to watch me lose. Dad hadn't even gone to Egypt. I remember telling him how sorry I was that he came all that way to watch me lose. He told me he was still proud of me, but I wasn't satisfied.

Back home, I was determined to work as hard as I needed to, and Jean was still emphasizing a high-volume, high-intensity training approach. He'd have our team fight two-on-one, sometimes three-on-one. The only rule Jean imposed was that the guys who were on a team couldn't kick to the face. To build my stamina, Jean also organized these sorts of relay fights during practice, in which I would fight four guys for a minute each with only a few seconds in between. By the time I got to the fourth guy, I was really tired and forcing myself to concentrate and not lose sharpness. We'd wake up in the morning, run to Kempner a mile and a half away, run a mile there, do sprints there and then run back home. We would do frog jumps around the block in my neighborhood during the dog days of summer. I wanted to do them perfectly. I expected to do them perfectly. Unless I was shooting a basketball with my brothers, I obsessed about technique when I did just about everything.

Jean had us doing squat jumps. It took a lot of muscle endurance to execute four sets of twenty-five jumps. I'd get after myself to do them perfectly, so Jean had no form adjustments to suggest. I think I had a higher pain threshold, being able to go higher and longer than all the other kids. Jean had us do hops while in the squat position, when we wouldn't fully extend our knees. He would have a mental competition with us and see who had the strongest mind to be able to endure the pain of doing that. If you can do that for a minute, you're in pretty good shape. If you can do it for three or four minutes, you're really in fantastic shape. One day, Jason Torres and I just kept going and going and we were doing it for fifteen minutes. Jean had to stop it because he knew we weren't going to be able to walk after we were done.

We jumped and did duckwalks with knees bent up a hill that we actually rented so we could train on it. In the summer, we would run five miles from Highway 90 to Kempner in the middle of the afternoon. At the end of some of those runs, I felt as if I were in the Sahara Desert. Jean and I would start our mornings with every intention of jogging a mile. By then we'd be sprinting. We just couldn't help ourselves. From a physical standpoint, some of the training was useful and some may have been overkill, but at least I knew at that age that there was no other kid anywhere who was training as hard as I was. I was pushing myself to exhaustion regularly. It gave me the confidence to believe that when that guy standing across from me in the ring was on his fifth or sixth gear, when he was practically maxed out, I still had a lot more to give.

The Olympic Games in Sydney were two years away, and I'll never forget the day Jean gave me some great news: The IOC had decided to add taekwondo to the list of medal sports at the Olympics for the first time. At last. It was invigorating, because I always loved competing against fighters from other countries. I loved traveling and seeing other cultures. I loved the way my sport brought people together at the same time I could test my skills against the very best in the world. We stood around saying, "Heck, yeah, this is what we've worked for. Let's do this." Nothing was guaranteed for any of us, but at least we were closer to realizing a dream. In those few weeks after the announcement, I thought a lot about what Jean had gone through and about what he was giving up for us. I thought about how this thing called the Olympics gave him the freedom to dream about something big when the rest of us never really knew what it was. I thought about how he was taking my progress as his responsibility for a second stage of his life, and how my own responsibility of looking out for Mark and Diana had helped me grow up and become a more mature young man. I never stopped thinking about my parents. Nobody knew if any of us would ever get to the Olympics, much less win medals, but any one of us who accomplished anything would be doing it for all of us. Time to let the Olympic music play in the background.

I had planned all along to get a scholarship to attend medical school and someday become a plastic surgeon. I was good at math and science, and several people on my mother's side were doctors. I knew all the bones, all the muscles. The body intrigued me, especially since taekwondo was such a physically demanding activity. Once we found out that taekwondo was going to be an Olympic sport, I was really conflicted about what to do. I went to Warren Junior College for a semester, and then I received a full scholarship to attend the University of Houston. But taekwondo isn't a college sport, like football or basketball. Granted, teachers are used to working with students in those team sports to help them manage their studies while still pursuing their athletics. But I didn't expect to get as much slack for training in my individual, lesser-known sport. With all of my travel and competitions, I decided to concentrate on training until 2000. Then I would stop and pursue my medical career.

After the 1997 World Cup, when Jean lost again to Marquez from Spain, I felt a little guilty because Jean was the reason I was winning; yet he never had a coach. He had to develop his own workouts, but he couldn't really push himself, since there was nobody overseeing him. You're always better if someone is there to pace you on your runs or double-check your technique in the gym. Jean was blackballed in the United States, and at the same time he saw me doing well. He gave himself a hundred percent to his siblings. In his gym I felt as if I were in Club Med, in the lap of luxury. We still didn't have mats—it was just carpet on cement—but we actually had a facility just for us.

It wasn't a washeteria/garage training facility. We felt like a real professional team: David Montalvo, Jason Torres, Angelo Decamps, Javier Bolivar, Paris Amani. These were good people. We couldn't even do certain kicks back when we were training in the garage. We'd have eight people in there. I look back at how ridiculous that was.

Paris Amani had been a member of the national team. By the time Paris came to Houston, he had already trained with us and knew what we were like, even though he was still training with us. Paris had moved to Austin to work with Dell computers. Jean asked if he was happy with what he was doing. Paris said no; he felt as if he were in a cage. Jean told him he was opening up the gym. He offered Paris a fifty-percent share if Paris would run the gym when Jean left to compete or train somewhere else. They were partners for more than a decade. It wasn't really a business for Jean; it was a place for us to train.

Our fighters still needed to qualify for the places for our country at the Olympics by winning either an Olympic qualifying tournament in Croatia or a second-chance regional qualifier in Miami. The athletes who gained spots wouldn't necessarily fight at the Olympics, because they would have to win the Olympic trials, but qualifying the place for the country was the first step for all of us. I'm sort of ashamed to admit this, but Jason and I partied in Croatia before we competed. I loved it there, and one night I planned to go to a club to release some energy for a few hours, and those turned into a few more hours. I shouldn't have been surprised that I lost a match to Germany's Aziz Acharki, a very good fighter, but one I knew I should have beaten. I was feeling pressure, and Jean and I were angry that the federation had told us ahead of time that he would be the team coach for the trip, only to replace him with Dae Sung Lee at the last minute. Jason and I felt betrayed by the decision and the drama surrounding it, but honestly, that was a poor excuse. I learned a good lesson, but I felt lousy afterward about the way I had to learn it.

Since I had been eliminated, Jason carried our hopes to get that first spot. He didn't secure the spot, but he also didn't lose a match. His courage at that meet was something I'll never forget. Jason was fighting Luis Garcia from Venezuela when he suffered a broken jaw. It happened in the first round, when Garcia kicked Jason in the back of the head. The momentum of the kick pulled Jason's head down, with his opponent's foot wrapped around Jason's head. Jason fell down on the other guy's knee, breaking his jaw. I didn't realize how bad it was, because the actual kick didn't look that bad. Then we all saw the blood and figured the match would have to be stopped. Maybe Jason didn't know how badly he was hurt. Maybe he just had it in his head that he was going to earn the spot in the Olympics for Team USA no matter what. But amazingly, Jason continued and somehow won the match. Our medical trainer, Trish Bare, was telling him to end the fight, but he wouldn't stop. Jason was choking on his own blood, and each time he bounced up and down, the displaced bottom half of his jaw was bouncing around on its own, because he no longer had any control over it. His unorthodox technique, just discovered at that moment, and his incredible will to win allowed him to prevail. Even though he couldn't fight in the finals, Jason deserved his own gold star for guts. That night they flew him to Italy for surgery. He was drinking his meals through a straw for a while and needed a second surgery when he got back to the States, because the doctors who performed the first one had misaligned the jaw. This time they put a titanium plate in his jaw.

In 1999, Mark and I went back to a university in Korea to train and learn. One day, I looked over and noticed Mark having a tough time with a guy named Sin Joon-sik, one of the local fighters there who was taking it a little rough on him. Nobody was wearing chest protectors or much other equipment, but the guy wasn't letting up. We were supposed to be having a friendly, low-key match, but it was actually very intense. I waited for a stoppage and tapped Mark on the shoulder, letting him know that big brother wanted to jump in. On our first exchange he did an illegal skip kick to my midthigh. On our second exchange, he did the same thing, only a little harder. Now I was getting irritated. I started tapping my thighs to let him know I didn't appreciate what he was doing. On our next exchange, we got into a clinch and he broke out of it with a kick that grazed my head. If I hadn't moved my face at just that moment, he'd have knocked me out. I was pretty ticked off now. I could tell this guy was a good technician, but he didn't seem like a serious fighter. By that I mean he didn't want our not-so-friendly friendly match to turn into a street fight. Too bad. As soon as we came together again, I started punching him as hard as I could until his chest was flattened and tenderized. He kept falling over after each punch, which was a cheap way of avoiding the real combat in each exchange. After one punch, I stood over him and moved my shoulders up and down as if to ask him if he wanted some more. The "friendly" match had gotten so fierce, fighters from our group and theirs stopped what they were doing to come over and watch. We put on a show, and it wouldn't be our last.

I didn't compete at world championships because of a broken arm I sustained during the Pan Am trials in March.

Lesson learned from Croatia, I was back on track at the Pan Am Games in Winnipeg just two weeks later. I faced Alejandro Hernando from Argentina and beat him in the semifinals, 3-1. In the finals, I defeated Luis Benitez of the Dominican Republic, 1-0, in a frustrating match that featured almost no action. Benitez spent half the bout going back, falling off the mat, getting his knee injured, his shin injured. He received five warnings and I kept getting frustrated, thinking, "C'mon, let's fight."

Soon after the match, I started getting some funding from the USOC, because they had a program to support their Olympic athletes for the Sydney Games. I was a step closer to fulfilling my dream of becoming an Olympian.

In October, I competed at the Olympic regional qualifier in Miami. If you didn't qualify at the world qualifier, first, second or third, you would have one more chance to qualify your country for the Olympics by placing in the top two at the regionals. I reached the finals there against Alejandro Hernando of Argentina again. Hernando was a Pan Am champ from 1995, but one I had now beaten several times. We were in the finals, so we were already guaranteed a spot. I had been in Argentina to do seminars for the national team, so I knew him well. Before the final, his coach came up to me and said, "Hey, Steven, congratulations. You know, you're both in the finals, so what's the use of really fighting?" I started taking my stuff off, and then the coach said that it would be a huge honor for the country if Alejandro Hernando could get the gold medal. I wasn't sure what to make of that, so I told him, "Let's just fight." I kind of egged him on by asking if he was afraid of my record. That got him to put his equipment back on pretty quickly.

I went in there without a lot of energy. I don't know what I was thinking, but in the first round, I went with an easy front leg and knocked him down. But as he fell, he threw a spinning hook kick and it hit me. I took a couple of steps on the mat and fell over. I can remember telling myself that I had to get up, but the next thing I knew, Trish was hanging over me, saying, "Steven, it's over." I tried to get up, but I kept seeing stars. Why was I on a stretcher? Why did I have a brace around my neck? Why were there three of everybody? What had just happened? Jean was going crazy trying to get to me. The Argentine coach was crying as he came over to apologize. People were saying they could have dropped a needle in that place because it was so quiet. Once I realized what had happened, I was completely embarrassed and I knew I had brought the result on myself by being cocky. My parents had flown in to see me fight. I knew how nervous my mom would get before fights, and I was sure I had her all worried. As the medical staff was looking at me in the back room, I turned to Jean and just said, "How embarrassing."

That was a good sign.

"Oh, Steven, if you're worried about your ego," he said, "then I know you're all right."

The rest of my body was okay, but my bruised ego stung for a while. The match was also pretty significant, because it reinforced the idea that I should never let down my guard, and because it would be a long time before we got my mom to a match again.

Now that the U.S. team had a berth assured for the Games, my next goal was to earn that place for myself and get on the Olympic team.

On May 20, I certified my spot on the team by beating Tony Graf at the Olympic trials. Tony is very strong and fast. He's a fighter who isn't afraid of battle, and it sometimes takes a while for other guys to figure out where his kicks are going to come from. Tony has a muscular wrestler's body, and I respect his courage. We've fought a dozen or so times and he hasn't beaten me yet. I like to get into his head by smiling at him, talking to him when we're in a clinch. I mean it as gamesmanship and not as a sign of disrespect, but I'll say things like, "You really tried that kick again?" or, "Now would be a good time to go for my face." I know he's thinking those things, but I'm letting him know I'm prepared for exactly what he's trying to do.

Once the clock ran out on the match, I gave Jean a huge hug and we both said, "We did it," a few times. I guess we were, um, speaking on each other's motion. It was the greatest feeling. Our family may have honed its skills in a garage, but we felt like we had just reached the penthouse. I won't say which one of us shed a tear, but his name starts with a J.

CHAPTER 9

Hey, Mom, Guess What?

by Steven Lopez

T he week before the Olympic trials, Jason and I were invited to the U.S. Olympic Media Summit along with other Olympic hopefuls from different sports on the U.S. team. The event just happened to be in Houston that year. The Summit was a relaxed opportunity for reporters to interview us away from the heat of competition, fill up their notebooks and get access to athletes they might not otherwise have a chance to speak with. Think about it: There are twenty-eight sports on the summer Olympic program, and the media outlets can't see competitions in all of them. Usually, this meant that athletes in track and swimming might get good coverage and those in sports like ours might get overlooked. Soon after we first arrived, Cecil Bleiker, the press officer for USA Taekwondo, set up a day of media training with practice questions for us. The next day, we would go into different rooms, sit at different tables and field questions from print reporters first and later from television reporters. Then we went into another room to pose for photographers. Over the next few months, profiles would appear throughout the country about America's Olympic hopefuls. That really helped us get exposure for ourselves and our sports. It was amazing how similar those questions were to the ones Jean would ask me around the garage: "How do you feel about what you've accomplished? What can you do for your sport? How did you get started in taekwondo? How did you become a champion? Are you nervous because it's the first time taekwondo will be a medal sport at the Olympics?" I remember how silly I thought those practice interviews with Jean had been. I always questioned him, but he was right-on. I felt very comfortable in that environment because of what Jean put me through when I thought he was out of his mind. What can I say? Jean was a genius.

Of course, the USTU didn't know this or didn't care. Even though I was the country's best hope to bring us a gold medal in Sydney, they didn't pick him to be the Olympic coach. The coaching selection was based on who was in line and who had paid the most dues. It was never based on merit. I felt cheated, because my brother would be sitting in the stands rather than in my corner, where he should have been. Young-un Cheon was someone I respected. I don't think he was the most qualified person to be the head coach, but I always felt that he wanted his athletes to win and that his heart was in the right place. If there was one coach from that culture I wanted in my chair, I wanted it to be him. Still, he wasn't my coach, he wasn't the man who knew me, and honestly, in spite of his age and experience, he didn't have as much technical knowledge as my brother.

We knew my mom got too nervous to watch us compete. Ever since she saw me get knocked out, she'd found reasons not to come to competitions. I understood that. I wanted her to be in Sydney, but I also didn't want to see her pass out from nerves in the stands. "Steven, I think I'll stay home. I'll be better off lighting candles, praying for you and taking care of Ninja. Who's going to look after Ninja [our dog]?" Of course, we had an entire neighborhood full of people who would have looked after the dog, but I wasn't going to push my mom to go. My dad tried. He bought her a nonrefundable plane ticket to Sydney. I hope it tasted good, because he had to eat it. Still, I understood my mom's feelings. I was okay with them, and I let her know I would still draw strength from her spirit and know that she and the people of Sugar Land were behind me.

On our way to Australia, athletes from all sports went through team processing in San Diego, where we received all our apparel. We had specific clothes for the team that we were supposed to wear at the ceremonies and during warm-ups. Then we also had our choice of T-shirts, sweats, hats, basically whatever we could carry. All of them had the USA logo and the Olympic rings on them. I wish I'd had a truck so I could have driven off with the whole collection.

The next day we were in the air, off to the land down under. I looked over at Jean just at the moment our plane landed in Sydney. He looked back and smiled. It was a just-pinch-me moment for both of us. The athletes received our official credentials, the laminated photo IDs that signified our access areas as athletes and let people know which sport we represented. Then we went to check in at the Olympic Village, the series of housing areas for athletes, coaches and support staff. It was a bit like the Olympic training center, except that this was specifically built for these Olympics, and it was like a self-contained town. On our way to our apartment, we saw a long line of roughly two hundred flags, one for each nation represented at the Games. Some teams that had already arrived had draped flags outside their balconies. The village was like the United Nations. Walk into the cafeteria and you could find even more types of cuisine than you'd see in the food courts at the largest malls. And this food was healthy food. Listen to the small talk in the halls and you could learn how to say "hello," "please" and "thank you" in virtually every language spoken in the entire world. You might see a three-hundred-pound weightlifter standing in line next to an eighty-pound gymnast. There were men, women, ten thousand athletes and coaches of every race, color, creed, religion and sport. I can't even think of a more inclusive group of people anywhere on the planet. These were the best of the best in every Olympic sport, and I was one of them.

The village had medical rooms, massage rooms, weight rooms, a library, a bank, an Olympic museum, a travel department, a post office, a translation service, a cinema, religious centers of different faiths, an Internet room where athletes could communicate for free with their friends and families, a photo store, an apparel store, an electronics store, a convenience store, a place for athletes to trade Olympic pins that our federations gave us before we arrived, an office to request free tickets for other events that were set aside for athletes, a TV room with satellite feeds from each of the stadiums and arenas that were holding events, a game room to blow off some steam and several places to pick up freebies from sponsors. The village was heavily fortified and surrounded by security. We passed through metal detectors when we went in and out, and the athletes had dozens of shuttle buses dedicated to taking us to and from our practice and competition venues. I walked through the village like a kid in a candy store, and as I was trying to absorb it all, I found myself smiling at nothing in particular.

I had a chance to attend the spectacular opening ceremonies. The Olympic stadium there seated more than a hundred thousand people. You know what it feels like when a warm front passes overhead and you just know a thunderstorm is about to hit? That was the feeling I had right before I was about to walk out. After all the athletes were in place, they played a song called "Heroes Live Forever," while volunteers pulled a huge white canopy above our heads. It covered the entire infield, so spectators could see only the shadows of our hands poking at the underside of the canopy. We couldn't see it as this thing was rolling on top of us, but they were projecting images of Olympic athletes from each sport onto the canopy. That was cool. I felt like a little kid. All the athletes were looking at one another because none of us knew what was about to happen.

Since my competition wasn't scheduled until near the end of the Games, I took one morning well before I fought to see a preliminary session of track and field, where I saw Maurice Greene burn up his lane the day before he won the gold medal in the hundred-meter dash.

Inside and out of the village, the Australian people were warm and welcoming to all us. If you've never been there, they really do say, "G'day, mate," to almost anyone.

The only tough part was walking past the pasta, pizza and Mc-Donald's stations, knowing I had to lose twelve pounds for the weigh-in before I fought. I did try kangaroo jerky while I was there. I don't even like beef jerky and this didn't taste much better, but as long as they weren't serving Benji from Korea, hey, why not be like the natives? I ate crocodile for the first time, too. It's tender like duck and probably a little greasier than chicken. I was used to having to cut weight, and each morning I would rub on baby oil, then throw on a tank top, long johns and a heavy jacket. In ninety-degree heat with a high sun, it's easy to drop weight when you're dressed for winter. I kept my meals to small portions of soups, salads and turkey without the skin. We worked out twice a day. Teams from several countries, including ours, had their own dedicated gyms and areas for workouts. I did double daily sessions in Sydney, just as I had at home, and a couple of the volunteers who saw the taekwondo athletes training at our area, the high-performance center, told me they were sure I had the best VO2 max (maximum oxygen uptake) levels of anyone they had seen.

As the days passed and more athletes finished with their events, I would look outside my room and hear people singing and celebrating. Think about it: You have ten thousand young, healthy, active people who have been living like monks for much of their lives for months. Many of them haven't been able to eat what they want, stay up as late as they want, see their families, pursue relationships, enjoy their hobbies, even keep what most people would consider normal school and work schedules, all because they've put those things on hold to train for the Olympics.

My family spent a lot of time at the special hospitality room that AT&T had arranged for the athletes' families during the Games. Mark was fattening up on alligator and shrimp. Yes, alligator. You know, tastes like chicken. For the first time, he also went to the casino, where the minimum age was eighteen, and won a hundred and fifty dollars at blackjack in about a couple of hours. Diana, my dad and some friends went to a zoo, where they got to see kangaroos and koalas. Then they walked around Sydney's famous opera house. Me? I was counting hours and minutes, just waiting to get busy on the mat. I was so glad I had Jean there as my training partner. Marky also prepared me for the fights in Sydney. He'd punch me, drive me and kick my butt. Sure, I'd face some tough competition once the tournament began, but I think Mark was the toughest and most skilled foe I faced all year, even if we were just practicing.

In the days before the competition, I took several requests for interviews from various media outlets. Each of the sports had its own dedicated media officer during the Games. In most cases, that officer was someone who worked in the office of the sport's national governing body. In the case of the bigger sports, the USOC might have an additional representative working with the athletes from that sport in order to sort through requests and schedules. That officer would also have to coordinate with however many sports agents represented individual athletes. In the case of the men's basketball Dream Team, for instance, this involved an entire roster full of agents. Almost every athlete in track and field had an agent, and a good number of them from the other sports did, too. Our team had Cecil, the officer and schedule juggler who took care of the entire team by himself. This may have been a manageable job during the winter, because we just didn't get very many requests outside our local area, but the Olympics were different. Including print and broadcast representatives, there were almost ten thousand reporters at the Olympics—as many people with media passes as there were with athlete passes. Every athlete in every sport was getting requests for interviews. Then we had local radio stations calling from back home. Every single taekwondo-related request went through Cecil. He tried to accommodate the big news outlets and people from our local area, like David Barron of the *Houston Chronicle*, who had spent time with us in the past. After all, it was the one time during the four-year Olympic cycle when we could really count on getting some exposure for ourselves and our sport. At the same time, he had to make sure not to overload us and interfere with the very reason we were there—to prepare for the biggest meet of our lives.

As great as the experience was, there were times leading up to the competition when I began to get stressed out. I started to keep a journal that Paris had given me a few weeks out from the Games, but I stopped writing in it about ten days before. I intended it to be a shorthand log about how I was feeling before and after workouts, how many hours I worked out, how many kicks I did at practice, what I ate, how many pounds I lost and how much I slept. But I also found myself writing about my nerves and therefore getting more nervous. The writing made the anticipation more intense, and I needed to be able to sleep at night and not burn up a lot of restless energy.

I didn't sleep well at all the night before competition. I had to make weight the next morning, and the nerves and weight cutting depleted most of my sugar levels. I went to sleep at midnight and woke up at four in the morning with a bad stomachache, mostly from thirst. I couldn't afford to drink because I didn't want to add water weight, so I tossed and turned for a while. Finally I woke up and walked to the gym while it was still dark in order to weigh myself. When I found that I was a pound underweight, I let out a big, "Yes," and started slowly drinking water, careful to monitor each tenth of a pound so I wouldn't exceed the limit of sixty-eight kilos. I stopped at eight-tenths of a pound and went back to my room to toss and turn some more. I never made it back to sleep.

I didn't feel as well prepared as I wanted to that day, so I was lucky that my first match against Claudio Nolano from Italy was pretty easy. He was much shorter and I had a huge reach advantage. His kicks usually fell short. I was able to keep my distance pretty well and defeated him 7–0.

In the second match, I had to fight Carlo Massimino from Australia. Those were always the toughest matches. I had been through many similar challenges of fighting the hometown favorites in their backyards, whether I was in Egypt, Cuba, Canada or now in Australia. The crowd there was really loud. They have a tradition at every sporting event in which half the crowd yells, "Aussie, Aussie, Aussie," and the other half responds by yelling, "Oy, oy, oy." I have no idea what it means, but it's their version of our fans yelling, "USA, USA." Each time he kicked, the crowd roared, even if I blocked the kick or it missed the target. In his previous match, the noise pressured the judges to award points, even if the guy hadn't actually scored, so Massimino might have expected me to keep my distance, as I had in some previous matches. Instead I attacked as often as I could. He was an acrobatic fighter who would try a lot of spinning hook kicks and other low-percentage kicks that got the crowd into the match but weren't necessarily very effective. Whenever he missed, he simply covered up his mistake by falling down and getting the referee to stop the action. We were even, 1–1, at the end of the match. These days, fighters can break ties by competing into a sudden-death period until one fighter wins by scoring the next point. But at the time, referees broke ties by evaluating who they thought was the superior fighter during the match. Not for a second did I have any doubts that I was the aggressor, but I was worried about not having the home-mat advantage. I stood in the center of the mat as the referee grabbed each of our arms and I waited for him to raise mine, until he did. There were a few whistles in the crowd, but even the fans seemed to know their guy had lost.

Even among all the screaming Aussies, I could still hear Diana. She had the guys with the bullhorns by an octave and a half. She's much more nervous watching than fighting, because she can't control anything. Back then she couldn't control her emotions, so she would say just about anything on her mind. She was yelling at the top of her lungs, and she tried to start a "USA" chant that never really caught on. She had the fake USA tattoo on her forehead. When you're emotional you don't really remember what you said, so I hope our relations with our good friends down under are still okay.

I had a long break before my next match, but I had the kind of awful feeling you get when you're cramming for an exam, like you're almost too tired to sleep, if that makes any sense. The feeling of physical fatigue was keeping me awake, so it wouldn't allow me to fight the feeling of drowsiness by taking a nap. Instead I sat in the middle of the training area and stared at a TV monitor. I munched on a peanut-butter-and-jelly sandwich and dozed for ten minutes before waking up again, worried that I wasn't sure if I had anything left for my semifinal. Even though he didn't have an access pass, Jean managed to smile, wave and talk his way into the holding area briefly, before he had to go back upstairs. I really could communicate my feelings only to him, because I didn't have confidence that anyone else on our staff would understand or know what to do. He told me to be strong and have faith, so that was what I did.

After Jean went upstairs, I let faith take over and just started praying. I had prayed for about ten minutes when I started to feel this rush of fresh blood running through my veins, almost like an infusion of strength I needed to sustain me. At that point I started to cry. Maybe it was because I felt God looking after me. Did I really deserve that? Was I actually worthy of that kind of help? Weren't there times I had done something wrong, like teased my sister or partied in Croatia or been human enough that I deserved the humanity of defeat? I didn't know how or why, but I really felt much stronger after that—calmer, more at peace, yet stronger.

I got up and started to walk around, still feeling some mild stomach pains even with the burst of strength. As I reached for my stomach, a member of the Australian delegation whom I had never met saw me and said, "Here, drink some Coke." Now, sugary sodas aren't always a good thing for you when you're competing, but with my low blood sugar and lactic acid building up in my body, the few sips of that syrup formula Coke has really helped me get rid of the ache. Hey, thanks, mate, whoever you are.

In the semis, I had a chance to avenge the loss I suffered to Germany's Aziz Acharki at the world qualifier in Croatia. He was the world champ in the lightweight division in 1995, and he was still fighting really well. He had just won his second-round match by a score of 15–1, so I knew I was in for a scrap. I was much more focused against him than I had been in Croatia. I fought pretty defensively against Aziz. I jammed, kept him away, caught him by going off the line and beat him 2–0.

Once I walked onto the mat, I saw Jean running around to get the best view of the ring. For the most part, it wasn't possible for him to give me any sort of coded instructions that I could understand from the stands once the matches began. But I could see him clap, pump his fists or put his hands in front of him, palms down, as if to tell me to relax.

At one point during the competition, the camera panned to me between rounds as I was nudging Coach Cheon out of the way in order to find Jean and see whatever signals he was giving me from the stands. I'm the kind of guy who wants to hear things as they are. Tell me what I'm doing right, what I'm doing wrong and what I need to fix in order to be at my best. Don't sugarcoat it; just give it to me straight. I don't need compliments; I need information. Coach Cheon meant well, but I think the moment was making him nervous. He was hard to understand anyway because of the language barrier, but he became more frantic once the match started, and he wasn't really able to offer any insights. It sort of came off as me saying, "Get out of my face and let me see my brother." I didn't mean for the gesture to be disrespectful, because Coach Cheon really had our best interests at heart. But these were the Olympics, and I didn't have time for niceties. I needed to win, and I needed whatever strength and instruction I could get from Jean at that moment in order to help my country win a gold medal.

An hour passed between the semis and the finals. I was already guaranteed a medal, but I wouldn't have wanted to face anyone other than a Korean in the finals, especially the one I had sparred against three years earlier in his homeland on the day our "friendly" match got nasty. Sin Joon-sik and I were on opposite ends of a warm-up area that was separated by a window. I noticed that each time I would get up to warm up or stretch, he would do the exact same thing. For some reason, the thought of him following my lead convinced me that I was going to beat him. I already assumed I was in his head earlier in the week when Diana had sent me a text message about an interview my opponent had done in a taekwondo magazine. They asked him what he thought about his chances. He said he thought they were good, even though he was still worried about facing Steven Lopez. I had this guy.

I took it to him, because I wanted to make it a real fight rather than a chess match. In the first round, I was inching in just before he countered with an ax kick. I didn't think he caught me, but I heard the crowd roar. I threw a three-kick combination, hoping the judges would score one if they scored the other. They didn't: I was down 1–0 after the first round. In the next round, I kept trying to throw my front leg, but Sin kept backing up. The referee motioned to him to engage rather than stall, and he gave the Korean a kyong-go. One more and we'd be even. At that point, I kept pushing him back with my lead leg, knowing he would fall back or go off the mat. I could tell the referees wanted to give him another half-point deduction that would have evened the match. But as much as they motioned for him to fight, they wouldn't give him the second kyong-go. By the end of the second round, I realized they weren't going to penalize him no matter how uninterested he was, so I had to score soon.

As I sat on the side, I really had no idea what I was going to do for round three. That was when I looked over at Jean, who was giving me a high sign, telling me not to worry. That one glance reminded me of something he and I had talked about a few days earlier. I knew that the guy had kept going to my backside with his right leg, which seemed like his only weapon. Jean had told me that if I fought him, I should try to trap his right leg by stepping forward to give him my torso as a tempting target, and then spinning around to throw a back kick just as he tried to go for the torso. I was running out of time, but halfway into the third round, the center referee finally gave Sin his second kyong-go, bringing the match back to 0–0. I was still waiting for the opening, but I didn't want to catch him with a lot of time left in the round. The way things were in our sport, I figured they'd give him another point if one of his kicks got anywhere close to me. I wanted to run down the clock. Finally, with less than a minute to go, the scene played out as Jean had described and I had pictured. Sin took a step forward and went after the torso. I countered with a left-leg hook kick I almost never use. It's odd to say, but I'll never forget how good it felt to feel his face against my foot. I was thinking, Please score the point, please, please. It may have been only a second or two, but it seemed like ages while we both stopped kicking and looked over at the scoreboard. We waited, waited, waited, and then finally saw the point go up for me. For two and a half rounds, it had been me on the attack. Now he needed to attack in the last forty seconds just to tie the match. He came at me with a kick that missed and another one I blocked. I stepped away from him twice until, with about twenty seconds left, he just stood, half-defeated, and waited for the final seconds to tick down.

I couldn't believe we had done it. No, it wasn't just me. I stood stunned for a second or two, crossed myself and fell to the floor. At first I was in a kneeling position and started to say thank-you. Then I slumped forward and put my head on the mat. The next thing I remember, I felt a tap on my shoulder. I was sure it was the referee, but it was actually Jean. Huh? "Jean, what are you doing here?" I said. "Aren't you supposed to be in the stands?" Those were the first words out of my mouth. He grabbed me, started making these shrill noises I had never heard before, composed himself for a second, told me I did a good job and then rushed away, as if he thought nobody would see him out there in the center of the mat. Not far away, Diana had also hopped the railing and was trying to explain herself to the two security guards who had grabbed her. "But I'm the sister," she pleaded. "I'm supposed to be like this." It's funny now. I don't think either of them realized exactly what they were doing. In the excitement of the moment, they must have thought they were on the moon. As the referee started raising my hand, I couldn't help but wonder if I was going to have to rescue Jean and Diana from prison somewhere.

As it turned out, cooler heads prevailed. Security sent Diana back into the stands and let Jean go after they were convinced that he was who he said he was. In the minutes before the medal ceremony, I was still trying to enjoy my emotions: not so much control them, but just let myself feel everything around me. I ran around the arena and saluted the crowd. Then I went into the stands and headed straight for my dad. I hugged him, told him I loved him and just said, "We did it. We really did it." I'm sure we said more than that, but the words just kind of got lost in the moment. On my way down from the section, I slapped hands with some of my teammates who weren't competing that day and with other members of the U.S. delegation who were sitting in the same section. I could tell that some of the meet officials wanted to make sure they didn't lose me, because we still had to receive our medals.

A few minutes later I was in the back, nervous and excited about being able to accept my medal and hear my country's national anthem. It was something I had been thinking about for so long that it was a lot like the anticipation I used to have on Christmas morning. When we went through team processing, the USOC had given us some really nice Team USA warm-up clothes. I wanted to change into them, but for some reason, the WTF is the one federation I'm aware of that doesn't allow its athletes to wear them on an awards stand. People sometimes use the expression "dreaming of" something when they don't literally have actual dreams about whatever it is, but I definitely had mornings when I would wake up after accepting my medal at the Olympic Games. It was like I had just hit the jackpot and won the lotto of life. My family was there with me, and everything in the world felt as if it were perfect at that moment, like you wouldn't want to change anything. Then I'd look around my room, recognize that it was a dream and realize that nothing could ever really be quite that good. Dreams are usually pretty silly if you think about them. Well, as we stood around in the holding area, waiting to accept our medals, I smiled and thought back to the aftermath of those dreams, only this time I didn't have to worry about waking up. This time I could just enjoy it, because it was all real. Of course, there would also be mornings when I would wake up after I thought I had lost at the Olympics, when I would have to watch the awards ceremony from the side while other athletes picked up their medals and I was left to think about what went wrong. I admit that in my sort of delirious state in the holding area, I had to ask myself for a moment, Steven, is this one of your good dreams or your bad dreams?

I remember being nine or ten, I can't remember exactly how old, when I watched athletes win their medals on TV with my mom. "Why do they cry when they get their medals?" I'd ask her. It just didn't make any sense to me. I cried sometimes when I was growing up, just like any other kid, but crying was something you did when you were sad. I had never cried tears of joy before. I had never been happy enough about something to do it. After I had my medal around my neck, I did all I could not to cry. Who wants to cry in public? I never wanted to cry in front of my friends, in front of my class. Who wants to cry in front of a billion people? I sang the words of "The Star Spangled Banner" as best I could. Man, that song goes by fast when you have a medal around your neck and you're choking up as you try to sing. People remember images of standing on the awards platform, and so do I, but it was over before I knew it. Then I went to the back and I cried. I was smiling and crying at the same time, doing exactly what those athletes used to do when I was watching them on TV with my mom. I cried for several minutes in the back. I just had to let everything go.

It was all good. Afterward I met up with Cecil, who was trying to round up my family while taking me to all my interviews. First, the three medalists all took part in a general press conference soon after we received our awards. Even with all the practice interviews I had done with Jean, it was hard to express my happiness to everyone. Sure, I knew the words I wanted to say, but even though you can practice words, you can't practice saying them while feeling the best feelings of your life. At one point a Korean reporter asked Sin about how he felt. After he answered, I listened to the response of the translator, who said he felt great shame in not winning, since he was the only Korean not to win gold. Shame? These were the Olympics. Nobody should be ashamed at being an Olympian. I responded to his answer by saying that if you fight for your country and fight with honor, there is never a reason to feel shame.

From there we went to the main media center to conduct some interviews with the likes of ESPN, CNN and others. We then went to the office of *Sports Illustrated*, which was almost empty at one in the morning. From there, we were invited to get on the phones to call back to Texas. Mark called some of his friends. Diana made a call. My dad laid my medal out on one of the tables and just looked at it, front and back. It was almost like a heater in the middle of winter. He was basking in the warmth of that medal for a long time. Jean was picking up a copy of *Sports Illustrated*'s Olympic preview issue, making fun of the fact that *SI* had picked me to win a bronze medal instead of gold. I called my mom. It was my first chance to speak with her all day. She was so, so, so happy. If you can picture the expression on someone's face from the tone of their voice, I could see my mom's smile, even eight thousand miles away. She told me my dog, Ninja, was noticing her excitement and giving her a look like never before—like, *My owner's gone crazy. What do I do now?* She spoke to me in Spanish, telling me, "I told you so. I told you so." Then I passed the phone around the room. My dad, Jean, Mark and Diana each took a turn to say how much we all missed her and looked forward to seeing her.

After we finished at the main press center, I went with my family to a restaurant in the Sydney Olympic Park area. It was really late, but I was starving after having to cut so much weight. After we sat down at the restaurant, Mark asked if he could borrow the medal. "Marky, why?" I said. "What are you going to do?" He insisted. After I gave it to him, Mark started waving the medal around, asking people if they wanted to come over and see what an Olympic medal looked like. It was amazing how many people just stared in awe at the sight of it, almost as if they were looking at a diamond. Other people asked questions and took out cameras. I mean, this wasn't a library; it was a restaurant. And yet we had this swarm of people getting quiet and gazing at this thing. It showed me what powerful, universal appeal an Olympic medal had for people. I put the medal in some socks, so I wouldn't scratch it up. I almost didn't know what to do the next morning when I woke up. Now what? Weren't things supposed to change after you won the Olympics? Maybe, but I didn't know how. So I guess I did what I would normally do: I went for a thirty-minute run around the Olympic Village and then worked out. It was one of the best runs I ever had. I was smiling the whole time, so at peace with what I had accomplished and been able to share with my family. Imagine everything we did in order to get to that point. Could anybody have been in a better place than I was? Could I have felt any happier? At some point that day, maybe in the middle of the run, I knew I was going to try to do it again. How odd. Before I actually went to Sydney, I just assumed all along that I would have one shot at an Olympics before going to medical school. That was the responsible, grown-up thing to do, right? Get a respectable job and make a living. This Olympic dream was only a temporary fantasy, wasn't it? As the Games were going on, I really never had the time to sit back and rethink that, because I was so focused on preparing for the matches. But on that day, when I had a chance to be with my thoughts and let the afterglow sink in, I went from knowing this would be my only Olympics, to knowing for sure that I would try to qualify for another one. That meant four more years of training, of early runs, sore ankles, a likely injury or two and maybe some disappointments along the way. But there was no way I wasn't going to do this again if I could. Just like that my plans had changed. Best of all, the next time I just might be able to do it with Mark and Diana.

Later that morning, I went to the arena to watch my teammate Barb Kunkel compete. Later that afternoon, Steve Fine, the photo boss at *Sports Illustrated*, picked up Cecil and me and took us to the Sydney Botanical Gardens for a photo shoot. The photographer Bob Martin wanted me to have a fierce, mean look on my face just as I kicked for his picture. The kicking part was fine, but I guess the previous few days had just drained all the ferocity out of me. He had to take the picture at least a dozen times, because I just didn't look mean enough. They wanted me to open my mouth, open my eyes and yell as loud as I could so the shot looked more authentic. They finally got the shot they wanted, but in the post-Olympic week, I wasn't the best subject for anything too ferocious. From there, we met up with my family at the AT&T Family Center to eat before we went to an interview on the set of the *Today* show. I don't have an exact transcript, but I'll give you a few highlight words from my conversation: "Awesome, cool, great, awesome, unbelievable, thrilling, incredible, and did I mention awesome?" After the *Today* show interview, we went to a big Olympic party that was taking place near Darling Harbor. When I arrived with Cecil, the doorman told me he couldn't come in. He was about to leave when I took out my medal, put it around his neck and told him I was taking him in. Cecil had been a big supporter of my dreams and deserved to be there, too. The bouncer then let Cecil in with his medal. Once we walked in, people started to surround him and ask what sport he competed in. Cecil was pretty embarrassed and gave the medal back. Again, it showed the magic of an Olympic medal.

I stayed in Australia for a week or two after the Games, stopping in Melbourne to see Kylie. We were just friends at that point, after a two-year distant relationship, but she had been so supportive over the years, it was good to share some time again. Honestly it was pretty hard for us to keep the relationship going, being so many miles apart, but we still had a lot of mutual affection left over. Kylie didn't compete at those Olympics, but she was so obviously happy for me and so proud that I was able to win in her country. If she had any mixed feelings about not competing or about the two of us not being together, I never sensed it.

I never really told my family about my decision to continue with taekwondo until I came back to Texas. Even then, we didn't really have a sit-down discussion about it; I just sort of went back to training as soon as I came home. At some point, my parents understood, because they saw how much it meant to me. I had never felt anything like the feelings I had at the Olympics: satisfaction, joy, pride in my country and my family and myself. Most of all, I felt really lucky. The world championships are great. Nationals are great. But I was going to make this my career. As long as my body allowed me to do this thing I absolutely loved, I was going to do it. Jean knew he'd be working with three siblings for four more years, and he never missed a beat. We all needed him. If anything, the idea of the whole family being in this together created a new goal for me.

I remember talking to one of the local reporters about getting back into training. Why go through the strain of climbing up the mountain again if you've already been to the top? For one thing, I still had a particular competition in mind in 2001: the world championships, which took place in each odd-numbered year. Jean had come so close to becoming the first American male to win a title six years earlier. Now, each time I competed, it was as if there were a piece of Jean out on the floor, his spirit and knowledge running through my body. Simply put, I wanted to win it for him. I had lost my first fight in 1997. I had a broken arm in 1999. This would be my year. I needed another one.

CHAPTER 10

The Best and the Worst

by Jean Lopez

O ur lives can change for better or worse in the blink of an eye. Sound like a cliché? I can think of two such days, the best and worst. Through the end of high school I had only had one serious relationship, with a girl named Shea Stevens, a local girl whose father just happened to own a taekwondo school. I had gone up to her at a club because she was wearing a large belt around her waist, and the first cheesy words out of my mouth were, "Um, are you a black belt?" Her answer, just as cheesy, was, "No, but my father is and he'll kick your ass." So how could we not start dating? That lasted until I was twenty. Then nothing. Nothing except that silly lingering daydream about a pair of emerald green eyes. I know, I know: Jean, geez, get over it. For a few years, I used to ask David Montalvo, a friend and teammate of mine, to say hi to Tabetha because they went to the same school. I found out later that he never did, perhaps because he had his own interests. I thought about looking her up, and Tabetha's sister, Brandy, even had a crush on Steven.

So I was at another club a few years later when I locked eyes with someone from across the room. I couldn't make out the face right away, until I got closer to the eyes. "Hi, Jean," she said. "It's Tabetha." No way! After ten years, are you kidding me?

I took her hand and walked her to the bar. I bought her a drink, because I thought it was the thing to do. I had never bought anyone a drink, because I didn't drink. When she walked out, she asked if I could walk her to her car. We traded phone numbers when I got to the car. Hmmm, no boyfriend? This was cool. Forget all those logical get-over-it notions; I was a giddy kid, at least on the inside. Then I misplaced her number. How could I? I had it right . . . Jean! You bozo! Where'd you leave it? Did you drop it? Where did you drop it? What did you do with it? Can you find it? Did you throw it out? Did you eat it? Are you out of your . . . Jean!

I might as well have misplaced my own brain. And, you know, maybe I did. I was kicking myself inside with one spinning round-house after another, when one day, David Montalvo, the same guy who never passed along my greetings to her, came into the gym and said, "Hey, you'll never guess who's outside in the reception area." David, excuse me, but do not get in my way.

This time, I made sure to take down the number again and copy it into, oh, thirty-seven other places where I couldn't lose it. I took her to a nice restaurant and we boiled ten years into a beautiful evening we both knew would be the first of many.

It wasn't long before I was showing off her picture to people I met in all corners of the globe. The Koreans proclaimed her "boo-tee-full." And I wrote her some of my favorite letters that still haven't seen the trash basket. In late 1997, I took her to a quiet area next to a pond in front of the Galleria, dropped to a knee and watched the tears drop from those amazing eyes. We were married on March 21, 1998.

Compare that life-altering day with another. . . .

On September 11, I was at the Olympic Training Center in Colorado Springs, getting ready to take the U.S. junior national team I was coaching to the Pan American Championships in Chile. At about seven a.m. mountain time I came down the stairs heading to the cafeteria where athletes often met and watched the large flat-screen TVs as they ate their meals. Before I really understood what was happening, I could tell that something wasn't right just by looking at people's faces. The room that often buzzed with conversation was silent, and all the heads, not just a few, were turned toward the monitors. At my sides, athletes who had gotten pieces of information about some horrible events on the East Coast were rushing past me to get to the monitors. Every face was glued to a screen. I looked at one of the screens and saw buildings on fire. What was this? Who did this? I remembered being in grade school, when the *Challenger* space shuttle exploded and my classmates and I watched a tragedy unfold in front of our eyes as we tried to make sense of it. But as we watched footage of the World Trade Center on fire, it was almost too difficult to let ourselves believe that this was worse, that it was actually a deliberate act against innocent citizens and against our country.

Steven was home eating breakfast, watching everything unfold on television. He saw the second plane hit the South Tower of the World Trade Center in New York and just kept staring at the screen, thinking he was watching a Bruce Willis movie that somehow wasn't real. How could it be? He reached me on the phone about ten minutes later and we mumbled a few things to each other as we watched events unfold on TV. "We're not invincible," we told each other, each wondering whether other attacks might follow these. Soon after, Steven called Papi, who leaves for work at six thirty each morning. They talked about what residents in Pearl Harbor must have felt when Japanese planes attacked that city sixty years earlier. Friends e-mailed Steven from Australia and Croatia, and he started receiving one text message after another. At different hours in different corners of the globe, everyone was trying to find details, seeing if friends were okay and if friends of their friends were okay. We were fortunate that we didn't have any immediate family in New York or Washington.

Meanwhile, Diana was at school in Houston, unable to miss any days from her senior year at Kempner. She was so eager to join us in Chile and compete in her first senior world championship that her bags at home were already packed, even though she wasn't planning to leave until the sixteenth. Instead, she and her classmates watched the events unfold on their television screens at the school. It was almost impossible for anyone to go about a regular school day or workday, because no one knew what would happen next.

Diana went home to sit with Mom and Dad and ask over and over what had taken place. It was impossible for anyone to process the events, but she took it the hardest of all of us. How could people be so cruel? Why would anyone think that they could be doing a good thing by hurting so many innocent people? There were no easy answers. Mark was already a regular watcher of TV news programs, so he flipped the channels and went from one political voice to another. As my family sat together in front of the TV, they talked about the country as a larger family and how someone had hurt our family members. New York and Washington may have been more than a thousand miles away, but they felt like next-door, and the aftermath would make it feel even more personal.

Of course, the trip to Chile was off. I talked to the fighters on the junior team and felt oddly powerless. About twenty teenagers between the ages of fourteen and seventeen were looking up to their coach to snap them out of their state of shock. Usually I either have answers to whatever their questions happen to be—about taekwondo, travel, friends, family, school—off the top of my head, or at least I can try to understand and offer some advice. This time, not only didn't I have ready answers for them, I was distracted by thoughts of my own loved ones. I wanted to catch a flight back to Houston, but planes weren't flying yet. I couldn't find a place to rent a car that afternoon, so I picked one up the next day and drove nine hundred miles back home, eager to see my family as we tried to go about our lives. Diana's classes observed moments of silence each day for the victims and their families, and many students at Kempner prayed on their own.

At some point we had decisions to make about our competitive future. The world championships were scheduled for early November in Cheju, Korea, making ours one of the first U.S. sports teams to travel abroad after 9/11. With the international climate the way it was, would a U.S. team traveling abroad be a tempting target, especially in a place where we weren't that popular to begin with? We didn't know if we would even be allowed to go. Would the State Department tell us we couldn't compete? Would the USOC keep us back for our safety? Would the U.S. Taekwondo Union say we should be better safe than sorry and wait for the next one? And did those of us on the team think we should go? Two weeks before we were set to leave, I held an impromptu board meeting at the taekwondo school. The group included Peter Lopez (no relation) and David Montalvo, two of our team members, and Steven and Diana.

My wife was very nervous and didn't want me to go. I didn't want to alarm her and wanted to keep my feelings to myself, but I kept hearing reports about other sports events being postponed or canceled because of security concerns. New York was supposed to host the World Wrestling Championships that fall, but after 9/11, the sport's international governing body moved the event away for the athletes' protection and divided the tournament between freestyle events in Bulgaria and Greco-Roman matches in Greece. The world championship in slalom canoe and kayak was scheduled for November on the Ocoee River in Tennessee, but it was scrapped because the U.S. Forest Service, which oversaw security for the area and the event, couldn't guarantee the athletes' safety. Even as far away as Melbourne, Australia, the World Squash Championships were canceled because of security alerts.

I had a different perspective from Steven and Diana. I had a wife and a two-year-old at home, and my instinct was to stay put, unless my siblings talked me into going. Steven made the strongest case for traveling to Korea. He had lost his first match at his first worlds in 1997, and was unable to compete in 1999 because of his broken arm at a time when we all felt he was ready to become the first American male world champion. On the heels of his Olympic title, his training was going better than ever, and the move up in class to lightweight suited him so well. He had never felt this fit and ready to fight. "Jean, this is our opportunity to show the world how resilient we are," he said. "We may have been punched in the stomach, but we're going to come back strong. If we don't go, we lose another year. We lose something we can never get back. We should prove to the world that we're the best and that we can come back from a catastrophe." Honestly, if Steven had wavered at all, I wouldn't have gone.

As emotional as Diana is, she really channels those feeling outward rather than inward. Just watch her cheer for her brothers at a competition. She won't take anything from anyone. Trouble may concern her, but it doesn't scare her away from her goals. "Jean, I could die tomorrow in a car crash," she told me. "I can't imagine terrorists are going to think to attack the U.S. taekwondo team in Korea, but if they do, I'd feel safest being around my brothers."

That was it. We were going.

Even though Mark hadn't qualified and had to stay behind, we knew he wanted to be on the trip not just to compete, but to be with us. He wasn't the same jumpy Mark who used to disrupt our ten-hour family car rides, but he was noticeably antsy, especially in the days before the rest of us were about to leave.

I went to my wife's parents' house and told everyone that we were still making the trip. My in-laws were worried, but very supportive, as they always are.

Mom was also behind the trip. "What can you do for your country from home?" she asked. "Ah, but what can you do in Korea?"

We never had the formal security briefing I was expecting, but our federation got word from our embassy that there would be plainclothes agents at the arena and at our hotel in Cheju, even though we didn't know who or where those security people would be. I remember looking around when we landed at the airport, wondering who was friend and who, if anyone, might have been foe.

Event organizers usually housed athletes at the same hotel and arranged for the teams to eat together in a ballroom they'd rent for our meals. Especially before competition, communication among teams usually stays at a minimum anyway, but our team members really felt like the plague during the first few days of those championships. Athletes from the other countries would just stare at us and whisper to one another as they were staring.

We walked in even closer quarters than usual during the trip and made it a point not to wear our Team USA clothing unless we were at the competition site. The feeling at the arena was almost spooky. I remember passing other delegations and watching as athletes and coaches stared back at us like we were ghosts. Were we supposed to just fold up our tents and stop living? Stop competing? Stop doing what we'd worked for? Steven talked about feeling an even greater sense of pride in Korea than at the Olympics in Australia. You always hear that America doesn't send athletes to the Olympics; Americans do. And whenever one of us stepped into an arena, we always felt in our gut that we were fighting for family. But I guess it felt like we were fighting for our extended families at this tournament, that we were personally representing people we had never met, even people who were no longer alive. And that feeling was about to get even more intense.

Steven rolled through his first three matches against fighters from Switzerland, Brazil and Chile, entering an anticipated quarterfinal showdown against Iran's Hadi Saei, the Olympic bronze medalist in 2000.

At most competitions, teams kind of create their own warm-up areas in the designated practice facility at the arena. When you put your equipment in one of the cubicles after you arrive, that space becomes your sanctuary. It isn't as if there are gates, guardrails and barbed-wire fences around those areas, but everyone recognizes the sanctity of another team's space. If you go to the beach and put down your towel, you know the next person won't put half of his towel on top of yours if he has fifty feet of unoccupied sand on either side. You don't need border guards and visas at international meets to realize that there is an understood, universally accepted respect for space.

Half an hour before Steven's match against Hadi, the Iranians blatantly invaded our space, taking gamesmanship to an intrusive level. We were minding our business, quietly going over strategy, when four men walked right in front of us. Two coaches brought up the rear.

Hadi was in front of them, staring at the floor and unwilling to look Steven or me in the eye. In the lead was the man we learned was the athletes' spiritual adviser. He carried an open Koran in his hands and began reading aloud from it a few feet in front of Steven. We froze at first, wondering how long this stunt would last. If this had been a state meet from our childhood, we would have spoken up and fixed this situation before it became a distraction. But the last thing we wanted to do was create an international incident at a time when we wanted to let a dignified performance speak for us. Steven and I were both stunned and steamed. We were fighting temptation to strike out and also to giggle. Instead, Steven threw on his headphones and started whistling to whatever tunes he could find. I wanted to say something to Hadi, not only because he understood a little English, but also because the act of poor sportsmanship was reflecting on him. But he averted his eyes and gazed at the ground or the ceiling each time we tried to make eye contact. Steven and I wanted to give Hadi the benefit of the doubt. I couldn't believe this scheme was his idea. He had to answer to people above him: coaches and officials who had been brainwashed into seeing the disrespect and hatred of our country as a responsibility. The nonsense lasted for fifteen minutes before the guys disappeared. The saying, "Keep your focus," is a cliché, but after they left, Steven and I were wound tightly into exactly what needed to be done.

"Steven, this is bigger than anything we've experienced before," I said. "More people are invested in this fight."

Steven said afterward that he felt very powerful walking into the arena. It meant even more than usual for us to walk in behind our flag. Around us we could sense the divisions among the crowd. People from Muslim countries who were making the most noise were definitely cheering for Hadi. Our supporters, if we had any, seemed to be too intimidated to say anything. Fans were breaking into songs and chants rather than just random cheers. We noticed the German team, which featured a number of Muslim members, joining in the loud cheers for Hadi. I usually wouldn't make note of the crowd because I didn't want them to distract my athletes, but I knew the way Steven responded to these type of challenges, the way he channeled a challenge into defiance. I pointed to the German contingent. Steven nodded. It made sense that the fight had a feeling of religious fervor. As we walked up to the raised platform in the center of the arena, Hadi placed a rug in one corner of the floor and knelt down to pray. Steven stood in the other corner and crossed himself, as he does before every fight.

Steven usually likes to feel out his opponents at the beginning, to get a sense of what they feel their strengths are, so he can attack their weaknesses. Hadi wanted to force the issue. He came at Steven quickly and got him into several clinches. Steven and I had talked about the way Hadi sometimes got carried away and made mistakes because of his aggression. Our idea was to fight with a sort of unorthodox finesse that Steven was comfortable with but that would confuse Hadi and leave him open to counterattack. Hadi liked to kick to the backside, which left his face vulnerable. Steven was patient enough to wait for that particular opening. At just the right moment, he caught Hadi with his face unprotected and took an early lead. After that Hadi started to panic a little and tried to do too much. It was like the baseball expression, "trying to hit a five-run homer." As a result of his aggression, he made the same mistake again. Steven waited for him to let down his guard and caught him with another clean shot. By the third round, Steven was giving Hadi that look he has when he has a fighter beat. It's a subtle nod of the head I've seen over the years, the I've-got-you look he has when he's at his best.

But give Hadi credit: Some fighters will let that get the best of them and they pretty much go through the motions and stop trying. He didn't become world champion two years earlier by giving up. Trailing big in the third round, Hadi began to figure out a way to score points against Steven. When Steven flicked out his left leg, Hadi would push the leg out of the way and kick around it. He scored with that tactic in the final round, but too late to overcome Steven's big lead. Of all the victories Steven has achieved in his career, this one may have been the most emotionally charged. There were hoots and whistles raining down from many places in the building, broken by a smattering of applause from our USA contingent that was mostly drowned out. Of course, that didn't mean we couldn't hear Diana. She would have taken on the entire crowd if she had to just to support Steven. Hadi didn't shake Steven's hand after the match, although we didn't take it personally. Again, we realized how closely his team's support staff was watching him.

Steven's energy was low after that bout. It was understandable. How many teams face their archrivals in a quarterfinal or semifinal that feels like a championship, then lose to a lesser opponent in the next game? Steven and I talked about guarding against that. It's the same thing in taekwondo. Two potential champions might draw each other in an early fight. Then the winner loses his next fight. Steven had fought maybe the most emotional match of his life, but he still had two more matches to go. The semifinal against José Luis Ramirez of Mexico felt like an anticlimax. Steven won the fight 4–0, but at times the bout seemed as if it were moving in slow motion. We were fortunate that Ramirez looked a little intimidated by Steven and didn't really have a good plan to attack him. Steven's defense wasn't as strong as usual, but we were fortunate that it didn't have to be.

In the other semi, Jesper Roesen, the quick and powerful Danish fighter who had been Steven's nemesis, defeated Athanasios Balilis of Greece 2–0 to advance to the final match. With victories against Steven at the '97 worlds and '98 World Cup, Jesper always came to fight with a good plan.

Steven and I talked about making sure he imposed his will on Jesper early, to make sure his opponent didn't start to build his confidence. I could tell Steven's energy was back up for the final. There was more snap to his kicks, and he countered Jesper right away to take a 2–0 lead in the first round. After that, Steven had the tired Dane backing up for a lot of the bout. Jesper stepped out of bounds once in each of the next two rounds, but wasn't penalized. Once, when Jesper fell, Steven reached over and slapped his butt so he would get up and fight. When Jesper tried two kicks to the head, Steven barely flinched. He looked for a counter, but Jesper squared up quickly, so Steven just waited patiently for the next opportunity. As I saw the seconds ticking down at the end of the bout, I began to get a heavy feeling in my stomach. It was the wrong time to get flashbacks, but I started seeing snapshots from my last bout in 1995, when I was moments away from becoming the first American male in history to win a world title in taekwondo and I let it get away in the last fifteen seconds. I never want to let my fighters see those moments when I have doubts or concerns. A coach transmits his energy to his athletes, and they translate that energy into their performances, positive or negative, whether they realize it or not. That's part of the reason I try to find the right times to keep an even keel and the times to give my guys a kick in the butt.

Those last few seconds of Steven's fight seemed to last an hour. I jumped and yelled when the time expired. Steven gave a hug to Jesper, who seemed to understand the moment and displayed excellent sportsmanship. I pointed up to the heavens and then embraced Steven for longer than usual. It was the kind of hug when you grab the back of someone's head like you really mean it. We both shed some tears. With no noticeable ill will from the crowd this time, you could hear the "USA, USA" chant from our delegation. Not that Steven and I paid much attention to the crowd. We just shared the moment and all its implications—national, historic, spiritual and, of course, personal. Steven understood mine. "I saw it in your eyes," he told me. "You were having flashbacks, huh?" He knew. Of course he knew. Even near the end of his match when he still had to concentrate on what Jesper might do for a final attack, he somehow sensed it. I laughed a little, sort of snorted through my nose the way you do when you laugh and cry at the same time. It was too much to process at that moment, too hard to find perspective in the middle of joy and chaos.

After I got back to our hotel room, I sat on the edge of my bed and just started to break down. I never told Steven about that. I didn't see it coming. It just hit me. It was as if I had put all those feelings into storage somewhere on the lip of a sieve that held them in place until I had to let them go. Really I had just untied a pair of boulders from my shoulders and watched them make a giant thud on the ground. It was everything I had wanted to accomplish as an athlete being realized as a coach. It was seeing my brother make history for our country. It was giving our country a lift in the face of tragedy and doing it with a strength and dignity that athletes from other countries could witness firsthand. It was the uncertainty of the board meeting a few weeks earlier. It was everything my parents had hoped for us. I thought about my parents immediately after Steven won gold at the Olympics in Sydney, too, but this was even more intense. All these emotions piled on top of one another were enough to break the dam. And once it was broken, all those stored-up feelings just poured out of me. That probably lasted for no more than fifteen minutes, but it felt like a week. As much as I replayed them in my mind, it was almost a lifetime's worth of thoughts.

Diana was fighting later in the tournament. She was the newbie on the senior circuit, and that meant she had to get used to a new class of experienced competitors and a more sophisticated style of fighting than she had ever seen as a champion junior. When she won her junior crowns, Diana was a terror. As soon as each match started, she'd be yelling and kicking almost before the other girls knew what hit them. This was an accepted style at a level that didn't have a lot of subtlety to it. Diana loved fighting that way. She loved letting the girlie shopper take off her makeup and morph into a tiger. As much as Steven and Mark were starting to intimidate opponents with their reputations and commanding generalship on the mat, Diana really scared the heck out of other junior girls when she went on the attack. When other girls tried to attack her, she'd counter with a roundhouse kick that was just too devastating for the other juniors to defend. She was a world junior champ, and she was unstoppable. As a senior, she would have to adapt. The most experienced women eat those ambitious juniors for lunch, because they know how to exploit every weakness and turn the juniors' jittery excitement against them. We had talked about how it might take Diana a while to get used to some more refined techniques.

She might do well, but she wouldn't dominate right away. It was like going from elementary school to junior high or junior high to high school. All that confidence you might have had as an older member of your previous school could disappear pretty quickly when the teachers were new, the kids were all new and mostly older, and the building looked more intimidating than it really should.

Diana was in for a learning experience. She fought a Polish girl in the opening bout and wasn't prepared for the girl's patience. Diana was used to street fights, and instead she was in for a chess match. Diana never got into a rhythm and she barely lost the match. Of course, she was disappointed, but she understood this would be a new chapter in her career. We talked about keeping this particular result in perspective. There was no reason she couldn't be successful once she learned some tricks of the more advanced trade.

Diana gave her best effort, but not every athlete in Korea was as lucky. One morning, a very strong Iranian featherweight named Babik was scheduled to fight Tal Moriah, an Israeli who drew him by chance in the first round. Instead, as Tal made his way onto the floor, he saw the Iranian crying in the stands and forfeiting the bout. Iran, like many Muslim countries, does not recognize Israel as a sovereign state, so its athletes are often compelled to withdraw from competition rather than compete against athletes from Israel. It isn't necessarily the athletes' choice. The next day, Tal passed both Hadi and Babik in an arena hallway and struck up a conversation with the Iranians in English. Both Tal and Babik expressed regrets about not being able to fight each other. The Iranian athletes had no choice but to take a stand for something other people imposed on them. But what would happen, Tal asked, if the athletes decided on their own to defy politics and put their competition first? What would happen if they decided they had trained for their chance to win a world title and they would fight anyway? "We'd be killed when we got back home," Hadi told him. It wasn't hyperbole. It wasn't a figure of speech.

Even though I didn't anticipate that an incident like that would take place, I had decided before the competition that I wanted to do something to bring the athletes together. Yes, Steven and Diana would be competing in order to show the world that we were strong, but it was also important to show people from other countries how much the United States valued peace and friendship. Earlier in the week I went to some of the local bars and restaurants, trying to find a place where we could host a party for the athletes after the competition was over. I knew a few Korean words, as most taekwondo athletes do because of the sport's origins and the commands we learn when we start the sport. But I actually found one place with an American owner who agreed to stay open late and let us have most of the establishment to ourselves. I told him I didn't really know how many people might show up, but it could be more than a hundred. I told him we would try to get there sometime around nine or ten, after the closing ceremonies took place on the final day. I wrote up a flyer about the party, made as many copies as I could and passed them around to athletes on each of the teams. It was a good way to break through some of the cold stares we'd been getting all week. The Spanish athletes told me they'd come, then the Dutch, then some others. I didn't anticipate how much I would remember both the ceremonies and the party forever for completely different reasons.

The closing ceremonies at an Olympics or world championship are supposed to be a celebration, a chance for the athletes to wave, thank the crowd and maybe get a little wistful because this chapter of their careers they've worked so hard to establish is over. For at least a few minutes it felt just like that. Music played, athletes marched and confetti came down from the rafters. As it did, I began to notice some paper airplanes that had landed in front of us. We all noticed them and didn't think twice about them. For all we knew, they might have had sponsor logos or the official championship logos on them. They could have been official souvenirs passed out at the concession stands. Then we took a closer look at them and froze. Written on several paper planes were *AA 11* and *UA 175*, the numbers of the planes that had crashed into the World Trade Center. The writing on another paper plane read simply: *Americans die.* My legs went numb. Steven, Diana and I all looked at one another and decided we should leave as soon as we could. We didn't wait for the ceremonies to end. Instead we ducked out the back exit and got on the first shuttle back to our hotel.

We were sitting around the lobby and talking just as other teams started to file in. A few minutes after the Mexican delegation arrived, one of their officials, Mr. Beltran, told us that our team should be careful, because he had heard there was a bomb threat at the hotel, even though he didn't have many details. What should we do? Should we switch hotels? Should we call the embassy? Should we skip our own party? I asked Steven what he wanted to do. He said that if something were going to happen to us, we'd be better off at the party anyway. If the athletes from the other countries were going, the party might actually be the safest place for us to be. Besides, we were the hosts. Diana agreed, so we changed, got out of the hotel as fast as we could and prepared for a long night. We knew we were through sleeping at the hotel. We'd stay until the place closed, come back in the morning, pick up our bags and head for the airport.

Steven and I were still reeling from the ceremonies when we arrived at the party. A hundred athletes? My estimate was way short. Several hundred people showed up, including athletes, training partners and even some coaches. People danced together, played together, joked together and did what people would do if there were no politics or political boundaries. It was exactly the sort of hopeful sight that could wash away some of the bad taste of the ceremonies from our mouths. In the back of the house were two pool tables. At one, there was a game involving Hadi and Babik, taking turns playing with Tal. Instead of feuding and dodging, they were shaking hands and complimenting one another on good bank shots. Hadi saw us from across the room. He was without his handlers, so he put his hands together, almost as an apology, and asked if we were okay. That was the Hadi we knew and wanted to see again. Those were the moments I was most proud of.

I don't think I ever remember being as acutely aware of our place in the world as I was during that week in Korea. It was a challenge for us as Americans and as a family to prove that we weren't pushovers, but that we also weren't bullies. Even as we were both worried and defiant, we were able to express sentiments that didn't have to be mutually exclusive: our willingness to represent and defend ourselves and our wish to reach out; our national pride and our desire for peace.

CHAPTER 11

Against the Script

by Diana Lopez

was growing up on and off the mat. I was a little more cynical now because of my experience in Korea. But I also looked like a more seasoned fighter, with my first hints of complex strategy. If some girl tried to kick me in the back, for instance, I knew how to spin back with a counterdefensive kick. I still kept going, but it wasn't just a race to see who could throw as many kicks as possible. It was hard to break away from the old me, the one who kicked and kicked her way to her second junior world title in Killarney, Ireland, in 2000. I was so comfortable in those years: I really never got intimidated by any situation. After beating girls from Chinese Taipei and Kazakhstan, I went down to the final seconds against a girl from Korea before scoring to advance into the medals, yet I was never worried about the outcome.

For the gold medal, I fought Sidel Guhler from Turkey. We fought our final contests on a raised stage, one match at a time, so all eyes were on me when I fought. I had fun. I felt I was supposed to win. I felt strong. I had great timing and I had her measured from the start of the match. I built a 3–0 lead in the first round, then relied on my defense to move out of the way so I could keep my lead. The match ended with the same score, and I raised my arms, feeling I had conquered this level of competition. A lot people came up to congratulate me and pose for pictures with me afterward. I felt great.

I was the captain of that team, traveling without my brothers or parents, and it was an awesome feeling to have everyone's respect. Even the boys asked me a lot of questions because they weren't used to traveling. Since we were still juniors, we still played a lot of pranks on one another. We weighed in on the day we fought in those days. One night after I was finished competing, I was up late talking to all my junior team friends. As the captain, I was the one in charge of waking people up in the morning. So those of us who were finished decided we'd start the process a little early, like around two thirty a.m. I told my teammates not to wake up the people who had to weigh in and fight the next morning. Everyone else was fair game. We actually videotaped one boy named Daniel Elkowitz who was convinced he was so late he was holding up the bus. You've never seen someone brush his teeth so fast. It was a good idea, except that we did wake a few people who were supposed to weigh in that morning.

I think sparring with the boys made me more confident in fighting people who were supposed to be stronger or somehow out of my league. I faced that when I went to my first Olympic trials in 2000 at age sixteen. Instead of stronger male opponents, I was fighting more experienced women who knew the ropes better than I did. I looked up to these women, and it was strange for me to be in their class. I was aggressive. I was never scared. I was a screamer. I was a fighter. I fought the exact same way as a senior, when I moved up from a hundred and thirty pounds to a hundred and forty seven. I'd still attack and score monster points, even though the girls were bigger and stronger than I was. I didn't put pressure in my head to make that particular Olympic team. I knew I was an underdog and I wanted to make sure I came out of there with more experience and a greater understanding of what to do so I could get to the Games four years down the road. I beat some women on the national team because I took it to them. I finally met my match when I reached the semis against Barb Kunkel, a thirty-year old veteran who had been one of the best in the county for seven years.

I hung with her in the fight, even though I could tell she was able to read me better than I could read her. I scored against her on a nada-bong and backed her up a couple of times. She won the match 3–2. I was okay with the result, because I knew how close I was to being the best in the country. That was when I really believed I was going to make the Olympic team someday.

Around that time, I started to study video. It's funny, because Steven doesn't like watching his fights. Our teammate Peter Lopez used to have people send him videos of our team, and I would ask to watch my fights, because I wanted as much information as possible. It wasn't an ego thing, because I'd watch the bad parts more than the good parts. If someone scored on me, I'd want to rewind the tape and figure out why. How could I have prevented that? What should I have done?

I borrowed some style elements from each of my brothers. Jean did a lot of spin kicks, and so I learned my spin kick from watching him. Steven doesn't do many spin kicks at all, but he does lead out with his left leg, so I learned how to kick that way, too. Marky does his fancy showman moves, and I've picked up on some of that. Mainly, Jean tells me to be aggressive and strong. If I fight my fight, he'll tell me, the other girl won't be able to hang with me. In other words, I need confidence. If I bounce and try to sneak points in, that's when I become vulnerable.

The day I lost my first senior worlds in 2001, I remember thinking, Wow, I didn't even get hit and already my championships are done. I realized then that it was more of a cat-and-mouse game at the senior level. My opponents slowed down the game so much at the senior level, and they were always prepared to use my aggression against me.

I won the Indoor Open in Brussels. We still had a bad taste in our mouth after what happened in Korea. The meet in Brussels wasn't as well run as the invitational meets in other countries, and it turned out that I fought only one match. It felt like a high school match, with a lot of rowdy teenagers in the stands. Brussels has a large Muslim population in a particular section of the city, and many of the kids had signs in Arabic. At one point, I remember spotting a guy who took out an American flag and made a gesture as if he were taking out a lighter to set it on fire. I felt sick. Really, cheer for your countrymen, even boo me as a rival fighter, but why do something like that? I wasn't interested in fighting people in the ring; I wanted to punch out the guy in the stands. Afterward, I noticed the guy coming up to me and asking for an autograph. Now, I was doing everything I could to keep my emotions in check. "Are you crazy?" I told him. "You make like you're going to light our flag on fire after thousands of people died in New York City and you want me to just smile and pose for a picture or give you an autograph? How do you think that makes me feel?" I spoke in single words of broken English, so he could understand. I don't think they were sincere about their response, but they tried to be sympathetic after they saw my reaction. One boy pointed to another and called him stupid. Another one put his hands together as an apology. Then another one started to give a thumbs-up sign when he talked about George Bush. Whatever. I told them this wasn't about politics; it was about respect for other human beings who were people just like them. I really don't think they knew why they did the things they did or why they bought into the whole death-to-America idea. I did get a sense that some of what I was saying was sinking in, because now they saw a real person in front of them. I wasn't some gunslinging cowgirl like they somehow imagined: I was somebody who was obviously hurt by what they did.

I'd like to say I shook the incident off, but it had a lasting effect on me. Until then I was pretty naive about my easy life. I trusted that everyone was good. Even people who tease me or try to kick me in the ring are not people who would want to hurt me. But after going through September 11, the ceremonies in Korea and the incident in Brussels, I really understood that there were people out there who meant harm to our country. I took that personally, because they meant harm to me, even though they didn't know the first thing about me. My parents began to tell us about why people would be jealous of us.

Some people don't care for freedom of belief and rules of law because they abuse those things at home. Other people stand behind a way of thinking that doesn't allow for any other way of thinking. So people in the United States who can believe what they choose and be whatever they want to be must be wrong. They must be defeated. It was hard for me to understand that kind of thinking, but it made me so much more grateful for the choices I had and the life I lived back home. It also made me a little less trusting of people who were acting nice to me. Were those people being honest or were they going to do something different behind my back? My mom had always told me to keep one eye open and one eye closed when it came to people I didn't know. There was a time when I never understood what that saying meant.

I had several experiences that introduced me to poverty around the world. I remember seeing kids in Turkey hanging out on the street and looking for fights to join. For five dollars, the kids would start to fight someone. They weren't fighting for a cause or a reason. They weren't fighting out of hatred or anger. They were fighting to put food on the table for their next meal an hour later.

Still, nothing prepared me for what happened when I went to Vietnam at the end of 2000 for a World Cup. People swarmed around our hotel, waiting for us to walk outside so they could sell us something. When we did venture out, always as a team, people on the street were poking me and asking me for money. I started to get a little worried about it, because we'd had to get our hepatitis shots before we came over, and I had no idea what they were actually poking me with. A man with no legs rolled up to me on a skateboard holding out a cup with some change in it. People pouted as they begged. But nothing prepared me for the woman who came up to me and a few members of our team. I guess she picked me out because I was young and female, and even though she knew only a few English words, she knew the words "baby" and "money," because she was offering up one for the other. No way! Her own baby? How could anyone even think of that? How could things be so bad that she would just offer her baby to a total stranger? Was it even hers? Did she steal it? I was so heartbroken. The baby must have been no more than a few months old. None of us dared to hold it because we didn't want the woman to run away.

I don't regret the experiences overseas, and I would really encourage everyone to have a passport and travel to other places, not only to see what other cultures are like, but also to appreciate our own a little more. I think we sometimes take where we live and how we're able to live for granted. My parents always instilled in us that we're here because of God, and we have to thank Him for everything we do. That's why we never take things for granted like the food on our table and the love of family. We pray at night and we share kisses when we walk out the door.

I think my travels left me with a healthy chip on my shoulder. I still wanted to trust people just as much. I still wanted to believe in people and think the best of everyone, but I understood now that there were times when I couldn't. That whole period was a transformation for me that was kind of like learning the truth about Santa Claus. That's also why I love traveling with my brothers. I can always trust them to look out for me. Seriously, if people gave out gold medals just for being a great older brother, they'd have to give one to Jean. In January 2002, the USOC gave him the next-best thing: their Rings of Gold Award, which goes to those who help others achieve their Olympic dreams. Steven sent in a nomination letter that read in part, *I could go on and on about the many sacrifices he made for me and all the hardships and trials he has been through to pave the way in gold for me. (He) is my unsung hero.* Jean received the award at a convention in Las Vegas and told people who were there from our Olympic family, "I cherish the award, and it motivates me to do other things for the sport. The purity of the sport is what motivates me." I second the motion.

Since I was the fourth Lopez to have interrupted her school schedule for taekwondo obligations, my teachers were used to the idea of someone in our family asking to make up a test or turn in her homework a little later because she had to go out of town. The people at Kempner were really great about it. Kids there used to call me Karate

Kid. "Taekwondo Kid" doesn't really roll off the tongue. I always got invited to parties, which I never really attended. I was usually fine just hanging out with Maria. Since I didn't have a serious boyfriend, when it came time for senior prom I went with Peter Lopez, one of my friends at the gym. I was friends with a lot of guys, but I was so in my own little world that I didn't know if anyone really liked me. I dressed up in sweats, went from class right to training and didn't get into the dating or social scene. I would go on dates in college, but I never felt strongly enough about anyone to take someone seriously or bring guys home to meet my family. I guess having three older brothers and training with guys a lot made me a little leery of what guys were really thinking—not as far as hanging out and joking around, but as far as relationships went.

When I wasn't in school, I would usually have time to just have fun and hang out with Maria. We always liked to go swimming at the public pool nearby, but my mom never let us go in until after six p.m., when the sun couldn't scorch our skin. Jean called us vampire children because of that.

I graduated from Kempner in 2002 and decided to follow in Steven's footsteps and put off college until after the Olympics. I sort of wish I hadn't. Having school *and* training would have been better for me, because I think I put too many emotions into having to make the Olympic team. Going to school gave me a schedule and something to fall back on during days that didn't go so well. My whole set of goals and sense of happiness didn't depend on just one thing when I was in school. It might have worked for Steven, but at times I thought so much about getting on that 2004 team, it overwhelmed me.

Not every bout was packed with pressure. I first fought Nia Abdallah in the finals of my last junior nationals, in San Antonio. I didn't know much about her, so I don't think I took the match seriously enough. I ate a cheeseburger before the match, which isn't something I ever do. I won the match 3–0. I had no idea then that it would be the start of a long rivalry.

In 2002, I won the Pan Am Championships in Ecuador. Marky

wasn't on that team because he didn't make it. Steven was letting some-one else go. I finally made a statement at a WTF-sanctioned senior open. I fought a girl from Ecuador in the finals. It was a slow-paced match. The girl was waiting for me, but Jean told me to just wait for her. He used to tell me to be patient, but it was hard for me to do. This time I was more patient than usual. She made one mistake as the sec-onds were ticking down: She led with her right leg. I went on her motion and just kicked her first. They scored the point and I was able to survive the last fifteen seconds. It was cool to be able to hear my national anthem being played for me. I had seen Jean and Steven win the competition, so I sort of expected that I would do it, too.

During the trip, we got to stand at the equatorial line, right in between the two hemispheres. It felt appropriate, because I was in be-tween two places, too, hoping soon to make the leap from being the newbie senior to the girl to beat. We all went up to a Latin lounge after our last day of matches. Even though I haven't been to Latin America or South America very often, it feels like home because of the culture and the familiar food. They fixed rice and meat, and I ate it up. It was nice, but I wanted a bigger show.

The Dutch Open wasn't what I had in mind, though it is a great invitational meet. We had a trainer working with us one year named Joe Rogowski. We got along well and kept in touch, even though he lived in Orlando. I always thought he was very cute and fun to talk to, but I wasn't about to date my trainer. After some time went by, he asked if I could go to a wedding in Orlando, where he was from, be-cause, he told me, I seemed like "a cool chick." My brothers all said absolutely not. Why? I wondered. It's just a wedding date. My brothers were pretty adamant that he had to come by the house and spend time with them before I went off somewhere with him. Joe was disap-pointed when I gave him the bad news. "That's my family," I told him. Maybe he shouldn't waste his time. That was a big test for Joe, a sort of commitment before any commitment. A lot of guys would have said, "Oh, this girl is too much work." He went to the wedding by himself, and he still stayed in touch. When I competed later at a meet in Atlanta, he came up to watch me and spent time with Jean and me. We were still friends, but Jean's objections were waning and eventually we were a couple. Oh, and I won the Dutch Open, too. Twice.

The next year I fought Nia again for a berth in the Pan Am Games. This time, the roles were reversed and I was on the losing end. She was unorthodox and frustrating to fight against. She fell often, especially right after she kicked. She frustrated me a lot each time she fell. She was unpredictable, which worked to her advantage, but she was an outside fighter. I lost by a point.

We had a competition at a hotel ballroom in Colorado to see who would go to Mexico to qualify within the region for the Olympics. The whole OTC was cheering for Nia and my team was cheering for me. It was an odd setup because there were no stands, just people standing and cheering on the side. I was getting frustrated, because I was kicking and not scoring points. So in between rounds, Jean told me to forget the score and go back out there and fight. Nia would move back each time I attacked. Then she'd counter and catch me before she fell, so I couldn't counter the counter. On one exchange, she punched me in the chin, which got me pretty annoyed. When I finally saw an opening, she fell again and this time I just snapped. I was determined to land a kick, so I followed her as she fell and caught her while she was on the ground. I shouldn't have done that, but I needed to get that out of me.

By the time of the 2003 Worlds in Garmisch, Germany, I was pretty comfortable in my own skin as a senior. Mark and I always fought on the same day, since we were in equivalent weight classes. This was sometimes a problem for Jean, who wanted to be able to coach both of us. As matches in the different rings backed up against one another, he couldn't always get in both of our corners for every fight. I was scheduled to fight my opening bout against Spain's Sonia Reyes, the same woman I had beaten at the Dutch Open a year earlier. I was feeling pretty confident about the fight, so I told Jean to just go with Mark, who was about to fight at the same time.

I kicked and kicked and thought I connected on several points, but in the end I lost 3–2. Not again. It was my second match at a senior world championships and my second loss. What was I doing wrong? I knew I couldn't sit around and blame anyone other than myself. I needed to learn more about how seniors fought, what kind of strikes the refs were going to count and what I had to do to be able to play the game better. That was why I immersed myself in video: to get used to patterns of what worked and what didn't and make myself into someone whose smarts could match her energy.

Of course, my disappointment could never match Mark's. He became disillusioned after coming out on the short end of so many close matches. In 2001, he won nationals in Cleveland as a featherweight. He wanted to continue Steven's legacy in that weight division, so he became more versatile. Before, he'd throw one kick and move out of the way. Now he was becoming more offensive, started punching more, tried to find the right mix of techniques. He was sparring with a guy named Jake Stovall, who used to throw an array of strong punches. Judges don't usually score those, but they could take their toll and discourage an opponent from attacking. It worked for Mark, and it convinced me to punch more often, especially against competitors who seemed to be easily intimidated.

At the world team trials in 2001, Marky fought a guy from the preferred OTC group named Jason Han, whom Steven had beaten before. Jason was fast and strong. He'd throw a good fast kick, a sliding front-leg roundhouse kick. He also had a good defensive roundhouse kick. Since Jason was faster, Mark tried to use his timing against him. Jason held a lot, and Marky felt he was playing to the refs, who actually gave a point to Jason for a punch. Still, Mark accepted Jason's victory that year. Steven always found a way, so Marky knew he needed to do the same.

There was a girl from Puerto Rico named Dagmar Diaz who came in and won one of the divisions that year. She and Mark didn't meet formally at that meet, but they talked for a while at the U.S. Open the next year. They started e-mailing, and it took a few months for her to call Mark out of the blue. They became a couple later that year.

Marky lost another close one to Jason again at nationals in Colorado Springs. I used to get emotional when Mark was getting screwed out of spots on the team. I was crying in the stands for Mark, because I sympathized with his disappointment. I wasn't sobbing, but I wanted to get the tears out of my system. As I did, I looked up and realized there was a guy there recording me. I didn't know who he was, but I looked over at him and totally lost it. I grabbed the camera and pushed it into his face.

Mark's head told him God did things for a reason. How else could he have met Dagmar? On the positive side, he could concentrate on school. After 2002, he thought a little for the first time about dropping the sport. He often asked himself whether, if he had put just as much energy into another sport, could he have been just as successful. He could be famous, have lots of money, and not deal with people who were big fish in the small ponds, abusing power and authority. He didn't feel appreciated.

Marky stuck it out and beat Jason Han twice at the 2003 team trials in Orlando to get that spot at the world championships in Garmisch. At that time things started to change a little bit. Things were getting intense within the organization. The old guard within the USTU was under investigation for the way it was running the sport and handling funds, and the victory was a big triumph for Mark. He doesn't usually hit face shots, but in the last round, he scored against Jason with a fast kick to the face, which turned out to be the decisive blow. That sent him off to Garmisch with Steven.

Ironically, Mark's first match in Germany was against Argentina's Alejandro Hernando, the same guy who knocked out Steven at the Pan Am qualifiers in 1999. When Mark saw that that was his first match, he said, "Yes, I get to nail this guy for Steven." Mark didn't knock him out, but he won pretty easily. He didn't score with any head shots, but it was pretty anticlimatic. Mark told Steven later he wished he could have knocked the guy out for him. I don't think Steven cared, because he knew the first match had been a fluke.

The mats in Garmisch were pretty slippery, and the fighters were falling a lot. Mark was only another deduction away from getting disqualified in his next match against a Mexican opponent. The guy was pretty strong and fast. Before the third round, Jean told Marky to stay on the ground and avoid throwing double kicks or spin kicks, in order to make sure he didn't fall. That took some weapons out of his arsenal, but he stuck to moving off the line and throwing out his left leg, just the way Steven does. The guy was very good at blocking Mark's kicks with his leg, but Mark knew his opponent was tiring and not taking any chances. Mark finally caught him twice at the end. It was a good test of stamina and discipline, because he had to be careful not to get that last deduction.

In the quarters, Mark fought a Brazilian guy who bounced around a lot and was pretty tough to catch. In between rounds, Jean was trying to pump Marky up and inspire him. He must have noticed that Mark was a little low on energy, because he reached into his motivational hat for something new. "C'mon, Mark," he said. "Do it for Dagmar." What? Mark hadn't heard that one before. Sure, Jean would invoke other members of my family, but this was new territory. That must have been his wild card. Mark protected his lead well and won the match, but the Brazilian and his coach were pretty upset that Mark was able to keep his distance, and not engage in closer combat. After the match, the Brazilian fighter sat in the middle of the ring in protest before officials came out and coaxed him to leave.

The crowd favorite, Germany's Erdal Aylanc, was next. Mark waved to the fans, even as they were booing him. He made sure to take a snapshot in his mind of that moment. He didn't mind the reaction, because we all sort of feed off it. "It's not like we're at war," he'd say. Compared to soldiers who go out there on a real battlefield in a foreign country far from home, we're really not doing anything that dangerous. We love competition, and we especially love it when the odds are stacked against us. We look at it not only as a chance to beat the person in front of us, but also everyone who is cheering against us. Marky used to look at it that way when he fought nationals against the guys from the OTC. Whether he was on the wrong side of politics or the wrong side of the crowd sentiment, he had fun when he could just say, "Bring it on." We watch the NBA play-offs and see the way certain players and teams lose their heart when they're on the road. Why? The court is the same length. The basket is the same size. The rules are the same. Sure, the refs will give one or two more calls to the home team because officials can be influenced by the fans, but why are so many guys intimidated by those moments? Yeah, your fans aren't there, but so what? Just go out and play.

God had given Mark the chance to be there, and he welcomed the opportunity. Aylanc was a little shorter than Mark, and he was pretty scrappy. It was close, and they were down to the last thirty seconds. Aylanc charged pretty carelessly to get that last point before overtime. Mark lifted up his front leg and caught the German for a two-pointer in the face. It was on to the finals, where he would face more than just his opponent.

Korea's Kang Nam-wong had been world champion in the bantamweight division the year before after beating Peter Lopez in the finals. Then he moved up a division to featherweight. He was pretty short, so Marky wanted to utilize his reach advantage. At first they traded points. Later in the match, Kang was falling just as he was throwing a back kick. Mark countered with a roundhouse kick and knocked Kang into next Thursday. He was on the ground and out. Done. Finished. Marky waited for the ref to start counting Kang out and declare Mark the winner, but instead the man started looking around at his fellow judges. Instead of counting the guy out, the ref motioned for the medical team to come out and help Kang. Fighters are never supposed to get more than a minute of injury time, and they are never supposed to have any additional time once they've been knocked out, but instead the ref motioned Mark to the side while the trainer took off Kang's helmet, sprayed him with water, rubbed his neck and moved his finger back and forth in front of Kang's eyes to see if he was tracking. Mark and Jean didn't understand what was going on. Kang eventually regained consciousness and stopped wobbling around. The referee then had a long conversation with the Korean coach, who was gesturing and pointing at Mark. After another few minutes, they brought the fighters to the center of the ring, where Mark waited to be awarded the bout by knockout. Instead, the ref stepped away to consult again with the Korean coach, then looked at Mark and gave him a gam-jeon, a full point off. Mark was stunned. He and Jean tried to ask for an explanation, but the ref told them to engage and start fighting again. Kang rallied to win the match by a point, and I will never forget the if-looks-could-kill glare on Jean's face.

Mark tried to laugh it off. In a way, this decision was so over-the-top absurd, it was easier for him to do that. He still did his celebratory round-off back flip after the fight, as if to show who really won. Even though people were booing him after the previous fight, they cheered for him after the bout against Kang. Nobody was going to applaud or cheer for us, especially since we're from the United States, unless they saw that a real injustice had occurred.

CHAPTER 12

Repeat After Me

by Steven Lopez

Why go through the strain of climbing up the mountain again if you've already been to the top? For one thing, I still had a particular competition in mind in 2001: the world championships, which took place in each odd-numbered year. Jean had come so close to becoming the first American male to win a title six years earlier. Now, each time I competed, it was as if there were a piece of Jean out on the floor, his spirit and knowledge running through my body. Simply put, I wanted to win it for him. I had lost my first fight in 1997. I had a broken arm in 1999.

It was great to feel the support of people in the local area in those first few weeks after I came home. I was one of several Houston-area Olympians who received proclamations from the mayor. In October, Sugar Land held a Steven Lopez Day. I rode in a yellow Hummer, escorted by police, family, members of Kempner's band, junior ROTC and drill teams that entered Oyster Creek Park. "If you really work hard for it, it will come to you," I told the crowd

"Steven is such a role model for Sugar Land," said Representative Tom Delay, who gave me a U.S. flag that had flown atop the Capitol. Officials gave me a key to the city.

I went to each of my schools (elementary, middle and high school) to talk to the kids there. It's also cool to give back to the sport by giving seminars, or give back to the community by going to a mall opening, but when I went back to the schools I had attended myself, I knew the kids could relate to me. They had many of the same teachers, walked the same corridors, ate in the same cafeteria and had dreams just as I did. Kids have people tell them what they can accomplish all the time, but it's easier to believe it when the person saying that was once one of them.

I would usually talk about my story for about thirty minutes and then take questions from the other students. The teachers loved having a young recent graduate come in and talk about the value of discipline, hard work, leadership and listening to your teachers and professors, and the importance of education. In my case, all of those things were true. If I didn't have parents who preached the value of discipline to me, for instance, I would never have become an Olympian. There was no way, I'd tell them, that I could have done that on my own. Some of the questions could be pretty funny. At each school I'd get the inevitable do-you-have-a-girlfriend question from a giggling girl. Usually the guys would want to know if I had used my fighting skills on somebody in a back alley somewhere. I told them truthfully that even though I had some scraps in my early school days, I was probably like a lot of Martial artists who gain enough confidence to stay out of trouble. Really a Martial artist's instinct is to find ways to avoid confrontation, even if that means walking away from a challenge.

In 2002, we went to Tokyo for the World Cup. I enjoyed the trip to Tokyo: the buildings, the architecture and the respectful Asian culture that was similar, in a way, to the Latin culture. The semifinals there shaped up as an Olympic rematch, with Sin of Korea and Hadi from Iran joining me among the final four. I caught Sin with a good kick that knocked him down in the middle of the fight. The referee looked him over and started to count, which should register as an automatic two points. Instead they gave none. Huh? If you kick a guy in the face or if you kick him to the body so hard that he falls down and they start counting, you receive two points. It's in black and white, right in the rule book, kind of like giving someone two points for a hoop in basketball. Did somebody not see what just happened? I guess he flew back onto the ground on his own. I guess he stayed there to admire the scoreboard or the girl in the stands. I was really angry. I know taekwondo is a judged sport, and sometimes you can split hairs when you disagree with a judge's decision, but this time I realized the only way I was going to win was to beat him up. So I started kicking and punching as hard as I could. I didn't care about the score at that point, because I knew the judges would have him ahead. Each time we exchanged, the officials broke the exchange to give one of us a kyong-go. At the end of the day, he had five of them, but I was disqualified with the maximum six. I was pretty furious with the whole thing. It was being officiated like a local tournament. Sin was in worse shape. He was too banged up to fight in his final match. He won a silver, I won a bronze and Hadi, the guy who was lucky enough to watch from the side, won a gold medal.

To an outsider, it may seem that our camp complains about officiating when things don't go our way. Sure, lose and you look for conspiracies rather than winning gracefully. Instead, I'll let Lee Chong Woo, a former WTF vice president, discuss it.

Lee was quoted in the April 2002 issue of *Shindonga*, a Korean magazine, as saying: "When I said to the judges/referees, 'judge fairly,' they understood what I meant. They knew that I was influencing them indirectly to show the Korean team favoritism. . . . Because taekwondo is originated from Korea, the manipulations were successful in benefiting the Korean competitors. In other words, if I had not influenced the judges/referees, Korea would only have received one or two gold medals." In the article, Lee said he encouraged the practice of "lopping off branches," in which the strongest rivals of Korean fighters would lose preliminary matches. For example, French heavyweight Pascal Gentil lost in a horrendous decision to eventual gold medalist Kim Kyong-Hun. Somehow, Flavio Perez, the Colombia referee for my gold-medal match at the Sydney Olympics, decided to judge fairly when he deducted a point from the Korean fighter for a violation. For that, the WTF suspended Perez for one year. Gentil came up to me after his fight and told me, "I wish I would have fought before you did."

USA Today reported similar comments from Lee: "In order to accomplish my intention, I had to decide whether this judge/referee can be used for the Korean team's benefit or not. . . . It was impossible for me to ask judges/referees to show their favoritism for the Korean team directly, but I did influence them indirectly through the assignment process. Those judges/referees who have a foxy sense figure out my intentions, but those who did not were not able to catch my point." *USA Today* pointed out that Lee once scolded a referee for giving a Korean female competitor a one-point deduction that caused her to lose.

I'll fast-forward to late in 2003, when the USOC finally decertified the USTU after an internal investigation discovered a pattern of financial mismanagement. The USTU also owed the USOC two hundred and six thousand dollars. Earlier that summer, the USOC's membership and committee chair Thomas Satrom wrote in a letter that the USTU had "an allegiance to Korea to the detriment of U.S. programs in the interests of U.S. athletes." The USOC also criticized the organization for having four executive directors and five finance directors since 1997. "We are clearly a dysfunctional organization," said Christo Lassiter, an attorney who appeared on behalf of the USTU's board of governors. "This dysfunction has gone back ten, twelve years, and we very much appreciate what the USOC staff has done to right the ship."

A few months later in Seoul, Kim Un-yong, the head of the WTF, was sentenced to two and a half years in prison for diverting more than four million dollars from the federation and other sports organizations. He was also accused of accepting roughly one million dollars as bribes from business contacts. That speaks for itself.

In 2003, the Pan Am Games were held in Santo Domingo, a hot place that could have laughed at the Houston summers. Our team worked out on the concrete floor of a dance hall, because the dojo downtown had what press reports described as "canine aromas." The hall had a bar in the corner, a stage and a fog machine, in case anyone felt like a Scotch and a dance in between workouts.

I had a good time there. I felt a little more experienced, like the veteran of the team. I knew the routine. I had won the Pan Am (tae-kwondo only) Championships in 1996 and 1998 and the (multisport) Pan Am Games in 1999, so I felt I had control of the fighters in the region.

This time I was going up another class, into the welterweight divi-sion for the first time. I felt a lot stronger and even, oddly enough, a lot faster. I was much happier because there were fewer restrictions on what I was able to eat. I didn't have to force myself to cut as much weight, and I wasn't forcing myself to have workouts on days when my body needed rest. I really felt good. I know some of the experts felt I wouldn't be strong enough, especially since I wasn't used to fighting at that weight, but as I was getting older, the change really suited me. I may not have been faster as a welterweight than I was as a feather-weight or lightweight, but I felt faster, because the guys I was fighting against weren't as quick. All those years of having to keep up with the guys who relied on speed really gave me a quickness advantage against the welterweight guys who were used to relying on power. Because they were slower, I also had that extra split second to read them, and it seemed like guys were telegraphing their attacks much more often. Yes, there are knockouts in our sport, but as a rule, speed kills, and I felt the weight-class change really gave me a great speed advantage. Yes, my bigger opponents would also be stronger, but I've never really wor-ried about not having enough strength to tangle with somebody. In the end, I beat José Luis Ramirez of Mexico in the finals to win my second straight gold at the Pan Am Games.

It was great having Jean in my corner full-time. Yes, I could train with him before, but it was a huge help to be able to have a dia-logue with him about strategy between rounds. The other guys who had been in my corner, even the ones who could communicate with me in English, weren't as familiar with what I was comfortable trying and what sort of moves worked for me against shorter guys, taller guys, quicker guys, slower guys, aggressive fighters and passive counterat-tackers. Jean had this mental Rolodex of other guys I'd fought, and he could just say, "Hey, Steven, remember the time you fought this other guy? His style is a lot like this guy's. Remember how you beat him?" We don't have a lot of time for lengthy discussions between rounds, and Jean could reset my strategy with a few short thoughts I was able to put to use as soon as we started fighting again. His instant advice was a luxury.

It's a lot easier for me to compete than to watch my siblings com-pete. I'm very different from Diana, who is a real cheerleader. I'm a nervous pacer. You wouldn't know I'm so invested in the outcomes of the matches just from looking at me, because I don't make a lot of noise. Inside, it's like there are fifty-seven taekwondo bouts going on inside my stomach. Having them around makes me feel like I'm at home. That's one of the best feelings I have when I'm away from home. Just seeing my siblings around makes me feel like I have home-court advantage even if we're on the other side of the world.

In 2003, that place was Garmisch, a beautiful small city in the German mountains that once hosted a winter Olympics in 1936. We were staying in a hotel that overlooked the forest in front of us and the mountains beyond that. From my second-floor balcony I looked down onto a pond where I could see goldfish swimming around. It felt like we were staying in a toy city, almost like a gingerbread house. My friend Peter Lopez was there, although he had since switched affilia-tion and was then competing for Peru, the birthplace of his parents. In 2001 he won a silver. In 2003 he won a bronze and my brother won a silver. We hung out together and were just really happy. I had been in touch often the previous year with a girl named Lana, my friend from the Croatian team. We hung out together in Garmisch, and, well, that started another long-distance relationship.

This marked my first world championships at the new weight class. I really wanted to win worlds for Mark, who had been cheated out of his rightful gold medal earlier in the week. In the quarters, I fought Rosendo Alonso from Spain, a guy who was always on the

Julio and his wife, Ondina, emigrated to New York City in 1972 in the hopes of a better life to start their family in the United States of America.
PHOTO COURTESY OF LOPEZ FAMILY

Diana has always looked up to her older brothers and tried to follow in their footsteps. In 1985, Mark was trying to be Superman and jumped off the bookcase. Diana (at only twenty-two months of age) of course followed but didn't land quite right and ended up breaking her left arm.
PHOTO COURTESY OF LOPEZ FAMILY

The Lopez siblings have always been competitive, whether it be at playing board games like Monopoly or collecting numerous Taekwondo trophies. PHOTO COURTESY OF LOPEZ FAMILY

Diana and Mark spent much of their early careers training in the family garage with older brothers, Steven and Jean, dreaming one day of representing the United States at the Olympic Games.

Steven does an NBC interview in the Athlete Village at the 2000 Olympic Games in Sydney, Australia, prior to winning his first Olympic Gold Medal.

The Lopez family was all smiles after Steven won the family's first Olympic Gold Medal at the 2000 Olympic Games in Sydney, Australia. Ondina didn't make the trip and instead remained home in Houston praying for her son's safety.

Steven Lopez being photographed by *USA Today's* Robert Hanashiro for an Olympic cover section for the 2004 Olympic Games in Athens, Greece.

PHOTO BY CECIL BLEIKER

Jean and Steven give NBC *Today* show anchor Matt Lauer a few Taekwondo tips during an interview at the 2004 Olympic Games in Athens, Greece. PHOTO BY ANN BLEIKER

Former U.S. President and fellow Houstonian George H. W. Bush demonstrates his punch to the Lopez brothers during the Olympic Games in Athens, Greece.

PHOTO BY CECIL BLEIKER

Steven and Jean give Katie Couric of NBC's *Today* show a tour of the Athlete Village at the 2004 Olympic Games in Athens, Greece.

PHOTO BY CECIL BLEIKER

Julio, Diana, Jean, Mark, and Steven celebrate Steven's second gold medal with close friend and colleague Cecil Bleiker at the 2004 *Sports Illustrated* party in Athens, Greece.

PHOTO BY ANN BLEIKER

On April 29, 2008, the Lopez family appeared on NBC's *Tonight* show with Jay Leno, marking one hundred days until the Opening Ceremony.

PHOTO BY CECIL BLEIKER

Ondina and Julio are interviewed by the media awaiting the arrival of their kids at the Beijing airport. A special thanks to Hilton Hotels for making their trip a reality.

PHOTO BY ANN BLEIKER

A throng of media welcomed the Lopez siblings to Beijing, their first Olympics experienced by the whole family, including their mother, Ondina.

PHOTO BY ANN BLEIKER

Steven, Diana, Jean, and Mark pose with USA basketball player Kobe Bryant prior to the 2008 Olympic Games Opening Ceremony in Beijing, China.

PHOTO COURTESY OF MARK LOPEZ

Julio and Ondina Lopez are all smiles as they make their way to their first ever Olympic Opening Ceremony, thanks to Visa. PHOTO BY ANN BLEIKER

Steven had always dreamed of one day competing with all of his siblings at the Olympic Games, and in 2008, that dream came true. He hopes to repeat that feeling in London in 2012.

PHOTO BY CRAIG SESKER

The members of the Lopez family are big sports fans, and following practice at Beijing Normal University, they spent some time with USA soccer standout Julie Foudy and NFL football player Tiki Barber, who both worked for NBC in Beijing. The Lopez family plays soccer and football to stay in shape. PHOTO BY ANN BLEIKER

Ondina and Diana Lopez pose with friend and colleague Ann Bleiker and the Beijing Olympic Torch at the Coca-Cola experience in Beijing, China. Coca-Cola presented the Lopez Family with their "Live Positively Award" on August 15, 2008.

PHOTO BY CECIL BLEIKER

Lopez family members and close friends made the trip from Texas to Beijing to cheer them to victory.

PHOTO BY ANN BLEIKER

Mark, Steven, Diana, and Jean show off the hardware they collected at the 2008 Olympic Games. Mark won silver, while Steven and Diana took home bronze.

PHOTO BY ANN BLEIKER

Sports Illustrated writer and coauthor of this book, Brian Cazeneuve has covered the Lopez family story beginning in 2000 at the Sydney Olympic Games when Taekwondo made its Olympic debut as a full-medal sport. PHOTO BY CECIL BLEIKER

In 2008, the Lopez family made history by becoming the first ever family to have four family members on the same U.S. Olympic team and the first ones to capture three Olympic medals in the same year. This would not have been possible without their undying love and support for one another. PHOTO BY SMILEY POOL

podium and usually won bronze medals at worlds. I beat him fairly easily. He's tall, one of the few guys I fought who was my height. He was also pretty fast, but I was much stronger. Fighting at the new weight class, I was often taking on tall opponents, guys who were my height. That was a disadvantage, because I no longer had as much of an edge in reach over most of the other fighters, but it was also an advantage, because I was able to open up my fighting approach more without worrying about the quick, short guys sneaking in for points. I always felt more explosive than the guys who were my height. I was able to aim for bigger targets, which allowed me to score off the clinch. In the past, those clinches always worried me a little, because the short, quick guys would sometimes score sneaky points against me once we broke from the clinch.

I won two more matches, including another in the finals against a hometown favorite, Mohamed Ebnoutalib from Germany. I had never fought him before, but I had trained with both him and his brother, Faisal, when I was in Europe. We kept trading points, and the match had a really slow tempo to it. I almost felt like we were in a training gym, the way we traded points. Fortunately, I got the last one and had my second world title. This one was all for Marky.

That fall, we knew the U.S. team would have two spots each for men and women at the Athens Games. The USTU would then have to decide in which classes the United States would enter fighters. The logical choice would have been to pick the two classes for Mark and for me, because we were the strongest athletes on the national team and the ones with the best chances to bring home Olympic medals. I remember Juan Moreno, one of the people who made the decision, telling me that it came down to a discussion about whether Mark's silver medal at the world championships was more prestigious than the gold medal that Tim Thackery had won at the Pan Am Games. For us it was a no-brainer that the silver at worlds was bigger, because everyone is there. But ultimately, they chose the fin- and flyweights because they considered Tim's Pan Am gold medal to be more important. That created a very unusual situation. Because there were only two weight divisions available to the guys on the team, and neither Mark nor I would jump all the way down to flyweight, he and I would enter the Olympic trials in the same weight class. In the end, Tim failed to qualify his weight class for the Olympics, so I was our only male taekwondo athlete.

Soon after the world championships, Jean told Mark one day that they hadn't picked his weight class for the Games. I couldn't believe that they made that choice. Of course, Mark and I were the two best male fighters in the country, but that wasn't the main consideration they used when they chose the weight classes. It pretty much ended Mark's Olympic hopes for that year. First of all, he would have to move up in weight to a hundred and seventy-six pounds, which was a huge jump to make in six months. And if he was actually able to get through all the other fighters in the challengers' bracket, that meant the guy he would have to face for his first Olympic berth would actually be . . . me. I know people would have loved to have that match take place, but I can't say he and I would have. We had sparred together for many years, but we had never actually fought.

Throughout the winter we prepared the way we always do. Yes, we were okay with it, but no, we didn't like the decision, because we couldn't be teammates in Athens. We really didn't discuss the possibility of fighting during our training. We just did everything we could to make each other better, and if we had to cross that bridge, we'd do it. We've had teammates who have had to fight. Chris Martinez and Mark fought at the 2008 Olympic trials. I fought Jason. I fought David when I was growing up at the U.S. Open, but never had two Lopezes fought each other. Had it happened, Jean had already decided he would not be in either one of our corners. That was a courtesy he always gave to one of our teammates if one of them had to fight one of us. It wouldn't have been right for Jean to coach someone like Chris all year, for instance, and then show up on the bench on the opposite end of the mat with a world or Olympic berth on the line. It's a testament to how Jean sees the team.

I knew all along that Marky was completely deserving of another

Olympic berth, and he wasn't going to stop training, because, God forbid, if I got hurt sometime in the next few months, he would try to earn the spot at the trials. Marky still had to win the portion of the Olympic trials that was before the Olympic fight-off, before the winner was set to face me.

Mark fought four matches in the first phase of the trials. He started with Josh Coleman, who was a lot bigger than he was. Mark was fighting at a hundred and sixty-two pounds, fourteen below the limit. Josh was six-four and was usually around one eighty-five for his natural weight. It was different for Mark to have to fight guys who were maybe a little slower, but definitely much stronger than he was used to. He certainly didn't have to cut any weight before the competition, so he felt pretty strong the day of the match. It was fun for him, because he was able to stay on the outside and throw a lot of different kinds of kicks he didn't normally try in competition. He even threw a quadruple kick a couple of times, knowing that most of the other guys wouldn't be able to catch him. He had to be smart with Josh, who doesn't make a lot of mistakes and is actually pretty athletic and quick for his size. Marky called on some of his experience fighting as a junior, when he was so much smaller than everyone else. It was exhausting for Mark, because he was always on his toes and jamming on the inside, making sure not to get pushed around. Somehow he squeezed in a point on a three-hundred-and-sixty-degree kick and managed to keep Josh away the rest of the match. It was satisfying for him to beat Josh, because he was the guy who had beaten Jean at his last nationals, so Mark was able to avenge another loss for one of his brothers. He was also sort of fighting strategically for me, because we really felt Josh would have been a tougher opponent than Tony Graf, the guy who was going to fight the winner of Mark's fight and could ultimately face me in the fight-off. I had Tony's number, and we couldn't see any way he would have beaten me. It would have been really hard for Josh to beat me, too, but Josh would have negated my reach advantage, and, like a boxer who can knock people out, he certainly had a puncher's chance against anybody.

Tony was up next for Marky. He's a powerful guy, but shorter than Mark. He thought Tony was going to be tired, but he was surprised that his opponent had so much energy. Mark had four fights before that, and I'm not sure he paced himself too well. He was down one and caught Tony with an ax kick in the final seconds. The referee went to check with the other officials about whether to award Mark the two points. They talked, came back and decided that Mark had scored after time had elapsed. It meant that Tony would be my opponent at the fight-offs in San Jose. Tony was pretty good about it. He came up to Mark later and told him that he had a lot of class and he enjoyed fighting him. I was excited just watching the matches. I really wanted Mark to make it to the finals against me, as weird as it would have been to have to fight him. He almost had the match against Tony, and I was very proud of his effort.

That left me to tangle with Tony at the final stage of the Olympic trials, the fight-offs in San Jose. When Tony kept going off the line to try to get a better angle against me, I would just pick up my left knee to thwart his attacks. I kept thinking it was time for him to come up with a better strategy. I had never lost to him, and I kept waiting for him to throw in a new wrinkle or something I didn't anticipate. Instead, he was just very predictable and easy for me to read. I felt very much in control, and I scored my points the way I usually do—with front-leg roundhouse kicks that gave me the match.

Of course, later in the day, Diana had to fight Nia Abdallah for her chance to get on the team. That one made me nervous. Diana needed to get down to one twenty-five, but she was struggling with cutting weight. She went to the sauna on the day of weigh-ins, and she was really very tired. I was still pretty confident in her. I wish Diana had taken it to Nia a little bit more. Diana held a brief 2–1 lead in the third round, but then gave up a tying point that went to sudden death, but Diana couldn't pull it out. I remember thinking Diana was hoping for the best, instead of taking hold of the situation. Nia got in the winning kick twenty seconds into overtime.

Jean was pretty good, telling Diana, "There's nothing you could have done. You did your best. You have to come back stronger the next time." It wasn't quite so simple. Sure, she lost in 2000, but that was more of a learning experience. She was prepared for defeat then and she was okay with it, because as young and inexperienced as she was on the senior level, she knew it would lead to better and better things. This time, she found herself questioning her whole future in tae-kwondo. Of course, she would rebound, but at the time she found herself asking, Do I really want to keep going through with this?

Fortunately, the new blood at what was now USA Taekwondo made its first important decision a good one: They picked Jean to be the head coach at the upcoming Athens Olympics. The change for us to the new federation was like night and day. For one, we were being paid the stipend money we were supposed to receive. They also chose the right guy to be the head coach and were in frequent contact with Jean. The new federation really did a good job of talking to Jean about a pre-Olympic training trip to Malta. How many days should we be there? How far in advance should we leave? They were much more receptive to asking us what we needed as opposed to dictating to the athletes and coaches and people who knew us best what they de-cided we were going to do. Our stipend money doubled from two thousand dollars a month in 2000 to four thousand a month in 2004. The USOC also stepped in and made sure we received our stipend money directly from them, so the funds that were earmarked for us weren't used up by the federation before they ever got to us. As soon as Bob Gambardella got in as head of the new federation in 2004, I finally got my bonus from the 2000 Games. In 2008 they raised my stipend to sixty-five hundred dollars a month, which was among the most generous stipends they paid any summer athlete. It wasn't really necessary to give that money to basketball players or track athletes, because they had their own sources of revenue.

In the weeks leading up to the Games, we were getting more and more media requests and opportunities. In May, I attended the Media Summit again. Jean was also invited, since he was the Olympic head coach, and I was proud to see him get some of the attention he deserved. It was gratifying to see some of the most prominent journalists in the country asking questions of the person who had the foresight to give me my first media training. During that trip to New York, I also got to appear on *Late Night with David Letterman*. It wasn't like I had a whole segment with him; it was actually just a line. The producers invited ten different athletes who were going to compete at the Games that summer to read one line each from Letterman's top-ten list. The topic for this particular show was going to be Top Ten Perks of Being an Olympic Athlete.

That was cool. As an Olympian, I was happy to be one of the ones they picked. It was an acknowledgment for me, but more for tae-kwondo. Our sport was still pretty new on the Olympic program, so it was an honor for a taekwondo athlete to be up there reading off a top-ten list along with athletes from the higher-profile sports.

I was way more nervous than I ever was before a fight because I was completely out of my comfort zone. I didn't know if the line they gave me was going to be funny. I was concerned about my delivery. I could tell that people in the live audience were being pretty support-ive, but I had this image of friends back home sitting around, looking at one another, saying, "Yeah, that's just not funny, Steven."

We didn't have much time to meet with Letterman personally, but he did come into the holding room to shake everyone's hand. "Have fun with this," he told us. "You guys are the guests and you guys are the stars, so just enjoy yourselves. We're privileged to have you here."

I felt like such an amateur. I can only imagine what it's like for actors who have to memorize their lines, or even newscasters who get to read from a teleprompter, the way we did. Essentially they lined us up and told us where to read from the monitor. I was looking at them, trying to gauge how nervous they were compared to me. Then the words scrolled down and we each waited for our number to show up on the screen. I felt like someone who was thrown into the ocean without knowing how to swim, or like the kid in school who had to perform in a play in front of all the teachers, parents and classmates.

My line had something to do with the lagging preparations that were plaguing the Greek organizers before the Games. The whole list was pretty clever. For the record, here it is:

No. 10: Win the gymnastics competition and you get to keep the pommel horse.

No. 9: After the closing ceremonies, I can let myself go for three and a half years.

No. 8: Serving as an ambassador of peace, spreading my harmony through strangleholds.

Me at No 7: When we get to Greece, we get to help them build stadiums.

No. 6: It's fun to watch the bellboy try to lift my bags.

No. 5: Every four years, people pay attention to me—kind of like Ralph Nader.

No. 4: Free admission to Olympia Dukakis movies.

No. 3: Having your life story turned into a melodramatic montage narrated by Bob Costas.

No. 2: I get to beat up people in a different country for a change.

No. 1: Let's just say you can't be the next American Idol without our approval.

Feel free to laugh about this one, because if you don't I will, but about six weeks before the Games, *People* magazine picked me as one of its 50 Hottest Bachelors. Really? For real? How did that happen? Did they confuse me with some other guy named Steven Lopez? They came down to Houston. I was only concerned that it might make me look as if I were showing off. I didn't want to look like a guy who was trying too hard to be sexy, because, well, that's not sexy. Not cool.

I was hoping they would ask me to pose in a way that would let me look natural. At first they didn't seem to know what they wanted me to do. They asked me to wear an unbuttoned black shirt, which right away started to worry me. Then they took me to a fast-food drive-through in Rosenberg, outside of Houston. I kept telling myself, Steven, don't worry. They're the professionals. They know what they're doing. We took a few shots at that location and moved on. The photographer then asked me to bring some of my clothes with me to another location. I put on black linen pants and a black V-neck and they drove us out to a ranch. We stopped in a field and the photographer told me, "Okay, do something." Hmmm, I needed a little more direction than that. Finally they told me to wave my arms around. It didn't seem like much, but after eight hours of shooting, that was the shot they chose. I can't imagine what professional models go through.

The week after the issue hit the stands, I was on a plane and I noticed two girls sitting in the row behind me reading the 50 Hottest Bachelors issue of *People*. I had this uneasy where-do-I-hide? feeling, because I was still pretty shy about the whole thing. After we took off, one of the girls came up to me and asked, "Excuse me. Is this you?" Of course, she said it while the flight attendant was passing by, so the attendant then made an announcement for the entire plane to hear. So much for being incognito. Later I went back to go to the restroom and the attendant gave me a piece of paper asking me to contact her daughter.

My "hottest bachelor" status continued later that year when the producers of the entertainment series *The Bachelor* called Cecil asking about my availability to be the male subject on the show. It's every guy's dream. You get placed with two dozen beautiful, eligible bachelorettes. They all want to kiss you, tell you their stories and compete for your affection in front of the world. And we turned it down.

It was actually a pretty easy decision, especially as our family sat around and watched a couple of episodes of the existing show to see what it was really about. First of all, it would have interfered with my training. But also, we wondered if it was something I would really want to be remembered for. The situations they put the bachelors in don't really paint a good picture: Kiss one girl, tell a second one you love her, propose marriage to a third and dump all the rest. That isn't me and it isn't any of us.

Around that time, I started a brief job with the Home Depot through their Olympic Job Opportunities Program, which enables us to earn a full-time salary while working part-time hours that make accommodations for our training and competitions. I was a customer service rep in the lumber department, so if you needed help figuring out what wood to chop, I had you covered.

At the time, Jean was also acting as my agent. He negotiated a deal with McDonald's to have my picture on their cups and bags. It was a weird feeling to be walking through an airport, for instance, and see people carrying something with my picture on it.

Jean once got me a deal with the local Mercedes car dealership in Sugar Land. They provided me with a Mercedes for two years and it was a great ride. I felt I had arrived when I drove around my neighborhood in style. Everything was pretty smooth. Um, almost everything. I was filling up the car with gas one day and I must have been lost in an Olympic dream, because I drove off with the gas hose still in the tank of the car and ripped the hose right off the pump. The station manager came out and started waving and yelling at me. When I stopped, he told me I would have to pay the $140 to fix the pump and get a new hose. I gave him a VISA card, picked up my receipt and picked up the gas hose. When he asked where I thought I was going with it, I told him: "I just paid you $140 for it, so I'm taking it with me." That might be my most unusual souvenir.

Leading up to the Games, there was some talk, though not very loud, about our athletes staying home from Athens because of security concerns. A Senate security committee held a hearing in Washington about it and invited me to speak as a representative of the active Olympians. I was actually invited by Steven Bull, who was the USOC liaison in Washington, D.C. I had gotten to know him from going to the White House in 2000. They also invited Carl Lewis, one of the

Olympians we really admired as kids because of his sustained excellence in so many different events; and Mitt Romney, the Massachusetts governor who had organized the Winter Olympics in Salt Lake City in 2002. I was pretty nervous. Jean came with me and we both talked to Cecil over the phone the night before the presentation to go over some talking points. Essentially, I tried to point out how badly we wanted to attend and how hard we had trained in order to have our chance at becoming Olympians. I made the case that it would be a huge disappointment for us not to go after what we had sacrificed to be there. Carl then got up to talk about being a member of the 1980 team that boycotted the Moscow Olympics, a decision that was made by former president Jimmy Carter, but not supported by the vast majority of Olympians. Some important USOC people attended the hearing, including Jim Scherr, the USOC president, so I really wanted to do a good job. I spoke from notes, but I also tried to speak from the heart. Afterward, Jim told me I had done a good job on behalf of all the athletes. Romney also came up and thanked us for being great representatives of our country. Whew. It really was an honor to represent thousands of athletes from the twenty-eight summer sports, to be chosen to be able to speak well and articulate proper thoughts. It was just another time I had flashbacks to the interviews Jean would conduct with us in the garage. As I get older, my brother gets a lot smarter, if you know what I mean. The committee made no recommendations for us to boycott the Games. We were good to go.

Before I left for Europe, Diana gave me a simple but wonderful card that said simply, *Do it for me.* It was the perfect inspiration. We first attended a ten-day pre-Olympic camp in Malta, a very relaxing place. Mark was my training partner, and we were able to take a few breaks from training. We went on Jet Skis, enjoyed the water and took away some of the stress right before the Games. Mark came with me as my training partner in 2004 and was looking for a way to pass the time one day. Across from my hotel along the bay was a plot of land that was connected to ours by a thin strait. Mark decided to swim to it, as if it were an island. It took him forty-five minutes to get there.

Nobody believed him when he told people about it, so Nia bet him fifty dollars that he couldn't do it again. I told him not to do it, because he might either drown or catch a cramp, but he took the bet, and this time, with people watching on either side, he got in his morning work-out and made fifty dollars.

We arrived at the Olympic Village in Athens a few days before the opening ceremonies. The village itself was similar to the one in Sydney. When I arrived in the village, I had a feeling of coming back home, of being in a place that gave me warm and comforting thoughts of a time in my past that was really great. The rooms had two beds each, but they were pretty small. If I reached out, I could touch the walls on both sides. Jean and I shared a room, and the badminton guys were in the adjoining rooms within our dorm. Other than the small rooms, the setup was similar to what we had in Sydney. It was fun to go to the cafeteria and see the athletes from other sports and other countries. Once you hear all the different greetings people have, the many ways people say "hello" around the world, you really understand that you're back at an Olympic Games. Pin trading was a big deal at the Athens village. I never really got into that, but I appreciated how much the athletes from the other countries valued pins with the USA logo on them. I usually gave away a lot of my pins.

During the day, the members of the U.S. delegation would take buses to the American College of Greece on the outskirts of the city. Security there was really tight, given some of the anti-American senti-ment that had been building around the globe, but the remote setting had a lot of benefits. We could work out at our own designated times, instead of those that were assigned to us, and we had a great group of medical and sports medicine personnel on site to look after us. We usually had workouts in conjunction with guys from the other combat sports, like judo, wrestling and boxing.

The Bush girls visited there, and one day so did the first President Bush, who was in Greece to support the team. With gun-carrying agents from the U.S. State Department patrolling the wooded hills and rooftops, the former president posed for photos with individual teams, including ours. We could sort of identify with him, because we were also acting as ambassadors for our country. We gave him a USA taekwondo T-shirt, as if the man were hurting for T-shirts. A week later, we saw a Greek newspaper with a picture of him throwing a softball and he was wearing the shirt we gave him.

I was ready to fight pretty quickly in Athens, and the days seemed to move very slowly before I could. Some days Jean and Mark would be holding a bag and I would be kicking so hard that Jean would have to tell me to ease up. Mark didn't have a pair of sneakers with him one day, so he started playing basketball barefoot with the judo guys. He had so many blisters on his feet that he had to go to our sports medicine people for relief.

As always, it was great to have my family along. My dad actually took out a second mortgage on our house to pay for the family's hotel and trip to the Olympics.

Diana had understandable mixed feelings sitting out the competition in Athens. She got to wear a funky red-white-and-blue outfit as she sat in the stands for the competitions. She'd have not only Mark, but also a much larger contingent of friends and U.S. fans to talk to than we did in Australia. She visited the Acropolis, ate gyros and even played volleyball on the beach with my father, Tabetha and Peter Lopez. It was a beautiful place, yet it also made her wish she didn't have to be there just for fun.

Diana was having a tough time watching from the stands. Nia made it all the way through to the finals, finishing with a silver medal. She had Jean in her corner coaching her and I'm sure that helped, but Nia deserves credit for getting that far and bringing home a medal. Jean remembers telling Nia, "I know you fought my sister, but I'm here as a U.S. national coach, not as a brother. I want the best for you. I know your game better than you know your game." Nia kicks really long. Sometimes she's unable to find the distance and she gets frustrated. She's unconventional. When she's tired, she gets into trouble. Jean maximized her strengths. That was what he and Nia did for the whole month. Nia thanked Jean afterward.

Diana was conflicted when she watched Nia. She had been on all those teams, fought in all those tournaments and now she was watching someone else win that Olympic medal with our brother in her corner. One day, she sat alone by herself in the stands and just cried. Maybe it was jealousy. Maybe it was disappointment. Maybe it was a missed opportunity. It obviously felt bad. It could have been her. She went over to Jean one morning and told him what she was feeling. "Well, Diana," he told her, "it really still can be you in four more years. Nia listened to everything and she did very well. Now you have to go back, train hard, forget about the past and look at the future." He was right. She really didn't want to hear that, but she needed to hear it. There was no way around the fact that she had to start fresh and go through four more years if she wanted her own Olympic medal. For the rest of her life, she would regret not giving it her all to get to that point.

Iraq had won a wild card entry into the tournament, and they chose to put one of their athletes, Raid Rasheed, into my weight class. Of course we drew each other for the first match. The Greek crowd was definitely supporting Rasheed. When the public address announcer said my name, I heard boos, whistles and people who spoke English yelling for the U.S. to get out of Iraq. It felt as if I were back to fighting an Egyptian in Cairo or a Korean in Seoul again. I guess I wanted to take the edge off the tension a little bit, so when I came out for the obligatory prematch handshake in the center of the mat, I handed him a gift, the same model of T-shirt we gave to President Bush back at the American College of Greece. I doubt he ever wore that shirt around the city of Baghdad, but I wanted to do it as a peace offering. I did get a few claps from the crowd. I did it because I imagined the people of Iraq, and for that matter the whole Muslim world, watching, and I wanted them to think of an act of friendship when they saw an American fighter. Again, sometimes you represent your country with defiance; other times you offer a handshake. I really wanted people who thought badly of us to remember the handshake.

Fortunately it was a pretty easy match. I hit him at will and knocked his helmet off with one kick that wasn't scored. Between rounds, I told Jean, "This is going to be another one of those matches. Maybe I have to knock this guy out to win." Of course, being the voice of reason, Jean shook his head and said, "Steven, calm down. You know you don't need to do that in this match. Just outclass him. He can't keep up with you. Nobody is going to cheat you out of that many points, and you don't want to get the crowd totally against you." Score another one for my older brother. I was pretty delicate about it. I scored with kicks, but didn't do any punching off the clinch. I didn't want the referees to be influenced by the crowd building up so much dislike for me that it carried over to the other fights. In the end, I won 12–0. I shook Rasheed's hand, patted him on the head and made sure to bow to him and his coach once we got to the corner.

I was really looking forward to my second match against Victor Estrada from Mexico. He was somebody I'd looked up to for a long time. He was thirty-two years old at the time of the fight, a real battle-tested veteran who had actually won a bronze medal at the world championships all the way back in 1993. He also won the bronze at eighty kilos in Sydney. I remember when I first made the national team in 1994, I'd watch him fight and think, Wow, that's where I want to be. Before going into that match, we were seated down in the waiting area and Victor was talking to two members of his support staff: his coach, who was seated off to the side, and another man, perhaps an assistant or performance coach, who was actually seated behind me. They were speaking in Spanish, but of course I could understand them. The guy behind me was telling him, "Victor, you know what you're supposed to do? You know the special plan we made?" I actually think he was saying those things less to reassure Victor and more to try to knock me off my game. I knew then that Victor was going to bring his best. It was a way for him to make history if he could win the tournament, and I took it to mean that he felt he would if he got past me.

Victor was pretty aggressive with me early in the fight. In the first minute, we broke from a clinch and he stuck out his right leg and pushed me over the leg onto the ground. He lost a point for it, but he wanted to let me know he wasn't conceding the match to me just because I had won the Olympics four years earlier. A minute later, I threw a nadabong kick at the same time he kicked. The kicks landed simultaneously, but they counted only his. Estrada was a very smart fighter. With his experience, he anticipated my moves better than other opponents. A minute later he scored again just as we both kicked. I trailed 2–0 (actually 1–0 with his deduction) after the first round, and I knew early it was going to be tough to come back against him. Jean was good at telling me to stay on him, that I could keep the pace longer than he could. "If you can keep your intensity level," Jean told me, "he will fall. He will crumble." Leave it to Jean to say just the right thing to fire me up.

The first ten seconds of the second round were huge. He came out and threw an ax kick at my head with his left leg. After I ducked back to avoid the kick, I countered with my right leg against the left side of his body that he had left exposed once he missed the kick. I had my point right away. Forty seconds later I scored on another counter, this time kicking my left leg over his as he tried to attack my right side. Victor still wasn't finished. With a minute left in the second round, he landed a kick to my backside. The kick wasn't within the target area, but he earned a point for it. In the closing seconds of the round, I backed him up and showed him my left leg, as if I weren't really going to use it. He hesitated, and that moment of indecision allowed me to flick the leg out and catch his rib cage. I was ahead, but we were in a tight fight with a round to go.

A minute into the round, I backed him up and looked for an opening. He might have kept track of how little room he had, but he left himself exposed right by the edge of the mat. I caught him with my left leg and knocked him straight out of bounds, down the ramped mat and onto the ground. He got up after rolling backward a few times, but the match was under control at that point. He received both deductions, so the match ended 4–2 in my favor, and I was through to the semis after what I considered my toughest fight of the tournament.

I was warming up before the next match and I felt a really bad cramp, like a charley horse, in the middle of my left hamstring, just as I was doing a lunge stretch. It calmed down again, but then I lunged with the other leg and the same thing happened to my right hamstring. I might have been dehydrated when I felt that cramp. Jean came by and asked how I felt. I told him I thought I was tired, but the turnaround before the next match was very brief and I remember him saying, "We don't have time for tired."

My next opponent was Youssef Karami, the Iranian I had bowed out to at the world qualifier, after I had already qualified the Olympic slot. Karami had won the other bronze at eighty kilos in Sydney, and was world champ in 2003 in Garmisch. There were too many points in the next match against Karami of Iran to mention them all, but I felt I had it under control even though the 7–6 final score didn't indicate that. Essentially, I took the lead and we traded points for the rest of the match. The referee scored points for each of us on a couple of exchanges. I remember how odd the final twenty seconds turned out to be. He was down by only one, but he seemed almost resigned to the outcome. I was waiting for one last desperate attack that never came. Instead he kind of leaned and hesitated and just let the clock expire. I'm not sure if he was tired and happy to make the match close or if he had too much respect for me, but he ended a good match on a pretty quiet note. I was one match away from another gold medal at the Olympics.

Bahri Tanrikulu was a very experienced Turkish fighter, with three world medals, including gold in 2001 in the middleweight division. (He later added a second gold in 2007 in the same weight class.) His sister, Arize, was also representing Turkey at the Olympics. I had heard rumors that he had hurt his arm in a previous fight, but he couldn't have been too hurt if he made it to the finals. Everyone is hurting by the end of an Olympics. I figured I might have trouble with him, because he was very fast. He liked to double and triple up with his kicks, something I had often faced when I fought at the lighter weights, but not so much now. I got off to a slow start in the match and we were even, 1–1, after the first round. By then I was starting to figure out his rhythm. I had already felt like the stronger fighter, and once I adjusted to his speed, I felt very comfortable. Midway through the second round, I backed him into a corner, then pushed him off me and caught him with a left-leg roundhouse, just as he was about to duck out of bounds. I let out a loud yell, as if to confirm the strike, and I had a 2–1 lead. In addition, the referee gave the Turk a kyong-go for going out of bounds. Now I was in control. After that exchange, we spent the next twenty seconds bouncing up and down, looking for an opening and not attacking. The referee gave each of us a kyong-go. With Tanrikulu's previous infraction, he now had a gam-jeon and was down 2–0, with a kyong-go outstanding for me.

Jean gave me a kiss on the cheek before the last round. (You need to be coaching your brother to get away with that.) He warned me to be careful of the two-point kick to the head and be sure to pick my spots. Once again, we came close to a clinch near the corner and I caught him with another left-leg kick that went under his right arm. I realized then that his arm was probably hurt, because he was so slow to get it back down to where he could block me. Again the referee warned him, which essentially meant I had scored a point and a half. I knew he wanted me to open up so he could counter with a two-point kick to the head. He was down by three and it was really his only chance to score quickly. I knew that and threw in a few fakes by twisting my hips and pretending that I was going to come at him with a roundhouse. I didn't need to score anymore, and that let me take some seconds off the clock until there was a minute to go. In the final minute I chased him out of bounds again, causing him to take a gam-jeon and leaving him with a negative point. He did a good job on the next exchange, knocking me off balance by kicking at my legs and then kicking me in the chest with a left-leg roundhouse. That brought him back to zero and left me up three with forty-five seconds to survive. At this point, instead of staying away, I came in close a couple of times, knowing that he needed to extend and go for the knockout. By now he was really tiring, and his kicks were slowing down so much I was having an easy time blocking them. With ten seconds to go, I could hear our U.S. contingent counting me down to zero.

Again I dropped to a knee, crossed myself and pointed to the heavens, just as I had four years earlier. I then looked into the stands for my siblings and blew them a kiss. I didn't have to worry about Jean getting arrested this time, because he was waiting for me in the corner.

As we hugged, I felt a completely different range of emotions than I had four years earlier. It wasn't new, but it was harder. I had fought three prior world champions out of my four matches. I had gone through similar, even more taxing physical tolls before, but the emotional challenge of getting up for one seasoned pro after another gave me one of my greatest days.

As I had in Sydney, I went to the post-meet press conference and gave several interviews before heading to the Main Press Center for a press conference and then to *NBC Olympic Late Night* with Pat O'Brien. Somehow Mark became Cecil's assistant with the media along with Cecil's sister, Ann, who was the diving team's press officer tour that night. After we finished at NBC, we again celebrated with *Sports Illustrated*, but this time we all went to *SI*'s amazing invitation-only party along the water. There was great music, great food and a large collection of athletes who had finished their events and were letting loose at the same time. My family, even my father, came along. We also invited Pano Iannakopoulos, a seventeen-year-old native Greek who had come all the way to Houston to train with us over the previous year. Pano's mother had given him a plane ticket back home to Athens for his high school graduation. Pano said he never expected to be able to attend such a great party in his home country. He wanted so badly to be able to learn from the Lopezes that he improved his English and finished his high school in Houston. I don't know how he did it, but Cecil was able to get our entire party of fourteen, including non-Olympians, into this most exclusive party. I'd heard they were turning away Olympians after it got really crowded, but we rolled up to the front gate at two in the morning in three minivans. In front of us they turned away a Ferrari, but let our three vans through. That made me feel pretty special. We left when the sun came out.

We didn't get much sleep though, as Cecil had me set up for several live television interviews beginning at eight a.m. Not much rest, but that's the price you pay as an Olympic champion. I couldn't tell Cecil I wanted to sleep. After all he was the one who worked so hard to get our whole group into the *Sports Illustrated* party the night before. Besides, it's nice to receive the attention after such a big personal accomplishment. Cecil also had me set to participate in the USA delegation closing press conference at the Main Press Center at eleven a.m. This time I was on stage with all of the stars of the U.S. Team, as well as Jim Scherr, the CEO of the USOC. It was very gratifying for me when Scherr recognized my brother Jean, who was in the audience at the press conference, for what he had helped me accomplish. Jean never got the recognition he deserved as an athlete, so it was great to see him finally being recognized now. After the press conference, Cecil took me to the set of The *Today* show, and I was in for a surprise. My family was there except for my mom, who was back in Houston. Cecil and Mark the night before had prearranged with the NBC producers for a satellite hookup with my mom back in Texas. I had no idea that was coming until they told me to watch the monitor, because they had a special guest who wanted to talk to me. Okay, I figured, who could it be? All of a sudden I saw her face and heard her sweet voice: "Hi, baby," she said. Wow, score one for Cecil and Mark. You guys got me. Given how shy my mom is, I was really surprised she agreed to do that. Seeing her made me so happy. It was a thrill to share that moment with her. I remember thinking she had overcome her shyness because she was just so proud. It was one of my favorite moments from Athens or any other trip. So that's why Cecil enlisted Mark to be his assistant.

I got back to Sugar Land and received another key to the city. It was great to have, although I now have a lot of keys that don't actually open anything. I had done a sponsor promotion that day, so I had my medal with me. That night I was at a club in Houston called Red Door and the E! network happened to be there. Of course, Mark and my friends let them know I was there, so I was interviewed on E! about partying in Houston. After an hour or so, we actually played a sort of joke on the people who were just coming into the club. We have a friend named Landry who is black and skinny. We put the medal around his neck and started spreading the word that the Olympic marathon champion was there all the way from Kenya. After a few minutes, everyone started chanting, "Kenya, Kenya." Word travels fast. Probably faster than Landry. A few days later we were at a club named Opus, where a local radio station held a "Welcome, Steven Lopez" night.

Again I had an easy decision to make about continuing. I never hesitated about it. I was definitely not going to medical school now, but the real incentive was a chance to go to the Olympics with Mark and Diana. I'm sure Marky would have been there in 2004 if they had only chosen his weight class. Diana lost out by a single point in overtime. We were so close that we knew it was a realistic dream.

CHAPTER 13

Good Things Happen in Threes

by Mark Lopez

'd like to say Steven, Diana and I were all in good places right after the Athens Games. But in fact, Steven was physically beaten up, and Diana and I were both dealing with the aftertaste of not making the Olympic team. The 2005 year was a test of our capacity—and Jean's—to build a family rally.

I really admired the way Steven had persevered over the previous few years. They had been difficult on his body. He cut weight a lot. He had broken bones. He had torn ligaments in his ankles. Throughout 2004, he'd feel a pain high on his left hamstring, near where it attaches to the pelvic bone. There were some things he couldn't do. If he did a double kick, he could go right-left, but he couldn't go left-right. If he tried ax kicks, he could try them only from certain angles. He could do sprints, but he couldn't do ten in a series.

Steven's new dream was to make it alongside us. He still needed a break after 2004 to try to rest his hamstring. The time off made much of the pain go away, but when he started to work out again, the discomfort came and went. He finally underwent an MRI at the training center, where they discovered a tear right at the attachment between the muscle and the pelvic bone. The doctors told him that if he had addressed it when it first tore, about eighteen months earlier, he could have had surgery then. But because the body was trying to heal itself as he kept putting pressure on it, he had built up a lot of scar tissue in the area. If he decided to have surgery at that point, it might get better, it might be roughly the same or it might get worse.

Steven didn't need to do as much grunge work now. Part of what Jean put us through was as much mental as it was physical. He would try to build up our will as he built up our technical knowledge. Steven was experienced enough that he knew a lot of what he should do, and he didn't have to prove any will in training. Of course, I still had to train in order to be physically prepared, but Jean began taking his foot off the accelerator with him, making sure he didn't come down with stress fractures or injuries that simply resulted from the overtraining that can take its toll on the body of a veteran athlete. Steven had once needed to run six to nine miles a day to lose weight. He used to do frog jumps, duckwalks, jump hops and other exercises with our teammates around the garage until only one of us was left standing. Those things were no longer possible if he wanted to keep his body whole. He still had markers for himself when it came to running the mile or riding a stationary bike. When he's in good shape, for example, the readout on the bike will tell him that he's riding at eighty rpms and he's lost four hundred and ten calories. When he's in good shape, he's close to breaking five minutes for the mile, something between 5:02 and 5:20. In taekwondo, you really don't have benchmarks to judge the speed of a kick, for instance, so he still needed to maintain some sort of quantifiable tests for himself. The bike tests cardio, and the mile run is a good combination of power and speed.

The previous two world championships were big wake-up calls for Diana. She had dominated her competition from the time she was five years old. As a senior, she had more adjustments to make and less certainty about her match results. After the disappointment of 2004, Diana came back home with a new determination. She had a strict schedule for herself. She wasn't just going to go home and lie around in between workouts. She had school to attend, and the balance really helped her get her mind off the disappointment of not competing in Athens. She felt as if she were bettering herself as a person.

She didn't cut weight properly. She wanted it so badly, she just worked out and went to the sauna all the time. She didn't eat properly, and she used to overthink everything. She had fun doing it, but she thought about it all the time. It was around that time that our teammate Chris Martinez told her to read *The Power of Now* by Eckhart Tolle. She always used to dwell on the past, and the message of the book is that it's important to live in the present, to make the most of what's in front of you. That really helped Diana live day by day and not worry about what she missed out on.

Diana started going to school at Wharton County Junior College near the house and took core courses for the first two years. She figured classwork would have overwhelmed her if she had gone to a bigger university. Instead she got to be a normal person. When she went to speech class, she would talk about the Olympics, but she also got emotional talking about the fact that she didn't make the team. This time she understood what she was doing, and everything was in place. She worked much harder in college than she ever had in high school.

She had to figure out her field of concentration, and two things helped her make the decision. First of all, she had been teaching little kids in taekwondo at Jean's gym since she was eighteen, and she was really enjoying it. Second, she watched her friend Maria get a degree in childhood education and saw how much she enjoyed it. That was it. Diana was going to study to become a teacher, too. These little kids brought joy to her day. They would be so honest with her, telling her, "Miss Lopez, you have big eyes." They would hug her after and make her feel so loved. She decided she'd be a childhood-education major. She'd make a difference in some young lives. Maria told her how she went about it, what classes to take and why it was worth it. She went to the University of Houston, so Diana applied there after junior college, and she declared her major in 2006. She took only a couple of classes at first while she was still training. For Diana, it was like being back amid the comforts of high school, but with an older crowd, and it was good for her to have some new people to talk to when she wasn't studying.

A month before the 2005 team trials for the world championships in Madrid, Diana went overseas and won the German Open. She didn't have to go there, but she told Jean she hadn't fought in a while, and she liked the more aggressive style of fighting they have in Europe and the way the judges score points more often when you kick. Jean was already going with a junior team. She fought in the hundred-and-thirty-pound division, beating two Turkish girls. A month later she went to the world trials in Dallas. In the best-of-three finals, she faced a veteran named Stephanie Beckel, whom she had beaten often over the years. Diana got off to a bad start and lost the first match. She went over to Jean and started recounting kicks she had landed during the match that hadn't been scored, and he told her to forget about it.

"Diana, that match is over," he said. "You know you can beat her twice, no problem, but you can't fight a match that's already over."

He was right. Between matches, Diana also called Chris Martinez, our teammate who wasn't at the trials, and he said roughly the same thing. "Diana, you know you can beat her ten times in a row if you have to. So just beat her twice."

She settled herself down, scored early in both matches and used her defense to get two victories and earn a trip to Madrid.

Things were good even before we went to worlds. Nia was on the national team in another weight class, and she and Diana both congratulated each other on making the squad. Nia came to the school to train with us one day. It was good for team morale, and it also confirmed for Diana when she saw Nia get tired that Diana had been training harder. Steven, Diana and I were all on the team, and Jean was going with us as the head coach. With new leadership governing our sport and the USTU out of the way, we sensed that this was going to be a really good year. Our family had a certain energy that summer. It was the first time we all made the same team for a major international competition, and we all fed off one another's enthusiasm. Nobody had to feel guilty about leaving anyone else behind.

Diana was also able to feed off of negative energy, or at least one comment that stayed with her through the championships. We were all training together at the Olympic Training Center one day when she went up to Juan Moreno and asked in passing if he had advice for ways she could improve.

"Actually, Diana," he said, "I think you're too slow for this weight class. You'd be better off fighting as a lightweight."

She didn't know if that had anything to do with his time working with Nia, but Diana looked at him and said, "Thanks," and in her mind she thought, Yeah, I'll never ask you for anything again. She went straight to Jean a minute later and mentioned Juan's comments.

"Diana, let him say what he wants," he told her. "You're fine. And you're working really hard, just the way we talked about after Athens. Keep it up."

It was quite a contrast from the punch in the gut from Juan to the pat on the back from Jean. I'm sure Juan didn't mean anything bad by it, but Diana was determined to prove him wrong. During that camp, she actually had a dream about losing her first match in Madrid, exactly the way she had at the previous two world championships. She never told any of us about it, because she didn't want us to think she was weakening or doubting herself.

Once all those crooked guys from the USTU were gone, I felt a big difference. We all did. When Bob came in and the other guys were kicked out, I felt I had a fighting chance. I was still young, still athletic and I still had my family to train with. My focus after 2004 was on being hopeful and positive and making sure they couldn't possibly pick another weight division.

I was becoming a more versatile fighter. Before, I'd throw one kick and move out of the way. Now I was becoming more offensive, started punching more, tried to find the right mix of techniques. I was sparring one day with a guy named Jake Stovall, who fought in a traditional style—the way we originally competed, where you just use your front leg and throw more punches. Punches didn't really score, but they could take their toll and discourage you from attacking. I didn't want to say anything that day, but it worked with me. He may not have had the WTF technique, but he was strong and he could punch. That convinced me to punch more often, especially against competitors who seemed to be easily intimidated.

I had some bad news: Because of the stress I had put on my left ankle in compensating for the nerve damage under my knee, I developed bone spurs in that ankle and had to get another surgery after the team trials. I felt fine, but I also had been training at only a hundred percent for a few months. Fortunately, I also had some good news that helped me get through the bad news: Dagmar had become a solid source of support for me through both good and bad times. Even in those early phone conversations I could see what kind of person she was, that she had good morals and ethics. She had my Latin background. She knew all the movies and shows I liked to watch. Back then we both liked comedies, like *Night at the Roxbury*, *Dumb and Dumber*, *Ace Ventura*, anything with Will Farrell or Jim Carrey.

She always had a willing ear and a kind heart. I remember the day we were driving around once and spotted a dog that was obviously overheated and emaciated. Dagmar made sure we stopped the car so she could rescue the dog, first of all to make sure it didn't get hit by a car and then to make sure it had some food. It didn't have a collar or any hint of an owner, so Dagmar took the dog to get some food, then took it to the vet to get some shots, and finally saw to it that the dog found a home.

It was ironic and sad that Steven's dog, Ninja, had died during the training camp before the world championships in Madrid. My mother and Dagmar had looked after Ninja in her final days. When Dagmar arrived in Spain, she wanted to wait until after the competition to tell me that Ninja had died.

Steven was set to fight on the opening night of competition. Diana and I were up four days later. We were nervous about Steven fighting a Korean in the first bout. I knew how much energy we, and especially Diana, could expend just cheering for him, and how that could tire us out. But with four days in between his fight and ours, we weren't going to stay back in the hotel. Diana wasn't so worried about losing her voice cheering, but she made an effort not to pace around as much, so she could conserve her legs.

Steven said he was pretty confident about worlds in 2005. It was his third year as a welterweight, and he was the defending world and Olympic champ. At those worlds, he made it more difficult for himself than he should have. Instead of fighting the way he usually does, he was trying out some things he didn't need to. Until that point in his career he had never had a sudden-death match. He had a couple that year, and he gave Jean a lot of white hairs.

Steven drew the Korean Chang-ha Jang in the first match. It was early in the morning and everyone in the stands from all sides of the arena tried to move over near our ring to watch. Steven had fun in that match. He did doubles. He did triples. He dipped into his repertoire to use an unusual nadabong trap hook kick, which is a really difficult technique he usually just messes around with in practice. Essentially, while he's in the air he starts into a nadabong, a kick that follows a three-hundred-and-sixty-degree turn. Instead, when he lands, he's in an open stance with his right leg forward, the opposite of the stance he usually takes. This time, he took a nadabong step, inviting the Korean to kick. As he did, Steven stopped and nailed him with a left-leg hook kick. They were even, 3–3, after regulation time. In sudden death, Steven did a sequence of five straight kicks, before one clearly got through and he won the match.

Two matches later, Steven won a lackluster match in sudden death against a competition from Brazil. After the match, Jean told him that if he fought like that again, he wouldn't coach him. Steven wasn't digging the way he can dig. Steven turned it up and fought his way into the semifinal contest against Rosendo Alonso of host Spain. That was one I'll never forget. With the match in Spain, we had some visitors whose presence we welcomed. They were plainclothes U.S. military guys from the U.S. embassy. We never got wind of any particular threats against us, but once our soldiers went into the Middle East, it never hurt for athletes or anyone else officially representing the United

States to have some people there to look after them. The crowd was pretty rowdy that day, and they weren't exactly supporting our team.

Steven was up 2–0 against Alonso after the first round, thinking of pressing the attack and keeping him on the defensive. Alonso was fighting very efficiently, and he countered Steven twice before sending the match into sudden death, 2–2. The match was in Spain, and Steven was thinking, If the guy kicks anywhere near me, the crowd will go crazy, as if he's just knocked me out. For that reason, he knew he had to fight smart. At the same time, he twisted his ankle, which was swelling up so much he was trying to hide it. Steven waited for Alonso to attack, avoided his kick, caught him off balance, scored with a counter and made a really loud noise so everyone would know he had scored. The referee gave Steven the winning point, to a huge chorus of boos and whistles from the stands. Maybe to cover his own rear end, the center ref called in all the corner judges to confirm, which they all did. As this was happening, the people who operate the overhead video monitor kept replaying the winning point on the screen. You could see Alonso falling over with part of his body obscured, so it looked as if Steven were kicking him on his butt while he was already down. Now the crowd was booing even more, especially after Steven's point popped up on the scoreboard.

An hour later, Steven came out for what he assumed was going to be his final match against Ali Tajik of Iran. But as he walked out, the guy coming out on the other side was Alonso again. Say what? The crowd started roaring its approval when they saw Tajik. Steven turned to Jean to ask if he had any idea what this was about. He had no idea either.

Finally, an official from the WTF walked over to them and started explaining. "Steven, you know taekwondo has given you a lot," he said, at which point Steven mentioned that he had given a lot to taekwondo, and what did that have to do with the fact that the Spaniard he had just beaten was standing across from us? "Steven, would you please do that over, just the sudden death?" Jean and Steven were stunned. Do it over? These were the world championships, not some local tournament where you made up the rules as you went along. There was nothing in the rules that called for the match—and certainly not just the sudden death—to be replayed an hour after the fact. "For the crowd, Steven," he said. "The crowd would like it."

Jean and Steven were dumbfounded. Why did the officials wait until they walked out to spring this on them? Now the crowd was in a frenzy again, and our team would look like bad sports if we didn't agree to something that wasn't even in the rules. Steven told Jean there was no way he was going to risk the match on a single point. For sure they would find a reason to give that point to the home guy. Instead, Steven said, if anything he'd fight the whole match again, leaving nothing to luck, and just go out and kick Tajik's butt. Jean didn't like that idea, so he, Bob Gambardella and Herb Perez, our taekwondo team's head of delegation, went over to the officials to state our case and stand by the rules. As they did, one of the arena cameramen was standing right next to Steven, getting a close-up on his face. As Steven's profile flashed across the overhead video screen, fans broke into a chant that I recognized in Spanish as meaning "son of a bitch." I have never had a problem with whistles and boos from fans, but that one made us think of our mom, and made us really take it personally. Steven was very close to making a certain gesture that he knew would have inflamed the crowd. He held back and controlled himself, but it was a hard thing to do. Honestly, at the moment the meeting broke up with the officials and Jean walked back to Steven I had no idea who was going to fight next. The resolution: Tajik from Iran . . . well, and the entire crowd, which was really out for Steven's scalp now.

Steven kicked and fell a couple of times because he just couldn't kick with his right foot. He still scored twice in the first round, and with a left-foot fast kick and a defensive roundhouse he basically looked like he controlled the rest of match. Steven finally drove Tajik out of bounds in the final round to secure the match. Afterward, the crowd was throwing glass bottles into the arena, and we were a little scared. Our military friends rushed us out of the building to the hotel before we had too much of an exchange with the crowd.

After Steven won, Diana and I turned to each other and said, "Yeah, okay, now it's our turn." It really was. We had both been though so many close calls and disappointments over the years: points we should have scored, matches we thought we should have won, teams we should have made. We kept telling each other that this was not a time for could-haves and should-haves. This was a time for us to be champions.

Later that night, Ireno Fargas, one of the men who used to coach the Spanish national team, came over and apologized to Jean for the behavior of his countrymen. Fargas had coached the guy Jean had fought against in the '95 finals. In Madrid, Fargas invited him to do a seminar in 2006 for kids with cerebral palsy at La Loma in Mexico. When they went out to dinner at a Chinese restaurant in Mexico, he told Jean that he had been the better fighter on that day in 1995, but he had been outcoached. When he said that, it gave Jean chills. It really hit him how close he had been. It was almost like he needed that to have closure. He couldn't stop thinking about it a couple of times a day for the next month. He didn't have the luxury of having someone to believe in him that he has given to us. If he hadn't made the decision in 1996 to open up his gym and dedicate himself to his siblings, we wouldn't have been where we were at that moment in Madrid, with one title in the bank and two more on the table.

Diana and I were set to fight on the last day. She told herself she was going to do everything I did in the days leading up to our fights. She ate what I ate. She trained and rested on my schedule. If we went to lunch and she was eating light in order to make weight, I might tell her, "Diana, we have a few days until we fight. You're only two pounds over. Just eat smart, but don't stop eating." We ate small portions in Spain, but we ate well. How can you not? We'd have chicken paella and *croquetas*, light pastries with cheese, chicken or beef on the inside. As long as she saw me doing that, she felt comfortable doing it. As long as she had me there, she didn't have to worry about whether she was doing the right things, because she believed in what I was doing and she just went along. I think for Diana her bond with me is even closer than it is with Steven and Jean. We're closer in age, and we always fight on the same day because we're in equivalent weight classes. I've always been more confident in her than she is in herself.

Diana could never sleep in late in the morning during the trip to Madrid. Each morning she'd go for a jog in the city plaza with some of our teammates. It wasn't so much to cut weight, but to relax and start the day.

We weighed in the day before we fought, which gave us the freedom to go out for a good dinner that night. We went to a steakhouse and really ate a good meal. If you've ever cut back on eating for several days and then broken the pattern with a big meal, you know how your body just exhales and wants to sleep after the meal. That must have helped her go to sleep that night, because she was out pretty fast, but she felt kind of sluggish the morning of fight day. She drank a Red Bull and a cup of coffee to wake herself up. That helped her at the start of the day, but she would pay for it later.

Diana likes to feel good in order to fight well. Steven can fight with a pulled hamstring and shake it off. If marching bands and fireworks suddenly went off in front of him, he probably wouldn't even notice. But Diana was in trouble. She was severely dehydrated. She had black tongue. Jean was telling her before the final round, "We're six minutes away. Dig deep. Muster any kind of energy and any strength. We train harder than we compete, so we're ready for anything."

Since my fights sometimes overlapped with Diana's, Jean would be the busiest man in the building, running from ring to ring all day. Diana fought Miriam Bah from the Ivory Coast in her first match. Athletes from African countries can be very tricky. They kick anywhere. It was a good start to her day. She was willing to kick to Diana's legs or anywhere, so Diana had to be alert. The woman used a few doubles and woke Diana's legs up. Diana was safely ahead after two rounds, so at that point, Jean ran over to help me.

The holding area was like a cold garage. I came back and put my legs up to rest. It reminded me of the junior worlds, when Diana and I were both fighting and both checking up on each other in between fights.

An hour after my victory, Diana had her second match against Zuhridinova Sayyorahon of Uzbekistan. She was much shorter than Diana was, but she was also very strong. She scored the first point, and she was very tough on the inside. Jean told Diana to take advantage of her reach advantage and kick on the woman's motion, because that way she'd beat her to the target. Diana kicked on her motion twice, scoring both times to take the lead. The crowd was loud all day, and Diana was very sharp during the whole match. She was ahead of her opponent on most exchanges, scored easily on defensive roundhouse kicks and pulled away to win the match 5–2.

Diana fought Maria Cabello from Venezuela next in the quarter-finals. Juan mentioned between bouts that Cabello had a very good front leg, which kind of fired Diana up. She realized once the match started that it was a very slow front leg and it was also just about her only weapon. Diana was able to read her opponent very easily. She scored off her motion, in the clinch, using doubles, just about any way she wanted. She won the match 7–0, and it felt like nothing was going to stop her. My dad would probably say it was like a batter who waits for his pitch and sees a beach ball floating into the strike zone. Diana knew she was just at her best, and it felt awesome. She had cinched at least a bronze medal, but she still wasn't content. She wanted to prove to everyone that she had what it took to be one of the best in the world, and that she could have won a medal at the Olympics.

Diana knew her next opponent pretty well. Karine Sergerie from Canada had come to the States to train with us for a while. She stayed with us and spent Halloween with my family one year, so she and Diana were familiar with each other in and out of the ring. She was also shorter, but very strong. She usually fought at a hundred and thirty-six pounds, but she had cut down to a hundred and thirty for that competition, and it took something out of her. They cut the competition floor down to one center ring for the semis and finals, and

Diana loved being in the center of everything again. Give Karine credit, because she stayed aggressive and made a fight out of it. They were even, 2–2, when Diana finally stepped up her game. She caught Karine in the head twice and really had her timing down. She could kick and move exactly when she wanted. She felt so in control that she wanted to make a show out of it, kind of like me. Karine never quit, but Diana prevailed and earned a spot in the finals.

Everything was great until the Red Bull started to catch up to Diana. Jean was asking how she felt before the final, and that was when it hit her. "I feel like I need to throw up," she told him. She was in the bathroom dealing with a combination of food poisoning and Red Bull for most of the next hour. Her stomach was screaming at her, as though she had been kicked by everyone in the building. She went to go lie down and passed out for about ten minutes before Jean came to wake her up.

"Okay, Diana, it's time to fight," he said.

Ugh, no, not now, thought Diana. I need to go throw up again.

Diana was set to fight Korea's Kim Sae-ron, who had also won junior worlds the same two years Diana had. Diana reminded herself that she needed only three more rounds of fighting to be recognized as the best in the world. In six minutes she and her brothers could all be world champions. C'mon, Diana, suck it up, she told herself. Win this and you won't even notice how your stomach feels.

Jean had told her to press the action before the fight. Kim was a good technical fighter, like many Koreans, he said, but she didn't like to get into a lot of heated exchanges.

Diana was pretty revived at the start. She let out a loud yell and she attacked Kim a lot in the first minute. She kicked her a couple of times in the side and back and finally caught her with a fast kick with her right leg to take a 1–0 lead. She wanted to keep pressing and engage her opponent as much as possible. Ten seconds later, they had a quick exchange in which both of them landed and both scored a point. Diana's blow had knocked Kim down, and Diana still felt as if she were solidly in control after taking a 2–1 lead to the second round.

Diana kept the pace going and caught Kim with a spinning round-house that knocked her down twenty seconds into the round. It was a good thing she didn't notice that they didn't score the point, because it might have distracted her from attacking. Midway through the round, Diana led with her right leg and caught Kim again. It wasn't as solid a blow as the previous one, but the judges gave her credit for it and she was up 3–1. Before the round ended, Diana pushed Kim back from a clinch, and caught her to go up 4–1. The ref cautioned Diana for holding and pushing before the round ended and gave her a kyong-go, but she still didn't feel like being cautious.

Diana looked over at Kim's corner and saw her coach slap her in the side of the head in between rounds, and she knew then that as tired as she was, she still had more left than Kim did. She stayed aggressive in the third round and got hit with another kyong-go in the final thirty seconds when Kim went down after a clinch. Diana was feeling the effects of the long day, and she put her hands on her knees while Kim was on the ground. That was when she really heard Jean scream-ing at her.

"Diana, stay on her," he said. "You're stronger. You know you're stronger. Just stay after her. She doesn't have it. You do. You're the best."

See, forget Red Bull. Jean is like a walking infusion of energy. She really connected with Jean in that last minute. She wanted this so badly. She had spent all that time training with guys, cutting weight, taking her lumps. She had put in all that work and now she was almost there. Diana and I can plug into Jean like an Xbox game. If we don't have anything left, we can lean on his energy. Those powerful words help us refocus and take us to a place where we can persevere.

Diana was determined not to get docked for stalling, so she kept after Kim as much as she could. She could hear her teammates in the stands start to count down the seconds, and she probably should have played it safe. Instead, the adrenaline kept pumping and she clipped Kim in the head in the final seconds. When she saw the ref put out his hand to signal the end of the fight, Diana fell on her back, looked up at the ceiling, raised her fists and just said, "Thank you." At last, after all those close calls, she was the best in the world.

She was so happy, as if she were about to float across the arena. She could have quit, but she didn't. She was thanking God for those bursts of perseverance that got her through the tough times. Yes, yes, yes.

Jean picked her up and spun her around. "Diana, you won!" he screamed. "You did it."

The one thing that did keep her from jumping out of her mind was my fight, which was still a few minutes away.

It's funny, but Diana told me she really didn't feel her stomach throbbing during that last round when she was kicking and getting kicked. She was too busy fighting for a world title to notice her physical condition. It was only when she started watching me fight that the nerves came back and she thought ten thousand people were kicking the inside of her stomach again. She didn't go straight back to the holding area; instead she sat on the side, where she wasn't really supposed to be. She gave me a quick wink and told me, "Now it's your turn, bro."

She also had a moment to look over at Juan and ask, "So, am I still too slow?" He laughed and told her she had proven him wrong. Sometimes doubters are the best fuel you can find.

Watching Steven and Diana inspired me to push forward for my own world title. I made my weight well, and felt strong. I was developing my front leg a bit more, the way Jean and Steven did. I could measure my attack, use the leg as a blocking tool, move back to create distance and almost have a third arm. I'm still working at that now, but I definitely improved in that area after 2004.

I was matching Diana victory for victory. In my first fight, I fought Germany's Rehman Moghal. He was feisty and strong, but I felt I had his game down, because I knew he liked to attack a lot and he was aggressive. In our very first exchange, I went off the line for a roundhouse kick and he scored a back kick against me, so he was up 1–0. I started throwing some double kicks and a nadabong that scored. I kept my composure and won the match.

I would give Diana high fives after she won. I didn't really speak to anybody except Jean on the days of competition. I just had my own little spot and kept to myself. I didn't actually watch any of her fights. I was in the holding area for most of them. I saw her final only because I was waiting on deck right there.

I fought Edgar Borja from Ecuador in the second bout. It was pretty easy, because he didn't have much skill. After the first round, Jean realized I had things under control and told me to save my energy. He scored twice, but the ref deducted two points for falling and I won, 3-0.

Ernesto Mendoza, my Filipino opponent, surprised me with his high energy and really good technique in the next bout. He was a little shorter than I was, and he really varied his game. He bounced around a lot, moving in and out. He was very quick on his feet. He'd inch in and move back. I'd have to pop him with my front leg when he got too close and then try to double up when I had him in range. I was stronger than he was, but he made it a real challenge to get to him. I won 3–0 and felt really good after that match, because it took a lot of energy and I still felt I had a lot left.

I fought Tamer Sayed from Egypt in the quarters. He looked as if he were worried about fighting me. One of his coaches was the guy Steven had beaten in Cairo years ago. I was pretty sure he was telling his protégé to watch out for my front leg, because Steven's was so good. Tamer was a little slow, and the match wasn't that difficult. On one exchange we butted heads, and he ended up with a bloody nose. I hit him with a lot of fast doubles he couldn't anticipate. In my aggression I gave up some points, too, and cruised to another win.

In the semis, I beat Dennis Bekkers from the Netherlands. He was inexperienced. He was leery of my front leg and of making a mistake, so every time I attacked he would jam me up, jam me up, jam me up. He was effective at shutting me down. On the inside when I was in the clinch he would hold, hold, hold. We were scoreless for most of the match. I really had to be strong in the clinch with him. When he finally decided to attack a couple of times, I popped him with two defensive roundhouse kicks and scored the only two points of the match. Guys like that are tough to fight, because I can't afford to make a mistake. I'd much rather get into an aggressive fight. When I spar with Steven, that's what I try to do. I try to jam him up, move out of the way and sneak in a point. Before the final, Dennis did a sporting thing: He came up to me and told me I would finally get my redemption for the title I deserved to win in 2003.

After Diana won, she had told me, "You'd better represent. Don't let your sister outdo you." I was pumped up for the final. This was the moment I had waited for since 2003.

There may be some coaches who don't like drawing Korean fighters. We love it. It's our chance to prove that we are the best and we have adapted our style to fit the sport. We have taken ownership. Jean reminded me of the match I lost unfairly at worlds in 2003 and told me not to let the same thing happen again. "If you were in fifth gear in 2003," he said, "I need you in sixth gear. Count on the Korean wearing out by the third round. For every kick he throws, I want you to throw two or three." During the match against Song Myeong-seob, I could hear Jean yell, "Too strong. Too fast, Marky. There's nothing behind his kicks. Very good job, Marky." I could also hear some chanting: "Ko-ree-ah, Ko-ree-ah." I like ours better. Song kicked me in the groin near the end of the first round. I walked it off and got pretty annoyed. On our next exchange, I nailed him with my right leg and knocked him down. Man, that felt good.

In the second round, I clipped him with a defensive roundhouse kick that backed him up. It didn't score, but I could hear Jean yell, "Beautiful, Marky, beautiful. He doesn't have it."

We exchanged again and each scored points with simultaneous kicks. In the crowd, you could hear simultaneous chants. I had no idea what the Koreans were saying, but my teammates broke into, "Let's go, Marky. Let's go."

We traded points into the third round and each had a deduction. The match was tied in the last thirty seconds when Jean yelled out, "Double or triple up. Everything nice and tight, Marky."

Song caught me with his left leg just as I tried to catch him with my right. I was down by one with ten seconds left. Nice and tight? Well, okay. I don't remember what I saw, but I threw a fast triple kick that caught him in the face and knocked him down. That was a career highlight for me: knocking down a Korean fighter with a two-point triple kick in front of a packed arena with a world title on the line. Now I was up one. I jammed him up one final time and the clock expired. I had my world title.

Jean started bouncing around like some overheated windup toy. He picked me up and almost threw me out of the building. He had really displayed his genius as a coach. He had just produced two world champions on the same day who had both beaten Koreans in the finals. All the hard work had finally paid off.

I jumped into Jean's arms. Then Steven and Diana ran over to join us. We spun one another around and probably banged heads a few times in our excitement. There were hugs, kisses and screams of joy.

"Wa-hah," Jean yelled, whatever "wa-hah" meant. Then we hugged again.

"Woo, three world champions, baby," I said.

"Thawazawesome," Steven yelled, cramming three words into one shout.

It was the best feeling, and it continued right through the closing ceremonies that night, when all the athletes circled around the arena—except for us. We were still hugging and celebrating, and everyone came up to us to shake our hands, bow to us and pose for pictures. I felt like royalty in a receiving line. I wish I could bottle that moment and go back and open it up now and then. In the days before the matches, I really didn't have time to put things in any kind of perspective, but almost as soon as the fights were over, Diana and I understood that we had become stronger people with stronger character and better discipline. We had changed for the better as people, learning the lessons of our sport with our family. Maybe it was good we didn't make that last Olympic team. Maybe we wouldn't have had that desire, that need to find our will to overcome our doubts. I may have different stages when I get complacent, but I was able to put those away because I still had a hunger, and because I had people close to me who understood that. Diana and I both said we were glad God kept testing us, because things happened for a reason, and we didn't know if we would have had that character and desire to achieve without the wait and the setbacks.

Later that day, Jean got on the phone to David Barron of the *Houston Chronicle* and told him, "When it seems we can't go any higher as a family, we do it. And the most beautiful part is, we did it as a family."

Once again, whole national teams kept stopping by at the after party to shake our hands. They especially stopped to congratulate Jean, who really deserved the pats on the back. Steven did an interview with two Iranian journalists in which they reminded him that he had now beaten six of their best fighters without a loss. I didn't know if this was a good thing, but the interpreter told him they had given him the nickname the Iranian Killer. He also said they felt the two reasons Steven was able to be successful were his closeness to his family and his obvious faith. Steven told him thank-you and that he was honored to fight athletes from their country. That's how you win not just medals, but also hearts and minds.

CHAPTER 14

First of Its Kind

by Jean Lopez

The day after we made history as the first family to have three members win world titles at the same competition, Diana was showing the intestinal scars of victory. She threw up on the way to the airport, in the airport bathroom and on the plane. We were driving her through the airport on a luggage cart. She kept asking the flight attendant for orange juice, and then she would excuse herself to get rid of the orange juice. She felt like death, but she had never felt so good in her life. When we got off the plane, she looked in the mirror and saw her giant black tongue. "Diana," Mark joked, "you brought back the foot-in-mouth disease." She started to giggle and told him, "Mark, don't you know it hurts when I laugh?"

I couldn't wait to see my parents and eat my mom's arroz con pollo and *tostones*. Of course, Diana had to wash hers down with some antibiotics. You always want to do things to make your parents happy, and the best part was being happy for everyone else.

My dad put Diana's and Steven's medals in a cabinet where he kept all the medals. Mark put his in his backpack. Dagmar later hung it on one of the walls in their house.

A month later, Mark graduated magna cum laude with a business degree. Mark had one internship his last semester, at Morgan Stanley. He would work for them later in the day after his second workout. It wasn't very exciting. He was doing cold calls to people, asking them if they had a retirement fund set up. One call was particularly lousy: He called a guy and his wife answered and told him her husband had recently passed away. Sorry about that one.

Mark later went to Puerto Rico to visit Dagmar's family. Her mother bought a huge amount of grilled meat, and he came back from the trip weighing a hundred and seventy-six pounds, most of it *churrasco*. That's like two of him.

After worlds, Steven went to Croatia for a while to visit Lana. It was an important time for the two of them, given the amount of time they had been spending together. She was twenty-one at the time and she was talking of moving to Houston. That was quite a commitment for her to want to make, but Steven didn't know if he felt comfortable with an arrangement that was basically one step short of marriage. She felt that after their two years of being together, even while they were apart, they had to make a decision about the relationship. By the end of the trip it was clear that they probably weren't going to stay together. It was difficult for Steven to go through that with someone he really cared about.

I had watched my brothers and my sister develop at the ideal pace for each of them, and it was important for me as a coach to make distinctions among them to suit their strengths and weaknesses. Mark was my soldier, and actually he would have made a great military man. He follows directions really well, which is hard to do when you have so much imagination and individual talent. It's been great to watch him evolve to learn to use his left leg as a defensive weapon, just as I did and as Steven does. Mark is like a crafty pitcher who may not have the speed to throw a fastball past the other team's best slugger, but he has such an assortment of curveballs and changeups that he drives other hitters nuts.

Diana has always had to do everything better and harder so she could hang with her brothers. She turned into the gym rat who loved it more than any of us. She'd wear her emotions, good or bad, on her sleeve. In my approach with her, I'd make especially sure to make her feel that she was an athlete, not that she was a girl. I didn't make any distinctions with her, even though I was conscious of phrasing things a certain way so she'd be able to receive things I was trying to tell her. I'd be very careful to broach the subject of cutting weight without being offensive. I was very conscious of problems that girls have, more often than boys, in regard to weight-cutting issues like bulimia and anorexia. I wanted to make her feel when she had to cut weight that she was trying to qualify for her division, not because it had anything to do with the way she looked. I could say, "Hey, Mark, you need to cut weight; your neck looks a little big. I can tell by looking at you that you're not at your fighting weight." Whereas with Diana I'd say, "You're looking great in training, but let's make sure you don't get too far away from the cutoff in your weight class. That's the nature of the sport and living the lifestyle of an athlete."

Steven had developed an aura about him. He was very quiet, not very expressive, almost at peace when he was training. When he won, he was very stoic and matter-of-fact, almost as if he were saying, Hey, this is what I do. Can I go play Nintendo now?

When I was first coaching him, I interpreted that as his not caring. I tend to be a lot more expressive, and the energy around me enhances my energy. I externalize. He's really consistent. When he was getting older, I didn't understand his lack of expression. I thought it was a weakness of his. I wanted him to yell in order to show spirit. He's a calm warrior. I'm a passionate warrior. It took me a while to understand his approach and how he deals with things. Steven used to be bothered when I would tell him he couldn't go out on certain nights because of training. By now we're on the same page. He's almost like a poker player who can look at his opponent and tell what kind of hand he has. Steven may look weak, because he wants his opponents to think he's weak, so they'll be too aggressive and make a mistake. If he's being aggressive, it's because he wants them to think he's being aggressive, when he's really being defensive, trying to keep them from attacking.

A complete monster would include Mark's gymnastic athleticism and strength, Diana's blackboard technique and Steven's sports intelligence. Let's see the Koreans, Iranians or Europeans cook up someone in their labs to beat that.

It's funny, because even though athletes from those places are our rivals, we actually get more fan mail from abroad than from the United States. We get mail from Germany, Austria, Poland, places like that. Some of the letter writers are collectors who make money off our signatures. Eh, whatever. We sign them. Some letters are actually really cool. Steven gets kids telling him they're doing school reports about him. He always answers those. If they have questions for him, he makes sure to give them good answers. You really appreciate the scope of what it means to be an athlete, a role model and an Olympian when you realize that people look up to you. It's awesome.

In 2006, there was also a guy who wrote Steven from prison. Our mom was very leery of the thing. "Steven, don't send an autograph to someone in prison." The man mentioned in the letter that he had been down in the dumps, but he looked up to Steven, his story and his faith in God.

Steven understood our mom's apprehension, but he showed her the letter and he said, "Mom, I mean, look at his words. They don't sound creepy. They sound like a guy who's trying to do better and get a second chance." Of course, we don't know what he did to get into prison, but Steven went ahead and answered him, telling him to hang in there.

A few years ago, Steven was in Brownsville, Texas, visiting a friend. They were eating sushi and a woman came over to introduce herself. "Excuse me, are you Steven Lopez?" He told her he was and she then said, "Oh, my gosh, my nine-year-old daughter is your biggest fan. We have our own taekwondo school around the corner. Would you mind . . . Could you . . . Do you think . . . You know, I don't want to bother you, but is there any way you could stop by after you're finished?"

They had plans to go out after the meal, but it was pretty hard to say no. Steven agreed, and in the meantime the woman called her daughter at the school and told her he'd be stopping by. By then it was about nine p.m. and the school's session was finished for the day, but the students and staff waited for Steven to show up. When he walked in, it was like they were welcoming the president. He was honored by the enthusiasm. It turned out the woman's daughter had written a report and painted a picture of him winning in Athens. The picture was really advanced and detailed. She actually received a little scholarship for her future education for the painting of Steven. That picture made him feel very special and humbled. Afterward, Steven was saying, "I mean I just do taekwondo, right?"

Steven has always lived a life of humility and integrity, which is why it was so gut-wrenching to see what he went through after a meet in Colorado Springs in 2006. The weather is very dry in the Springs. We're used to the humidity of Houston. Many times when we go to the OTC, we'll acclimate ourselves to the dry air by buying humidifiers and turning it on in our rooms for the first couple of days to put some moisture in the air. Without that, Steven starts to get nosebleeds. One of his childhood friends told him that he used Vicks VapoRub to avoid the nosebleeds. So Steven decided he'd try that, too. He fought only one match at trials, because for some reason several of the other fighters bowed out to him.

A few days later I was taking a break from playing soccer outside when I got a call from a woman at USA Taekwondo stating that there had been a positive drug test. I called my team in to ask if anyone had taken anything. Everyone insisted they hadn't. Okay, so we wait, I figured. A few hours later, a representative of the U.S. Anti-Doping Agency (USADA) called to say that Steven had recorded a positive test. I took down the details as stoically as I could and went in to call him.

"Shut up, Jean," he told me, figuring I was playing a joke.

"No, Steven, it's for real," I said.

"Really, for what?"

"Amphetamine," I said.

It took me several minutes to convince him that I was actually serious. We still couldn't make sense of it all. After we hung up, Steven wondered if somehow somebody had given him something without his knowledge. That wasn't possible, was it? Was anybody so desperate to see him lose that they would spike his water bottle when he wasn't looking? No, it couldn't be.

With all the talk going on about steroid use in baseball, we hated the way it sounded, because it sounded like a deliberate use of something that could actually help him. The way the newspapers put it out there made it sound as if he were using a drug to enhance his strength. When something bad happens, you realize how quick people are to find out the scoop about something that's negative. I don't think Steven and I ever received so many calls for interviews.

Steven started looking up methamphetamine and what it was supposed to do. It was supposed to keep you awake. He slept like a baby that night. It was supposed to suppress your hunger. He ate like a horse after the match. How could this even be? He called his doctor, Joe Anzaldua, to ask a bunch of questions. He felt as if he were in *The Twilight Zone*.

I took Steven to the local CVS and had him look at the shelves. "Steven, look around and tell me if you see anything you might have taken." Steven told me he'd taken only the same multivitamin he'd been taking for years. "Steven, look again," I said.

He looked around the shelves, figuring it was a useless exercise, until finally he spotted the Vicks VapoRub. "Well, I took this, but . . ."

I grabbed it and started reading the side of the bottle. Sure enough, it listed the amphetamine Steven had tested for. I started looking for a lawyer after that. Then we contacted the USOC and told them what it was, an over-the-counter medication. With that information, the lab was able to examine the remainder of Steven's sample, the B sample they use to confirm the initial findings, with a more critical eye. They were able to confirm that he had applied the specific rub that he had described. That allowed them to confirm that the amphetamine came from the Vicks.

At the end of the day, Steven received just a three-month suspension because the use was not deliberate and it could not have enhanced his performance the way, say, a steroid could have. Steven lost his stipend money for three months, and he had to take a drug-awareness education course over the Internet, almost like an online driver's-education course. Then they asked if he would volunteer to speak about his experience to other younger athletes in the USAT program. It was not a required stipulation of his suspension, but he did it, making the point to the younger athletes that ignorance is not a defense, and that before taking anything new, you first need to consult the USADA hotline, which can confirm whether that medication might contain something that could lead to a positive test.

The incident made us even more eager to return to what we do best in 2007, which we looked at as a very important year. We were headed to Beijing not only for a world championship, but also for a preview of the city that would host the Olympics. It was still our dream for all the Lopez siblings to be there in an official capacity. We had been there before, but in 1999, the place was full of bikes and there weren't many tall buildings. This time, the city was rife with cars, skyscrapers and dense, thick pollution. The city just looked bigger. The place seemed more technologically advanced. The rooms were neater and more like a hotel room at home.

Besides that, they really understood the sport much better. In 1999, Jason and Steven went there to give some instruction. The Chinese had eight men and eight women on that team, mostly taken from state-run basketball and volleyball programs, and each one fit the same prototype. Every male athlete was the same height: tall with good reach, but clumsy. All the females were the same height, too.

We could really feel the buzz about the fact that the Games were coming to China a year later. I could sense it. A lot of other world championships had sponsors, full arenas and good opening ceremonies, but this was a show. The arena was packed. The crowds were very into the match. The ceremonies were over-the-top with lights, dancers, dragons and acrobats. Wow, if they put that much work into a world championship, imagine how the Olympics were going to look.

We knew it would be a tough world championship for us, even as Steven was eyeing a share of history as the second athlete in history to win his fourth world taekwondo title. How could we even hope to approach what we did in 2005? The Chinese were really intrigued by our story. It seemed like we were doing press conferences every day, even before we competed. We seemed to sign more autographs and pose for more pictures than we had before. We really felt welcomed in China, and in all our interviews we let people know that we felt it and appreciated it. People there seemed to love us. It was pretty cool.

The venue for the championships was different from the one they were planning to use for the Olympics. This one must have been newly constructed, because there was an odd white powder that was circulating in the building and was getting everyone sick. Diana was having trouble breathing, but so were athletes from many of the teams.

Diana got through two easy matches, outscoring Suzana Dimovska of Macedonia and Thamae Likelei of Lesotho by a combined score of 13–0. That set her up for another showdown with Iridia from Mexico, the Olympic silver medalist from Athens.

Diana had beaten Iridia before and maybe by now Iridia had a mental block against Diana. I know Diana felt she could get into Iridia's head and break her. She was able to use not only her skills, but also her fortitude in that match to shut down a great rival she respected. The 1–0 score didn't reflect the control Diana had by the end of the match, when she just needed to prevent Iridia from scoring.

The way she beat Iridia may actually have worked against Diana in her semifinal match against Lee Sung-hye of Korea. Diana thought she could fight technically and sneak her points in, but the Korean was clinching her up and countering Diana's defense with patience. Lee held and Diana pushed. I told Diana to attack more, but she didn't follow my instructions.

Diana scored early with a left-leg fast kick, and Lee took a while to build some kind of rhythm. It made Diana think she had the fight. While Lee was still struggling, Diana didn't really press the issue. She gave Lee a chance to stay in the match and sneak in some points during close exchanges. When Lee connected as they broke from the clinch in the third round, Diana found herself down 3–2. Lee already had a half-point penalty, but Diana couldn't catch her or force another deduction in the closing seconds.

Marky didn't have his best tournament. He didn't make weight very well that day, and the chicken sandwich he had for lunch tasted less like chicken than like some of the alligator they served in Sydney. Mark beat Tamir Hasham of Egypt in the first fight by forcing Hasham into frustration and deductions. Then he defeated Azerbaijan's Ilkin Shahbazov, who won the world title in 2001 in Korea. He was shorter, so Mark used his front leg on him. He was feisty, but Mark picked him off pretty easily. Next Mark beat Guatemala's Gabriel Sagastume, a savvy veteran with a good defensive game, in the next fight. None of those fighters were the aggressive types Mark likes to fight. Only Shahbazov really wanted to engage him for any length of time.

Mark fought Song Myeong-seob again from Korea in the quarters, and Mark was pretty determined to push the pace. He scored first and kept attacking. They got to the third round and Mark was trying to punch out of an exchange on the inside. They docked him first for pushing and then for holding. Song scored when Mark tried to block his roundhouse with his leg. That gave Song a 1–0 lead in the final forty seconds. Mark went after him with time running out, but Song scored a point against him with a defensive roundhouse in the final five seconds.

That left Steven to fight for his share of the record. I wanted Steven to set a tone for the rest of the day in his first match against Carlos Rodriguez of Andorra. Steven got to him quickly and often. The ref was being merciful when he scored a TKO for Steven midway through the contest.

He beat Craig Browning of Great Britain and Carlos Izidoro of Brazil in the next two matches, intimidating both guys into taking deductions for stalling and holding so they both ended up with negative points.

The quarterfinal against Carlos Vasquez of Venezuela was much tougher. The Venezuelans have Korean coaches, so they are very technically proficient. Vasquez was a clever, sneaky opponent whose tight style didn't allow Steven to open up. He did whatever he could to jam Steven. That's the strategy against us now. Smart fighters will try to find ways to prevent us from using our reach. Instead of going forward, Steven adjusted and kicked on the motion to score his points. Still, Vasquez kept matching Steven point for point until they ended up tied after time was up. In sudden death, Steven made a conscious effort to speed up the tempo. That put Vasquez on his heels until Steven started to get more aggressive. Then, as Vasquez went off the line, Steven caught him coming in with his left leg for the winning point.

Canada's Sebastien Michaud is always an odd guy to fight against because he is so unconventional. He walks around in these funny shoes, his hair is shaggy and his fighting style throws people off. Before the fight, I talked to Steven about dictating the early pace. "Don't dance to his rhythm," I told him.

Steven did a good job of drawing him out. I told Steven to make sure Michaud didn't get off his own rhythm. He stifled Michaud, who lost a pair of points by deductions. Michaud held a lot so he was frustrating to fight against. Steven finally scored twice against him on defensive roundhouse kicks and then shut him down. Since Michaud's offensive game wasn't very good, the frustration wasn't so bad once he was the one trying to catch up to Steven. Once Steven had the lead, he was able to keep him away and hold him off, to get himself safely into the finals.

Steven was low on energy at the end of the semis. He sometimes suffers from dehydration because he loses so much water. Before the final, I told Clay Barber to come over and talk to him to shake some life into him. By then Clay had returned from his time as a stuntman in Hollywood and was working as one of our national-team coaches. Juan Moreno also walked over and said, "Hey, Steven, you know, these are the times that make you you." They weren't in Steven's face, but they were very positive.

Steven wasn't quite able to take the nap he wanted, because security in the holding area was very poor, so the ring girls and some of the volunteers were coming up to him asking him to pose for pictures after almost every match. One of the Chinese ladies gave him a teddy bear. Each time he went by, she would cover her mouth and have that shy look-away look. Ladies and gentlemen, meet my brother, the rock star.

There was one incentive, however, that neither of us could ignore as he awaited his final match against Jang Chang-ha of Korea and a chance to win his fourth world title. Only one other athlete had won four world titles in the sport. Jae-kyu Kyon was the Michael Jordan of Korea. His game of brilliant attack and defense was what we admired and respected so much about the Koreans of the eighties and early nineties. He was sitting ringside, and he was asked before the match if he wished Steven well in his quest to equal the total of four. Give him credit for his honesty, but he said, "I don't want Steven to win. I want the pride of the sport to remain in Korea."

That's when I told my brother, "Listen, Steven, this means a lot more than you. You need to have enough for Diana, Mark and the country."

Steven walked out to begin the final match and got to the raised platform before the referees. As we were waiting and stretching, we noticed the Iranian coach making eye contact with Steven, nodding his head and making a fist. It wasn't a negative fist; it was a go-out-and-win kind of gesture. I don't know why, but considering it came from the Iranian coach, that really meant a lot to us. They may have been our rivals and enemies on certain levels, but the fact that Steven had earned enough respect from their team for him to do that was one of the most memorable compliments any of us had ever received, even though it was pretty subtle.

Before the opening seconds, Steven let out a loud yell, which he rarely does. He started taking deep breaths and opening his eyes very wide and quickly. That yell seemed to get him going. He took it pretty quickly to Jang, who used the same tactic as in 2005, putting out his left leg and trying to draw Steven out. Almost every Korean he has ever fought has tried to counter Steven's raised left leg by sliding to the right, spinning and kicking to his backside. Jang tried to do that the entire match.

From that point on, he also tried very hard to score on the clinch, but each time Steven blocked it, Jang seemed to get frustrated and tired. All throughout the second and third rounds, whenever he spun and tried to kick to Steven's back, Steven would lift up his leg and jump up in order to make sure Jang's kicks would catch his butt, in the nonscoring area, and not his kidneys, in the scoring area.

The match went to sudden death. Before the overtime, I told him, "Steven, you can hit him with your front leg as hard as you can. That will set up a fast kick for your second exchange. I want you to look at this moment. Either you'll see it like woulda-coulda-shoulda, or you'll feel like the happiest man alive. Which do you want? I need you to be efficient, so your energy level doesn't go down."

Steven used the same defense against Jang, but instead of just blocking, he moved forward for his own counter. It's an unorthodox kick, a cut kick, that doesn't usually score, but Steven kicked him so hard that he launched this Korean into the air. He flew back several feet before making a thud on the mat. Steven raised his hands and the judges had no choice but to award the winning point. People have criticized it and said it doesn't belong in taekwondo because they want taekwondo to be more of a back-leg confrontational game. I think the front leg, our family trademark, is effective in the way a boxer's jab is effective: It keeps the opponent honest and sets up the rest of your game. It's bad if everyone fights the same. A few months later, Clay was looking around on the Internet and found that some taekwondo fan in Mexico had put together a Claymation version of the winning sequence against the Korean. The clay figure even does the cross, just as Steven does. It's funny and it's pretty cool. I grabbed Steven— history-making Steven—after the match and hugged him for a long time. I felt he came through again for the family.

It was a great moment for us not only because of the people in attendance who were displeased, but because of people who were elated for Steven. Peter Bardatsos, Clay and Juan were people we'd grown up with and started training with. Some were veterans of the Lopez garage who were having their own successful careers now as coaches. These were Steven's teammates on the national squad. These were friends. They were there to see history, and we all shared a few tears.

After worlds, our family honed in on the goal we had set years ago when I opened Elite Taekwondo center in 1996: to make history by getting Steven, Mark and Diana on the Olympic team together. It seemed like a sort of fantasy back then, but it was something I honestly believed in. Our qualification system for earning Olympic berths was pretty detailed. There are eight weight classes for men and women at most competitions, including the world championships, but because the IOC allots only a hundred and twenty-eight places for taekwondo athletes at the Olympics, the competitors are divided into four weight classes (flyweight, featherweight, welterweight, heavyweight) for the Games, with a maximum of four places (two male and two female) allowed per country. The U.S. team members were picked through a series of competitions. The first set of Olympic trials took place at the training center in Colorado Springs in August. The winners there could then represent the U.S. at the World Olympic Qualifier in Manchester, England. The top three finishers in each weight class in Manchester would earn automatic places for themselves in the Olympics and did not have to fight again until they got to Beijing. Those who didn't place among the top three would have to go to various sites for regional Olympic qualifiers—ours was in Cali, Colombia, in December—to qualify for a spot for the country with a top-three finish. If you finished out of the top three in Cali, your Olympic dream was over. If you made the top three, you qualified only for your country's place at the Games. Cali winners would still have to compete in the final round of the Olympic trials the next April in Des Moines, Iowa. However, the winners in Cali would have the advantage of waiting until all the other national competitors fought to determine a trials challenger. Cali winners would face the trials challenger in a best-of-three competition, already leading one match to zero. Challengers, in effect, needed to beat all other comers and then defeat the medalists from Cali twice in a row to get on the Olympic team.

The results from Manchester were pretty mixed. Steven advanced, placing him straight onto the Olympic team. Mark and Diana lost in the quarters, which meant that they would still have to advance the place in Cali and then actually earn the spot in Des Moines the next year. Mark dropped an overtime decision to another Korean, Son Tae-jin. The tournament was pretty noteworthy for both Steven and Diana.

Steven had a tough draw and got stuck with Karami of Iran in the first match that really should have been the finals. Karami was pretty tentative and Steven beat him 4–1, doubling up often and using a speed advantage. After that, he cruised through his next few matches, including a fairly decisive victory against Mauro Sarmiento of Italy in the semifinals. It was Steven's first time facing Mauro, who was about six-five and had an obvious reach advantage. He really didn't seem to know how to make the most of his height. In order to beat him, Steven would have to creep in and jam up against him so Mauro couldn't extend his leg to score on him. Mauro wasn't quite quick enough to get a kick in before Steven would be up close to him. That was when he would score off the clinch. Again, we didn't think much of the match at the time, since Karami was the main guy we worried about that day. Once Steven beat him, he cruised into the finals, drawing Michaud from Canada again in the last match. But once the top-three finish was secured, I suggested Steven bow out to him, since Michaud might have benefited more from gaining experience against Steven than Steven would have gained from fighting him. Instead, Steven and I stayed around to accept the second-place award and watch the final for third place and the other Olympic berth. It was ironic that the match involved Mauro Sarmiento.

In 2006, Mark and Steven had gone to Italy as guests of their federation to give a seminar to many of the top Italian fighters, including Mauro. They traveled to Florence, Milan, Naples and other many places, giving seminars about tactics, feint motions, check motions.

About ninety-five percent of points that score in taekwondo may be scored with the basic roundhouse kick, but you can use it from so many different setups and angles that a simple roundhouse can be harder to read and therefore that much more effective.

In Manchester, there was a repechage, or second-chance match, involving Mauro and an opponent from Puerto Rico. Since the Italians knew Steven fairly well, their coach felt comfortable enough to approach him and ask him for advice on how to fight the next match. Mauro's opponent was only about five-eleven, so Steven's advice, which he gave directly to Mauro, was pretty simple: "Use what God has given you, the reach advantage you have. Take one step off the line and kick with the left leg. Just move quickly, so he can't jam up against you." If nothing else, Steven gave Mauro a level of confidence that, if he stuck to the strategy, he'd win. Oddly enough, the Puerto Rican coach came up to me and asked for similar advice.

Steven joked with me that we'd see how good his coaching really was. Mauro was down in the match, but he rallied—using the strategy Steven gave him—and he won the match to earn his berth in the Olympics. It was a nice gesture on Steven's part, but our mom has a saying for things like that: *Cuidado, hormiga se hace elefante.* (Be careful. One day, the ant can turn into an elephant.) In other words, if you have a guy down, take him out. If you allow the ant a little help, one day he may be big enough to step on you. We didn't think it applied in this case.

Diana started off feeling really well in Manchester. She was really on, and she was managing her weight right. She first fought Austria's Lisa Weinzierl and got off to a great start, building a 3–0 lead in the first round. That was when she got into trouble. Weinzierl was very aggressive, and she landed a sharp kick to Diana's groin late in the round that caused her to start bleeding pretty badly from a hematoma in her leg. Diana won the fight handily. She then went to do some maintenance in between fights, but the bleeding just wouldn't stop. She didn't have any changes of uniform pants, so she had her teammates buy them in the arena before each fight because she didn't want to go out there with all that blood on her. Diana doesn't compromise. She really wanted to win that spot for us, so she didn't want to quit. She took some pain medicine and got ready to go back out. It was pretty embarrassing for her, because we had a male trainer and Diana is pretty shy about some things. She wanted to explain the details to him, but she held back, mainly because she didn't want to show it to him. Diana felt terrible. Each time she fought, it felt as if she had a ball of blood on her leg that kept her from kicking.

She fought through two bouts against Lailatou Amadour from Niger and Zarina Shamshatkyzy from Kazakhstan, but she was very tentative in both fights because she was worried about kicking too hard or getting into too many close exchanges. Diana won both bouts, but she finally lost in the quarters, 3–2, against Chonnapas Premwaew from Thailand. By that match, she just didn't want to lift her leg up to kick. She was bouncing straight up and down, being tentative and trying to counter the Thai girl, but she wasn't a hundred percent.

She and Mark would have to go back to Houston and prepare for the second-chance qualifier in Cali, Colombia, the last opportunity to cinch an Olympic berth for the U.S. team at -57 kilos.

Diana had to go to the doctor when she went home. Fortunately the swelling in her groin went down and there was nothing broken. She was back to training almost immediately after that for the tournament in Colombia. With two regional berths on the line in Cali, she knew everyone figured she and Iridia were the strongest competitors, so people were hoping they wouldn't draw each other in the first match.

Diana didn't attend the draw with me, but as soon as I walked into her room the day before the match, she could see the look on my face.

"I know, I know," she told me. "I'm fighting Iridia in the first match."

I looked at her and said, "Diana, I haven't even said anything."

She told me, "You don't have to."

It was a shame. If they had been on opposite ends of the bracket, they could both have qualified for Beijing. That was how it should have been, but that was literally the luck of the draw. Diana felt God was testing her again. If she wanted to get to the Olympics this badly, it couldn't be easy. She still had to go through Iridia at the regional qualifier and Nia at the Olympic trials. She was really going to have to earn her way to Beijing. She prayed before going to bed that night, and tears were running down her cheeks. I think so many years of pent-up emotions just started coming out of her and she had to get them out of her system the day before she fought. Diana slept well that night, believing she could take that next step.

It was very hot and humid the next day. The arena doors were open, but the building was not air-conditioned, and Diana was feeling a little light-headed from dehydration. Her match was very tight. Iridia is a very smart fighter and she changed her whole style of fighting against Diana. Usually they both fight with their left legs in front, but once they started fighting, Iridia was leading with her right leg, with an open stance, so now Diana pretty much had to throw out the mental scouting report she had on Iridia. Neither fighter did very much for the first couple of rounds, because each of them wanted the other one to make a mistake. Diana kept waiting and waiting for that opening, and she wasn't sure when it would come. In the final round, they came to close quarters when Diana let go with a double kick and finally scored on the inside with ten seconds to go. She threw up her arms and bounced around for the last few seconds until time expired. Diana was ecstatic, but torn. Iridia was someone she respected so much. She was a huge hurdle for Diana to overcome on her road to the Games. She could really start to taste it now.

Diana still had to fight Doris Patino, the hometown girl from Colombia, in that tournament, which always carries a risk because of the way fans can influence officials. The crowd went crazy when Doris scored the first point, but Diana knew she was the more accomplished fighter. She went off the line and caught Doris several times to build up a 5–1 lead and score a much easier victory than in the match against Iridia.

Mark had an easier time of it in Cali. He was on opposite sides of the bracket with our friend and training partner Peter Lopez. Mark won four bouts and reached the finals against Peter, a bout neither of them needed to win because they were both assured of advancing. Mark stood down, at Peter's request, so he could have the honor—and perhaps a bonus from his federation in Peru—of winning the region.

Now Diana and Mark each left Colombia with only one more hurdle in front of them before joining Steven on the Olympic team.

As this was happening, in late 2007, a number of international referees met in Korea to discuss a possible change to the rules that they were thinking of implementing after the Beijing Olympics. During the discussion, the officials referred to it unofficially as the Steven Lopez rule. The rule essentially would prohibit a fighter like Steven from raising his legs in a defensive posture to strike a blow below the waist with the blade of the foot—essentially using a defensive cut kick. Steven may have been one of the first to perfect that technique, but many other fighters, including Hadi Saei from Iran, have adopted the strategy, too. Depending on how the rule might be applied, we realized, it could take away one of Steven's greatest weapons: his ability to keep opponents away by balancing on his back leg and using the front one as a jab. If they voted the rule in, our defensive strategy would have to change. At least we wouldn't need to worry about it until after Beijing, because the officials never adopted the rule. Not a problem, right? Right?

Speaking of adoptions, the family grew by one that year. I gave Steven a black lab for his birthday on November 11, 2007. The dog's name is Sydney and, yes, the dog is named for the Olympic site. Toss a ball and Sydney will slip, slide and crash into anything to track it down for you.

My own family was growing. Maybe it's because I'm an Olympic dad, but my wife and I had a baby each quadrennium: Alyxandra (May 21, 1999), Diego (September 19, 2003), and Andres (November 1, 2007).

When Alyxandra was born it was the most surreal thing I've ever experienced. From one moment to the next, my life changed. The doctor was playing music in the room, and the first thing that came on the radio was the line "I believe the children are our future," from the Whitney Houston song "The Greatest Love of All." I felt like I held my breath for a few minutes after the birth, even though I'm sure it was only seconds. Once they poured water on her, she started crying, and it was the most beautiful cry I'd ever heard in my life. I had heard stories of how moody women can get through pregnancies, but Tabetha was a trooper. She never complained.

I was giddy when Diego was born. My first boy was so special. He looked so much like my dad; I thought I was going back in time, getting a glimpse at what my father must have been like when he was growing up in Nicaragua.

It almost felt like déjà vu. I was a father figure to two boys and a girl in my life once before. I was getting to be a kid again and escape all the pressures of doing what I do professionally. I could talk to them about things that are important to kids. I could spend hours with them. Sometimes I'd get in trouble because I'd turn off my phone and lose track of what I was supposed to do, because I'd get lost in their world. It was so much fun. I'd sometimes call Diego Mark and Alyxandra Diana. Alyxandra's mannerisms and body type were becoming so similar to Diana's. Diego was adopting Mark's features and Steven's demeanor. I was able to relive all that joy, but with the perspective of a thirty-five-year-old. I love playing soccer with them, watching cartoons with them and being able to laugh at silly things the way grown-ups forget to do.

My two oldest had already started taekwondo classes. We have Alyxandra on tape at age four saying she wanted to be in the Olympics like Steven. She won her first tournament, a couple of years later, so look out, world.

We were in a restaurant when Alyxandra was nine years old and she told Steven, "You know, Steven, you're going to have to settle down one of these days. You know you're going to have to get married. You're going to have to get serious, because it's the circle of life." I'm thinking, Where does she get this? Steven doesn't blush easily, but he was a tomato that day.

Diego wants to do things only on his own terms, like Steven. We were excited about competing in one tournament, until he got cold feet in the way that only a toddler can. As he was about to go out for battle, Diego turned to me and pouted.

"What's wrong, son?" I asked.

"Daddy, my tummy's telling me not to fight today," he said.

Hmmm, as an Olympic coach, I usually have an answer for a lot of things. "My tummy's telling me not to fight" isn't really one of them. "Tell your tummy it's going to be okay and you're going to go out there and have a lot of fun," I said. A minute later, Diego went out there and fought like a little rooster.

His intestinal fortitude was the kind of spirit our family would need as we entered the most important year of our careers.

CHAPTER 15

Sharing the Dream

by Mark Lopez

Everything speeds up once the countdown to an Olympics begins. There are more interview requests and sponsor opportunities, and seemingly fewer and fewer days to prepare for what could be the most memorable day of your athletic life. Steven had been through more of this than Diana or me, but now, with no quirky selection of weight classes, no major injuries and no political hurdles on the domestic front, people could really grab onto the thought of three Lopezes being on the Olympic team together.

Before the Olympics, sponsors started grasping our family story and the fact that Steven would be trying to win his third Olympic gold medal. We took on Cecil and Ann as our full-time agents and they helped us navigate our growing world of sponsorship opportunities.

VISA was one of the first, signing Steven as one of its gold-medal athletes through the 2008 Beijing Games, and the VISA people would come through for our family down the road.

In 2007, Coca-Cola signed Steven as one of six people that would become known as their Six Pack athletes.

As part of the Coca-Cola sponsorship, Steven had a chance to do a photo shoot in Sacramento with LeBron James. It was in November, when his Cavaliers were playing a road game against the Kings. He and Steven were two of Coke's six-pack of prospective Olympic athletes they were featuring in the lead-up to the Games. The others were gymnast Shawn Johnson, swimmer Natalie Coughlin, runner Sanya Richards and triathlete Andy Potts.

Steven arrived first for the shoot. Everyone was very relaxed, just joking around and chatting. As word spread that LeBron was about to arrive, everyone started to jump. "Do we have his specific candy ready for him? Is his specific music on?" Steven saw firsthand what it must be like for Hollywood stars. LeBron was the star of the day. He was pretty cool with Steven, but my brother said he felt oddly sorry for him. When people kind of fall over you like that and you've been a multimillionaire from such a young age, how do you have any perspective on how to act or on how other people usually act around so-called "normal" people?

The shoot itself was pretty simple. Steven was sitting down holding a Coke, and LeBron was standing over him with his elbow on his shoulder. After a few poses, Steven tried breaking the ice by telling LeBron, "Hey, don't get me wrong; I don't usually look up at a guy's eyes and start smiling." LeBron cracked up about that, which, in turn, meant that everyone around him cracked up after he did. That's star power, huh? The photos ran next to Coke displays in stores around the country.

At the end of 2007, we secured our first family sponsorship with AT&T for an internet program they were doing entitled Tips and Training. A film crew working on behalf of AT&T came to both Elite and Plex and filmed us incorporating fifteen fitness elements of our training that the public could also use in their general workouts. I did one that involved building up my abs, so people wanting their own six-pack could check that out. The shoot took two days and kicked off what would become a great relationship with AT&T.

In February, Steven traveled to New York for an appearance on behalf of VISA along with other Olympians, such as Michael Phelps, Nastia Liukin and Allyson Felix. Their group went to see a show,

Steven's first time seeing a performance on Broadway. It was *Spamalot*, a funny spoof on *Monty Python and the Holy Grail*, starring Clay Aiken, the former winner of *American Idol*. Steven said it was pretty fun and he would go to another show sometime. The group went out to a club afterward, and Michael Phelps introduced Steven to his friends by saying, "This is Steven Lopez. He kicks butt for a living."

Also in February, we were able to take our AT&T partnership to the next level. We signed on with them to be featured in a total of five commercials—two in English and three in Spanish. We were thrilled with this as it really showed their belief in us and would take our family story and our sport to a level it had never been. This wasn't a local car dealership we were involved with. We felt we had really made it, shooting a commercial for such a major, respected company as AT&T.

We had a lot of fun with the commercials. They gave us the red-carpet treatment, including our own trailers, though we pretty much hung out in one trailer the whole time. I loved the commercial that involved the whole family. The spot began with Jean using his computer in our living room, when the phone rang and he tried to keep me from getting to it before he did. As this was happening, the announcing voice in the commercial was saying, "The Lopez family stays connected to Team USA, the Olympic Games and each other with AT&T." I was wearing a harness for the scene and I did a backflip off the kitchen counter and beat Jean to the phone. When I did my stunt, I guess the guy didn't pull hard enough and I hit my head on the edge of the counter. It stung for a minute and I had little bump, but my hair covered it up.

As the scene was happening, the announcer in the background talked about the services AT&T provided: phone, high-speed Internet and advanced phone or wireless. Then Diana walked in and was sneaking up behind my dad while he was sitting on the couch watching TV. He tried to shoo her away, but she flipped over the couch and grabbed the remote as she landed next to him. My mom then came in, talking on the phone as she walked through the door.

Steven and I were involved in the final scene of the commercial.

For that scene, the producers put Steven in a harness at a gymnastics school in Houston that they rented out for us, so he could learn how to jump over a pool when he kicked. They also flew in some of Clay Barber's stunt friends. We shot it at a mansion that had the perfect pool they were looking for. They gave Steven a mark, an X where they wanted him to land. In that scene he was cooking barbecue when I yelled out, "Steven, the phone." At that point, I did a nadabong and kicked the phone over the pool. Steven turned around while he was flipping burgers. Then he jumped, kicked the phone in the air, jumped over the pool and then the phone fell into his hands before he answered it.

They also filmed one commercial with just Diana and Jean at the George R. Brown Convention Center. They were talking about Internet and phone speed, describing the services they provide. In the ad, Jean and Diana start sparring without landing any kicks until Jean stops her and asks: "So, Diana, how fast is your new broadband from AT&T?" Then they spar some more before Diana lands a kick. Strapped to a harness, Jean flies backward onto a mat. Then Diana walks up to him while he's on the floor and says, "It's about that fast." After the announcer explains some of AT&T's services, Steven walks up to Diana and asks the same question: "So, Diana, how fast is your new broadband from AT&T?" At that point, the camera shifts to Jean, who just shakes his head and looks away. It was a cool concept, except for one thing: If anyone wants to guess how many takes it took Jean to say his one line, well, guess a higher number. Then round off to the nearest hundred and you'll be within a week. It was hard for Jean. He hadn't actually done kicks like those in several years. It would crack Diana up when he'd say, "Diana, I haven't done this in so long and they're making the old man kick again." He was getting such a workout out of it. Sometimes he substituted the word "Internet" for the word "broadband." Even when he had the words right, he would emphasize the word "new" instead of reading it straight, and the director was getting frustrated with him. "Okay, Jean, just relax," he'd say. Jean finally pulled it off before we missed the Olympics.

Seriously, the commercials looked great. AT&T did a terrific job, and this was exposure for our sport that we never thought we'd see. The first time we saw the final ad was when we were doing an event for AT&T in Dallas. We were all in the same room watching TV when the commercial came on. We all shouted when we first saw it, but we were in awe for most of the spot. Imagine, our family in a cool commercial.

Those ads were awesome. Even people who have no idea what we did in the Olympics remember us as the people in the commercials. The Spanish ones were great, too, because they involved more of my mother and father. There were long days, but we had so much fun. We had our own masseuse, our own RVs, whatever food we needed.

The *SportsBusiness Journal* ran this excerpt as part of an article that mentioned our ties to AT&T and Coke: "The appeal of the Lopez family has been less about punches and kicks, or even gold medals, and more about target marketing. High-profile sport or not, Steven Lopez and his siblings have the ability to reach America's increasingly prosperous Hispanic demographic, which makes up about 15 percent of the U.S. population and is growing three times faster than the nation's overall population. 'The fact that it's taekwondo, for us, did not play a role,' said Laura Hernandez, executive director of diversity marketing for AT&T. 'For us, we didn't have a concern about the sport because of how dynamic the Lopez family is.' . . .

"For Coca-Cola, Steven Lopez is 'our main ambassador in the Hispanic market,' said Reinaldo Padua, assistant vice president for Hispanic marketing. 'We have a disproportionate size of our sales coming from Hispanic consumers. [The Lopez campaign] is really a key driver for plans and future growth in the market.'"

Jean was at home one day and got so excited when he heard "the Lopez family" on the screen, he started screaming, "Look. Look." Too bad there was nobody in the house and he was the only one looking. Soon after the commercial aired, Jean recalled people staring at him when he was eating and he'd think: Do I know him? He'd try to put the name to the face. Then he'd realize the person probably just saw the commercial.

Following those commercials, AT&T flew us to Austin, Texas, to shoot a music video they were filming with Three Doors Down in which we put our uniforms on and did a few kicks. Their producers sprinkled in clips of us working out into their video that was released as part of AT&T's Soundtrack of the Games.

Before the Olympic year, a young fighter from California named Charlotte Craig was emerging on the scene. Charlotte trains with Jimmy Kim in California. Jean coached her at the Beijing worlds in 2007. It was the first time she had made the national team, and she beat some good people on her way to winning the bronze medal. She is a sweet girl on the outside and a tiger on the inside. She sends more text messages to her family and friends than the rest of the planet ever could. Charlotte was born with just one kidney, and doctors told her parents to keep her away from strenuous physical activity for her own good. See why we like her? She hit it off with our family and almost became another family member herself. Diana took her on as a sort of younger sister. Charlotte said she admired our group and wanted to learn from the best, so she came to Houston to spend time with us. She was instantly hardworking, dedicated, fearless and easy to deal with. At one point she started telling people, "Haven't you heard?" she joked. "I changed my last name to Lopez." So it's official. We went through the adoption process and Charlotte became the fifth Lopez. Could all five of us end up in Beijing?

Because Steven earned the berth at the world qualifier, he had assured himself a berth at the Olympics, and he didn't have to fight at the Olympic trials. I fought Chris Martinez and Diana fought Nia. Having won the first stage of the Olympic trials, Diana and I entered the Des Moines matches with a 1–0 lead in the best-of-three series. This was a chance for us not only to fulfill our lifelong goal of making the Olympic team together, but also to make history. Only once before had three siblings ever qualified for the U.S. Olympic team. But those were only the third modern Olympics, and those Games were very different. When Edward, Richard and William Tritschler competed in gymnastics at the 1904 Olympics in St. Louis, the Games were staged as part of the World's Fair, and not every sport included international athletes. There were thirteen teams in that gymnastics competition, and all of them came from the United States. The Tritschlers competed on the team from St. Louis that finished fifth, so they didn't win any medals.

I made my weight okay in Des Moines, but I ate like a madman afterward. I ate part of Tabetha's steak. I ate mashed potatoes, an appetizer. I made weight at a hundred and forty-nine pounds and weighed one sixty-five after one day. Yes, that's sixteen pounds in a day. I wasn't fighting until eight thirty in the evening, so I didn't think I'd feel superfull. As it turned out I was. I was too stuffed to eat breakfast, so when I actually fought, I felt strong, but really sluggish.

I came out aggressively and scored with a fast double kick in the first round. I kept attacking and tried to keep Chris on his heels. He tied the match with a good fake-out in the second period. He started in as if he were going to kick. I kicked on his motion and left myself exposed. He got out of the way and scored to tie the match. It was tied throughout the match until there were about seven seconds left. Chris jammed me up. I pushed out and scored a quick point with my right leg from the inside. I was in. But here's the funny part: Even though I had accomplished my lifelong dream, I felt just as nervous as I had before I started to fight. That's because we still had one more Lopez to go.

Chris and I stood on the side and watched Diana fight Nia. I was nervous for her, but she looked pretty calm. She made weight pretty well the day before. She brought her friend Maria along to be her roommate on the trip. Steven stayed in the room for several hours keeping Diana calm by talking about his girlfriend and taking her mind off the big moment in front of her. Steven isn't the type of person who shakes you by the shoulders and says, "Are you ready, Diana?" He just kind of goes with the flow.

Nia started off using the same tactic as Iridia, changing her stance and trying to take away the way Diana uses her front leg. Diana felt a little awkward, because she hadn't trained for that, but she remembered the match in Cali and she felt more comfortable with the switched stances. She knew how Nia was going to fight. She's still unorthodox, and this was going to be a messy fight. Again it went down to the end tied, and Diana was determined to score a point no matter how. She did a quick slide and kicked Nia in the side and heard a pop. For an instant she was thinking, Please score the point, please, you know I hit her; please give me credit for that point. We took that one instant, held our breath and looked at the side scoreboard to see the zero under Diana's name change to a one. That was it. She had done it. We had all done it. Diana was going to the Olympics. All of us were. Three athletes and one coach. History. We were like little kids. We were giggling, joking. It was seriously the best day of our lives. Flashbulbs seemed to go off everywhere. After drug testing, we went out to one of the few restaurants that was open late in Des Moines.

After the match, Nia came up to congratulate Diana and wish her good luck at the Olympics with the other four Lopezes (yes, Charlotte won the fourth spot on the team). Then Nia started talking to the press afterward about how the refs had always favored the Lopez family. Are you serious? After everything we went through over the years with the OTC group and the USTU that got decertified, was she really serious? What kind of sportsmanship is that? I couldn't believe it when I read those things.

Sometime after the match, Diana called my mom to remind her about a promise she had made to us a while earlier. She made a deal with us that if we all made the Olympic team, she would go to Beijing to watch us fight. She knew what an incredible feat that would be. Of course, she was going to be nervous as a cat, but one of the first things we said to her after we all made the team in Des Moines was, "Well, Mama, get your passport ready." She said, "I'm going. I promised."

Later that night we went out to a steakhouse as a group. While we were eating, we glanced at an overhead TV that was tuned to ESPN and saw them scroll the notice that said, *Historic moment in taekwondo—three Lopezes on Olympic team.* That was cool. We all let out a big shout. We ate; we reminisced. We felt like kings and queens, and at least for a day we were.

Jean is the one who always puts things in perspective. We went out for steak that night and he told us, "Guys, do you realize what we all just did? We're here. This is the lifelong dream and we're living it in front of our family, our friends, the Olympic world. We made it."

A few weeks after trials, we attended the media summit in Chicago, where we had a lot of interviews and generated a lot of hype. We posed for some photos with the Getty Images agency, and Michael Phelps was in front of us. That meant we were among the best of the best.

We had a lot of media attention over the next few weeks. Jean tried to make sure none of it interfered with our training. *USA Today* spent a day at our gym. NBC came by.

Since 2000, Cecil had been in touch with the casting director of the *Tonight Show with Jay Leno.* When he was the chief media officer for our federation, Cecil had tried to get Steven or us as a family booked on the show. Once the three of us had made the team, the *Tonight Show* producers took us up on it. They flew us out to L.A., picked us up in a limo and brought us to the studio the next day.

Jay Leno was very nice to all of us. He came into the waiting area known as the green room and sat with us for about ten minutes before the show. He asked where we were from. He told us he had done Martial arts himself. He told a couple of jokes, of course. At one point he looked at Jean and said to him, "Hey, you and I have the same chin." He talked about his collection of cars and bikes and then told us to have fun and enjoy ourselves. Once he left, Diana said she was surprised he had blue eyes. I mentioned how personable and down-to-earth he was, and Jean insisted he did not have anything close to a Jay Leno chin. Diana and I were so nervous. In fact, Diana said to me, "Mark, what if I trip on my high heels?" she asked. I reminded her that even though she's had some clumsy moments, an Olympic athlete couldn't be that uncoordinated. "The tripping thing is all reputation," I told her. "You'll be fine."

The producer, Steve Ridgeway, let us know what questions Leno was going to ask. We had our own green room that said LOPEZ FAMILY on the front. The staff had little gift bags for each of us. On the way in to the studio we saw one of Jay Leno's classic 1950s cars. They picked us up in a limo from the hotel. I was pretty starstruck. Steven was cool. Diana was nervous. The producer asked me a question about what kind of clothing we used. I explained we had forearm protectors, the chest protector and a protective cup. The producer said, "Okay, make sure you mention that." I had it in my mind that I would really make the crowd laugh. I went out and blew a kiss to the crowd. It was surreal, because we hadn't seen the studio before. We went out there and the lights were right in our face. We couldn't really see the crowd. I felt the way I did in theater class when I couldn't remember my monologue.

Jean took his place in the audience, and the three nervous Olympians waited by the curtain to be introduced and, ironically, sit on the couch next to Dr. Phil, who was Jay's guest before us. We had sort of delegated who would answer which type of question, since we weren't sure if he would direct particular questions at each of us. It was a lot of fun. We walked out, and, well, Diana did trip, but she caught herself before she fell over. Good save. I was really impressed with how laid-back Leno was backstage, and yet as soon as the lights turned on, so did he. At one point Steven mentioned Jean, and the camera went into the stands and acknowledged him. As nervous as she was, Diana brought Dr. Phil into the conversation, telling Jay she'd been getting beaten up for years, since she was the young one, and, well, maybe he could help her out. At that point Dr. Phil put up his hands as if to say, "You're on your own on that one." The whole thing felt a lot easier once we got out there.

As I was answering a question, Steven cut me off and started talking to Jay. I had it in my mind that I had to mention the line about the cup, so I sort of blurted it out awkwardly: "Of course, you need your growing cup." It kind of got lost in the conversation. I was happy with the show, but not too happy with my performance. Sure, a few of our friends said I was funny, but I was still replaying that line over and over. It felt like a bad fight and I was watching myself get kicked. After our segment ended, we got to watch Natasha Bedingfield perform from our chairs onstage.

We went to a nice Italian restaurant after the show. Diana ordered the most expensive and elaborate meal on the menu. She needed food after draining so much energy out of her body. She's still hoping to go on *The Ellen DeGeneres Show*.

In May, Steven did another appearance in New York with the other Coca-Cola six-pack members. They made an appearance on the *Today* show and Steven got to meet Henry Winkler, the guy we had known as the Fonz on the reruns of *Happy Days*. Steven was surprised to find out Winkler knew who he was because he was writing a children's book in which one of the kids was learning taekwondo. Winkler mentioned something about having Steven write a chapter in his book. Nothing ever came of that discussion, but he told Steven he understood how taekwondo teaches kids about confidence and discipline. Hey, maybe the Fonz *was* cool.

We also did a very practical pre-Olympic promotion with Hilton Hotels at the OTC in Colorado Springs. They called it their Be Hospitable Program, an initiative designed to teach proper protocol for visiting various cultures. That was actually a great learning experience for us, too. We tend to talk a lot with our hands, but Jean was telling me, "Don't point with your chopsticks. Don't stick chopsticks into rice. Don't give books, clocks or umbrellas as gifts. Don't wear a green hat." I wouldn't have thought of those things. Tea drinking is very traditional in China, but I hadn't realized that when pouring or sipping tea, you are not supposed to point the spout of the cup at anyone in particular. When you're eating as a guest in a group of seven or eight people, it's pretty tough to look for the gaps among the seated guests.

Right after that trip, Steven, Diana and I made an appearance in New York for the Hilton family of hotels, and we spoke to children at a Build-A-Bear Workshop. It was fun talking to kids with Steven and Diana. We talked about discipline and dedication, but the part the kids really loved was the moment we told them they could let out a taekwondo yell. I'm not sure the parents and teachers loved it so much, but anytime you can actually encourage kids to make noise on command, you've got them.

There is a funny story to tell about another sponsorship event Steven attended in May. One of Steven's friends from the Olympic world was a Des Moines native, Shawn Johnson, the world all-around champ in gymnastics, who had come to the trials in her hometown with her agent, Sheryl Shade. Shawn and Steven were both members of the Coca-Cola six-pack of athletes they picked. It was funny to watch them hug after the meet, because Shawn isn't quite five feet tall—proof that Olympic athletes come in all sizes. Just hugging her, Steven said he felt like Yao Ming, the seven-foot, six-inch Chinese basketball star.

Who knew he would soon meet Yao and end up feeling like Shawn Johnson when he stood next to him. Steven and Yao were both spokesmen for Coke. They were invited to a NASCAR event, the Coca-Cola 600 in May at the Lowe's Motor Speedway in Concord, North Carolina. Their appearance was billed as a sort of East-meets-West theme. We would see NASCAR on TV and wonder why spectators would sit around the infield areas for two, three and four hours just to watch cars keep going around the same track. Actually, Steven said he was amazed at the energy of thing. It was a real event, with people crowding the place as far as you could see. They held barbecues next to their RVs. It was just a huge party for them. He met drivers like Dale Earnhardt Jr. and Tony Stewart. Steven felt bad for Yao, because every time one of the drivers came over to shake hands with him, they would say something about his height. None of the comments were disrespectful, but he must hear the same thing over and over every day. Steven didn't actually get to drive a car, but he rode in one of the lead trucks at a hundred and twenty miles per hour for a while. He didn't realize just how curved the track was, kind of like a cycling velodrome. It had to be shaped like that in order to compensate for the speed of the cars, but you don't realize how sharp the curve is until you see it firsthand.

Before the race, organizers let Yao and Steven see what it was like to run a pit stop. They watched how fast the pros did it and then tried it themselves. Yao filled the gas tank while Steven changed the tires. As fast as they both tried to make their changes, they probably would have cost their driver the race. The crew there let Steven hop into one of the cars, too. Since the cars don't actually have door handles, you sort of make like the Dukes of Hazzard and lift yourself in through the window. It was awkward for Steven, being six-three. No, Yao didn't try it. Steven also got to wear the team headphones while sitting in the pit and listening to the instructions to the driver, Kyle Petty: "Okay, so-and-so is coming up on your left." Yao and Steven didn't get a lot of time to talk, but Yao did tell him he liked watching taekwondo because one of his countrywomen had won gold medals at the last two Olympics. He also mentioned that, as exciting as it was to play for the Rockets during the NBA season, the thrill and the pressure would be nothing like playing for China at the Olympics.

We all later appeared on the Cartoon Network in a show that was hosted by Jonny Moseley, a former Olympic skier. The premise of the show is that kids write in about a hero they have and why they look up to him or her. The show's producers then invite the kid to meet the hero without actually telling the kid that the hero is waiting for them. One boy named JaWaun Stanley, who did taekwondo in his hometown of Leesburg, Georgia, wrote in about Steven, so they flew him into Houston, telling him he'd get to train in a good taekwondo gym. After he arrived, they hit him with surprise number one, telling him he would actually be training with the Olympic coach. After he started training with Jean, he was surprised again. Steven, Diana and I all sneaked up behind him and Steven tapped him on the shoulder. It was priceless. He put his hand over his mouth and his eyes got as big as saucers. His mother started crying just from seeing her son so happy. That was great. Great, great, great.

With all of our obligations, we actually had to turn down an invitation from the First Lady. As a fellow Texan, Laura Bush invited our family to the White House for Cinco de Mayo after reading about us in *USA Today*. We actually couldn't go because Jean was in Turkey coaching the junior national team and the rest of us we had a scheduling conflicts with our team. Bummer.

Between April and August, we did more interviews than I can remember. We also found out that VISA was going to feature our whole family in one of their Go World Olympic commercials with the voice of Morgan Freeman in the backgound.

The sponsorship ride was fun, but I was really looking forward to competing at my first Olympics. I was excited to leave for the first stage of our big trip: team processing in San Jose, a team training camp in Singapore and then on to Beijing, but I had also made another very important decision about a very important day. Dagmar had been with me through thick and thin, always as a supportive ear who would laugh with me, cry with me and do everything she could to cheer me up. I had been thinking for a while that she was the person I wanted to spend the rest of my life with, and I was going to ask for her hand before I left for Asia. On one of my last days in Houston, I made some special plans for us that evening and I sent my family a text message telling them what I was planning to do. Only a few seconds went by before Diana sent a text back wishing me luck and asking for an update. My parents, of course, were thrilled for both of us.

I took Dagmar to a nice restaurant in Houston called Mark's (no, it's a different Mark). I told her I wanted to take her out for one last special dinner before I left for the training camp. I knew she was planning to come to Beijing and watch me, but we wouldn't have much time to see each other there while my focus was on training and competing. She wasn't necessarily expecting anything. I had the ring in my pocket the whole time, and I was thinking of proposing at the restaurant. I couldn't quite find the moment to do it, because of all the people around. I know I'm a showman in the ring, but Dagmar and I are both pretty quiet and private people in normal settings. I was so nervous that I wasn't concentrating on my food or our conversation as much as I should have, so I figured I'd wait until later. I hadn't told her yet that I had also reserved a room for us at the Hotel Icon, a really nice boutique hotel in downtown Houston. We checked in and settled down, and that was when I found the moment to drop to a knee, hold out the ring and tell her how much she meant to me and how much I wanted to spend the rest of my life with her. It was a perfect moment. She started crying and accepted right away. Even before I left for my first Olympics, I already felt like the biggest winner of all.

I was on cloud nine in those last few days before we took off, but we still had things to do. The USOC had given us some sports performance money, which really came in handy on that trip, because we were able to bring along our choice of training partners. Under different circumstances, Nia would have been a great choice for Diana. She's good and she's a little awkward, which is something that would have been good for Diana to get used to before an Olympics, because she was likely to see a lot of different styles at any major international meet. Unfortunately, it really wasn't possible after the comments Nia made after the trials. The scene would have been too ugly. The job of a training partner is to want the best for his or her teammate and work unselfishly toward that goal. Diana wasn't sure whether Nia would have done that, so she picked Chris and Pano as her training partners.

Steven brought along Tony Graf as a training partner. Tony really deserved it because of how hard he trained and how close he had come to being on so many teams. Jean and Steven sat and talked with him to make sure he was cool with the role of training partner. As with any athlete who goes along in that capacity, you want to make sure the athlete is going to put forth full effort in training for the benefit of his teammate, but also not try to take the teammate's legs out so that he can get on the team himself as a last-minute replacement. Tony was once disqualified for trying to go after Steven's knees at one of our team trials, so there might have been some concern. Jean first talked about it with Juan Moreno, who was Tony's coach, and then he and Steven had a phone conference with Juan and Tony, in which Tony convinced them he was the right guy for the job. Tony told Steven in that phone call that he had helped make him a better fighter. He was very humble and he understood what he was supposed to do. He lived up to it, too. Steven really appreciated Tony's work ethic during training. His relationship with Tony has always been the kind of thing you would expect between two rivals, but ever since Juan took over part of the national team, along with my brother, it has been getting better, and Steven's respect for Tony certainly grew after Tony helped him out in Singapore.

Diana was too excited to sleep the night before we took off. She walked around and reread some cards that friends had written for her before she left on the trip. She held the special necklace that Joe had given her before she left. It was one his father gave to him when he was an athlete at St. Joseph's, so it was very personal to him—and very special to Diana.

We went to team processing in San Jose, which was a shopping frenzy. All shopping should be like this. It was like a big department store, and we were allowed to fill one cart with anything we wanted: T-shirts, sweatshirts, shoes, socks, caps, pants, blazers, you name it. I picked a great Olympics to attend, because everything was by Ralph Lauren. Diana tried on everything, and could have stayed there for a week. She told us she should have tried things on as if she weighed her regular one thirty instead of one twenty-five then, because everything would be a little tight after she got back. She had to send a few clothes back home, but, she insisted, a girl could never have too many Ralph Lauren polos. Arnold Schwarzenegger was there, too, and Steven and I took a picture with him. I wonder what size he would have taken. Here's one jacket for Arnold and another one for his biceps.

Singapore was a place I really liked. It was clean, warm and had a mix of cultures there. I remembered learning in a world geography class just how strict they are there. There was an American kid who wrote some graffiti on a wall and got four lashes across his bare back as punishment. They also lash people for spitting out gum and littering. They have a death sentence for drug users. An Australian kid showed up at the airport a few years earlier with a marijuana joint in his bag and was hanged for trying to bring drugs into the country. No second chances.

We were staying at the Shangri-La Hotel, the same hotel as the U.S. swimming team, so you know it was pretty nice. Our federation has really come a long way since the USTU days, when that organization didn't do anything for its athletes. The swimming pool was amazing. The food was delicious, even though I had to watch my weight and couldn't really take advantage of it. Again, Diana followed my lead for making weight during the two weeks before the Games. She went to get a pedicure at a local shop, where they put the USA flag on her foot, and once photographers found out about it, they were asking to take pictures of the foot.

Diana and I had time to take in a cool ride, a sort of reverse bungee jump, in which they strap you onto the ground with bands; then they place two sets of bands around your body. The bands are also attached to the top of a tall pole. When they release one set of the bands, the contraption propels you straight up in the air. You bounce around for a while before settling down. It was a really exhilarating adrenaline rush. I remember the convenience stores there did sell cigarettes, but instead of the usual cancer warnings you see on boxes in the States, they had pictures of a mouth with gum disease. Gross. You won't catch a Lopez smoking. No, thanks.

We went to a beach in Singapore that was the southernmost point in Asia. We passed a seriously weird medical-themed restaurant where you could sit in wheelchairs, order fake eyeballs and drink out of blood-collection vats. Ah, no, thanks on that one, too.

Since our competition wasn't scheduled until near the end of the Olympics, we flew from Singapore to Beijing a few days before the opening ceremonies. We had a big surprise in store for us when we got off the plane: Our parents were waiting for us at the airport. We hadn't seen them in almost a month. We were told some delegation people would be there to meet us. Getting duped never felt so good. It felt great to hug my mom, because I knew how queasy she gets about making a trip to watch us fight. The next day our local paper, the *Houston Chronicle*, ran a cool picture of me hugging my mom. My dad gave me a video camera at the airport that Dagmar and her mom had bought for me.

We got on the bus and rode to the Olympic village with Cecil. The Chinese government was supposedly going to stop construction a week before the Games began in order to improve the air quality, but the place was so polluted it looked like the moon from a distance. I pulled out my brand-new camera and started recording.

The village was well organized. I checked out the dining hall and started my camera rolling. In the first few seconds, you can clearly hear me saying a few "oohs" and "ahhs" as I'm rolling. I know what you're thinking: What were their names, what did they look like and where were they from? Their names were éclair, ice cream and chocolate cake; they were at the dessert table, and they looked fantastic. Okay, so swoon, pant, drool and pan camera to the frumpy salad bar, my dance partner until the morning of the weigh-in. The cafeteria was huge. They had an Asian-cuisine station, an international-cuisine, station, a Mediterranean station, a pasta station for carb loaders and a station for fruits and veggies. They had a McDonald's and a McCafé, where you could get coffee, espresso and cappuccino. Most of the athletes couldn't enjoy it until they were finished competing. It was great to see the variety of athletes there: Yao Ming was there, walking past Lionel Messi, the great Argentine soccer player, and Ronaldinho, his Brazilian counterpart. Michael Phelps saw some friendly Americans and asked to sit and eat with us. I talked to Terrence Trammell, the hurdler, who was conducting his own pep talk in the dining hall, talking about gold medals and world records to anyone who would listen. Maybe Terrence did have that espresso after all.

Even when I wasn't filming our family's every meal, we were often followed by a Chinese film crew that was looking into our story, as they were putting together the official film of the Games. They had visited us in Sugar Land, too. Jean will certainly never forget a meal they shared with us on our previous trip to Beijing. The crew took us all to a duck dinner one night. Jean is a very finicky eater, so he wasn't too eager to try new things. At one point I tasted something that had the consistency of cartilage. It was duck feet. I don't recommend it. They had duck feet, duck skin, duck tongue. Every part of the duck was there. At one point I said, "Jean, try the duck heart." I put one piece on his plate and watched as everyone at the table nodded with approval, since he was our group leader. I mean, Jean barely eats shrimp, so it was pretty impossible for me to keep from laughing inside while he tried to get through that bit of duck heart. Hey, if I can fight three guys at once, run eight miles and hop around with my knees bent until I can't hop any longer, well, I nominate my older brother to show our hosts how much he loves duck heart. Eat up, Jean.

Okay, back to the camera again. We were in the Olympic Village, putting on our team outfits as we were getting ready to march out for the opening. Diana helped Jean fix his tie. Steven walked around in a T-shirt, because the city was a walking sauna and nobody wanted to sweat into their uniform shirts. "It would be easy to be a forecaster in this town," Jean said. We opened a copy of *Time* magazine to a picture of our family. I looked into the camera and said, "This is the moment I've been waiting for my whole life: walk out in front of millions of people. Billions."

Our sponsors really came through for us in Beijing. Hilton put my parents up in one of their hotels during the Games. Coke arranged hotel rooms for Tabetha and some of Steven's friends. AT&T made sure my parents had tickets to whatever they wanted to see, including non-taekwondo events on days we didn't compete.

Michael Lynch from VISA brought my parents along to the opening ceremonies, so the whole family was able to experience that great show. That's huge, considering a billion other people would have liked to be there.

In midafternoon, we started walking toward the first building that would serve as a staging area for our team. Somebody turn down the heat outside. We got to a large hall where the U.S. athletes, all five hundred and ninety-six of us, plus officials, were being processed and told where to line up before we marched out.

Before we did, the nation's number one fan walked out to address us. "Congratulations for representing the finest nation on the face of the Earth," President Bush told us, as his father, George H. W., stood on his left, and his wife, Laura, stood on his right. "I wasn't sure what to say to you except, 'God, I love this country.'"

As the president started mingling and posing for photos, his wife, Laura, came over to remind us that we had declined her White House invitation. We explained that we'd had to fight that weekend. She said she understood, and she and the president then posed with us for a picture. We took another picture with Dana Perino, Bush's press secretary at the time. We took another shot with Coach K from the basketball team, and many others with Kobe Bryant, LeBron James and Chris Paul.

Soon after that address, we walked outside again to the arena that would serve as staging area number two. On the way, we saw Kevin Han, an Olympian in badminton, who had since retired and was now working at the OTC in Colorado Springs. He was one of the people helping our delegation that day. "It's good to be on the other side," Kevin told us.

I know there are a billion people in China, because most of them seemed to be lining our route in their red-and-white volunteer outfits as we moved from venue to venue. We'd tell them, "*Ni hao*," Mandarin for "hello," and they'd smile, wave and repeat the phrases they'd learned when they signed on as volunteers: "Have a good time," "Welcome to China," "Enjoy your stay."

We were among the athletes that NBC was planning to follow during the ceremonies. On the way into the arena adjacent to the Bird's Nest Stadium, Brett Goodman, an NBC executive, told us to stay to the right as we marched into the stadium so the network's cameras could follow us.

Inside, we again ran into Terrence Trammell. He saw my camera and told me: "When I get back, I'm going to get me an AT&T commercial." We then started marching right behind the men's basketball team as we edged closer to the entrance of the stadium. I knew Dwight Howard already because Joe worked for his NBA team, the Orlando Magic. It was obvious from talking to them that the guys cared about winning, especially after 2004, when the team didn't win and a lot of the players were criticized for not giving it a hundred percent. With my camera rolling, Chris Paul, a friend of ours from the basketball team who usually plays in Charlotte, started talking: "Go, Hornets, not Rockets," he said. "It's all good. We're all Team USA. It's a four-year thing. I'd much rather have a gold medal than an NBA championship any day." Good call. We passed LeBron James, who saw Steven, took off his headphones to speak into my camera—do all the superstars have headphones?—and told us: "Representing Team USA. Team USA basketball, the Lopez team. We're all bringing home gold medals, baby."

We had a different perspective from what viewers saw on TV and what my parents saw in the stadium. Because our team stayed in different holding areas, we missed a lot of the performers while we waited to march out in the parade of nations. AT&T gave us cell phones, so we were calling our friends back home and giving them a play-by-play on our cells. The Chinese did an amazing job with their signature venues for the Games. We were walking into the main stadium they called the Bird's Nest that would be used for track and field. It was also within walking distance of the Water Cube, the venue for swimming and diving, which had giant reinforced-plastic water-bubble shapes on the outside. They changed colors at night, and the whole thing looked pretty surreal. Shawn Johnson spotted Steven and got on his shoulders for a while, so she could actually see something. I'm guessing the balancing part was not a problem for her.

We still had a while to wait before our competition, because we didn't actually fight until the second week. Each day, we'd wake up and take our team bus to Beijing Normal University. We trained at roughly the same time as the NBA guys. It was cool to be getting my knee iced while I was looking over and seeing Kobe Bryant being adjusted by the chiropractor. If anyone doubted how sincere the basketball team was about wanting to win, I can tell you they were pretty serious about it. We would eat a meal at Beijing Normal. Some days we'd play *Guitar Hero* or watch different competitions on TV. Steven did go watch the U.S. basketball team beat Greece one night, and he went to a day of track and field when the U.S. men swept the four-hundred meter at the Bird's Nest.

Charlotte fought first. She had a great first match, beating Manuela Bezzola from Switzerland 4–0 and looking like she had a medal in her sights. She reached the quarterfinals and fought a tough match against Dalia Contreras from Venezuela. She fought her heart out, which is all you could ask of a seventeen-year-old, but she dropped a 3–2 decision, missing out on a bronze medal by one point.

Diana's first fight was against Chonnapas Premwaew, the same Thai girl who nailed her in the groin in Manchester. When Diana fought her this time, it seemed Chonnapas had lost a lot of weight too quickly before the competition, because she didn't have a lot of energy. The Chinese crowd was very polite. They cheered for everything. Diana caught her opponent on a spin kick, and the crowd erupted because it looked cool, even if it was not an exceptional kick. It was good for Diana to fight in front of an international crowd that wasn't heavily against her. The Thai didn't have much of an attack that day, and Diana won the match 2–0. It was one of the day's first matches, around nine a.m. Diana always prefers fighting matches one after another, but she didn't have to fight again until four, so she ate, slept and almost felt as if she were fighting on a second day.

When she came back, she was fighting Azize Tanrikulu, the sister of the Turkish guy Steven beat in his final match at the Athens Olympics. Diana felt pretty confident and comfortable fighting someone who used a typical European attacking style. The Turk fought okay, but it seemed like Diana had used up a lot of her adrenaline in the morning. Just when she tried to pick up the pace, she fell, hurt her knee and went out of bounds. She went to overtime tied 1–1. She tried one attack in the extra session that fell short. Then Diana saw Tanrikulu coming with the front leg and tried to slide back in time to avoid it, but she just wasn't fast enough. Tanrikulu had the point and the match.

That left me rooting for Tanrikulu to advance to the finals so Diana could still fight for a bronze medal by advancing through the repechage. Fortunately, she pulled out a come-from-behind 5–3 win against Martina Zubcic from Croatia. That allowed Diana to keep fighting.

She had a pretty easy match next, beating Teo Elaine, from Malaysia, 3–0. The last fight was much tougher. Veronica Calabrese is a tough Italian girl who was very efficient even though she basically kicks with only her right leg. She and Diana traded points until overtime, and Jean had the perfect plan for Diana to score the golden point. He told her to wait for Calabrese to lead with her right leg to the backside. Diana knew she was coming, so she slid back and scored with a defensive roundhouse.

Diana jumped up and ran over and hugged Jean. Yes, she had wanted to win a gold there, but she knew she'd be coming home with an Olympic medal. She was so wrapped up in her fighting that she didn't think about the pain in her wrist that started to increase after the last match was over. She had actually torn a ligament and, like me, would need surgery on her wrist when she got back to the States. She had her press conference after the match and then stayed around to watch mine.

As she was fighting her matches, I was fighting mine throughout the course of the same day. Fighting at the Olympics was challenge enough, but it took just one kick for something to go wrong. I drew Nesar Ahmad Bahave of Afghanistan in the first match. I don't know what I expected from him, but on our first exchange, he threw a kick at me that I blocked fairly easily with my left hand. Ouch! That one hurt more than usual. I could still lift up my hand to block, but I didn't really want to. Even lifting it with no resistance caused a big pinch in my wrist. One kick. Something was wrong after just one kick.

Soon after that, I did score once with a defensive roundhouse. He tried to use his height to his advantage, but I was very conscious of giving him just the right amount of reach. I caught him with one roundhouse, but then stayed on the inside as much as possible, so he couldn't extend his legs when he kicked. I caught him twice off clinches to build a 3–0 lead I maintained.

After the match I showed the hand to our team doctor. He knew right away that it was broken. He wrapped me up and gave me a shot for the pain. My mobility was severely hampered, but I'd have all of September to think about it. The trick was to hide the wrap so my opponents either weren't aware of it during the fight, or at least weren't aware of it until the fight began.

I knew my next opponent, Germany's Daniel Manz, from a trip that his national team had taken to train with us. I was pretty far ahead of him during that camp, and I didn't have much more trouble in this match. He didn't have a lot of respect for us as a team. He was a bit like me in that he wanted to be aggressive. Each time he kicked, he did a double or triple. I knew his timing, so I knew how to back off and then counter or clash and disrupt his techniques. He was still able to catch me once above the spot where I wanted my hand to be in order to block his kick. This hand injury was severely impairing my defense. I got by for a 3–1 win.

The next match was going to be very difficult, because I was going to fight my good friend Peter Lopez. I thought about the fact that Peter and I have been in the same division since 1999 and yet we had never fought each other. We know each other's game. Peter is fast and intelligent, but gets frustrated easily. I had to respect his face kick, because it's a real weapon. I went off the line against Peter to get a better angle and scored just away from his reach.

When I was up, I knew it was the last round, and I knew he'd open up a bit. I moved around, jammed, and lifted my front leg. I was aware of the hand injury, but I didn't want to let on to my opponents that I might have an injury.

I was just one match away from a gold medal. My opponent was going to be Son Tae-jin, the same Korean who beat me in overtime in Manchester. I remembered how much he pressed the end of the match there. Jean wanted me to attack, but be careful of Tae-jin's right leg, which was very quick.

As soon as the match started, I began moving forward a little too quickly. He kicked to my backside, an attack I would usually block with my hand. This time, I couldn't lift it fast enough and he grabbed a 1–0 lead. He must have been aware of my injury, maybe even more so than I was, because he scored on a similar sequence just twenty seconds later to put me in a 2–0 hole after the first period.

I was composed as I went back to the chair. I looked up at my supporters in the corner of the crowd and tried to stay aggressive without being careless, as Jean had told me. I went after him twice more, but this time made sure to follow up with fast double kicks, and tied the score 2–2.

As we went to the third round, I sensed that I had to score decisively in order to get credit for a winning point. Seconds ticked away. We clinched and nothing. We exchanged and nothing. We were down to ten seconds left in the regulation six minutes. As I inched closer, he kicked to my backside again and I caught him with a defensive roundhouse kick. I fell back as I delivered the kick, but I was hoping they would score my point and not his. By the time they flashed a go-ahead point for the Korean, there were just two seconds left. Son jumped away and the match was over.

I smiled in disbelief, put my hands on my head and did my best not to express outward disappointment. I bowed to Son, shook hands with his coach and waved to the crowd. I was that close. I had been that close before. This was heavier. These were the Olympics.

Before they called my name at the awards ceremony, I walked onto the first-place stand for just a second or so. I was acting as if I were confused, but in fact I wanted to feel what it was like to stand there, if only for a second.

I could tell Diana was sad for me, not just because I came so close to something again, but because of the wrist that wasn't healthy enough for me to block properly. I know she would have given up her medal to move me up to gold.

Steven was fighting the next day, so Diana and I went to an athletes' party to do some interviews, but stayed for only an hour. You don't think so much about yourself when you have three siblings you care so much about. I wore my medal to the party, because a lot of Olympic athletes were there. Diana didn't really want to show hers off, so she actually gave it to Joe and let him wear it around.

We got back early, ready to give our full attention to Steven. If he won, he'd have an astounding three gold medals at three Olympics. Even a medal of any color would enhance the feat of history we had already achieved just by being there.

Steven won his first match 3–0 against Bahri Tanrikulu from Turkey, his opponent in the finals during the 2004 Olympics. One of the Turkish reporters asked Steven about his arm injury from 2004. Did he think this match would be tougher?

It started out that way. Steven was down by two points early in the match, until he caught Tanrikulu in the head with an outside-in ax kick to tie the score. That seemed to take the fight out of him a bit.

Steven drew Mauro Sarmiento of Italy again for the second match. He hoped it would be a lot like the match he had fought against him before. Steven was ahead going into the third round. At the start of that round, Steven thought he had blocked one of Mauro's kicks with his arm, but the ref saw it differently and gave him a point. In the last forty seconds, Mauro went off the line and kicked. Steven lifted up his knee to block the kick and they slapped him with another kyong-go. That was the unofficial Steven Lopez rule at work, the one that wasn't even on the books. The violation may have been someone's imagination, but the deduction was real. Mauro had tied the score in the final minute and sent the match into sudden death. Steven was the aggressor. He went for a fast double and kicked. Mauro sidestepped, fell down, kicked as he fell and scored a point. Steven put his arms to his sides, sat down and just grinned. He couldn't believe it. Just like that it was over. It didn't feel real. He stayed composed and then he walked off. I could hear the silence in the arena. In the back room, people were saying they were sorry, but it didn't really make him feel better.

Jean filed a protest, which we were allowed to do within the rules, but the WTF refused to look at it. The experience was pretty disillusioning, and a couple of people in our delegation suggested Steven shouldn't fight the second-chance repechage, which could get him into the bronze-medal match. Steven took a deep breath and remembered that there were issues here that were bigger than he was. He needed to behave like a champion and continue to fight. People would have looked at our team and our country as sore losers, so Steven chose to fight and try to win a medal for our country. He fought the next two matches against Sebastien Konan from the Ivory Coast and Rashad Ahmadov from Azerbaijan. Both matches went pretty smoothly, and he won his third Olympic medal. People were very complimentary afterward, knowing what had happened regarding a rule that didn't exist. Mauro went on to the final match against Hadi Saei, whom Steven had looked forward to fighting all week. Hadi prevailed, winning his gold medal, although he said in the press conference later that he wished he'd had the honor of fighting Steven.

After the match, we walked into a mixed zone, where reporters could go to get quotes from us as we walked off. I was talking to David Barron, saying that I couldn't believe how they could do this to Steven after all he'd accomplished and done for the sport. As I was talking, I just broke down and started to cry. It was okay when I lost my bid for a gold medal, but watching my brother lose like that was too much.

I could imagine Steven being sore about losing. Unlike Diana and me, he didn't have a mark on his body. He looked like he could have gone back out there and fought five more times. He let out little hints of disappointment, but never anger. That isn't Steven. If he had been the only one fighting, it might have been different, but I could tell he didn't want to take anything away from our moment and the medals we won in our first Olympics. Steven could have blamed everyone around him, but he chose not to. He was very complimentary toward

Hadi, calling him a great rival and deserving champion. "There were some things I couldn't control," Steven said, "but in spite of them, I went out there and did my best." That was the epitome of everything Jean groomed him for since he was a kid. It was the interview practice in the garage shining bright in something less than a moment of glory.

It's funny, but as we walked back to my parents' hotel that night, we found strength and perspective in something bigger than each of us. Each member of the Lopez family was thinking to him- or herself, I can't afford to spoil the good I feel with the bad I feel, because I don't want to dampen my brother's happiness, my father's joy, my sister's achievement, my mother's pride. For our whole lives, we haven't had far to look for these deposits of inspiration we could always draw upon under any circumstances.

We made history in Beijing, but we built it long before we arrived. It's amazing how high you can reach when you stand on the shoulders of someone you love.

Epilogue

by Jean Lopez

A few hours after Steven won his bronze medal in Beijing, our family walked back to the Hilton, where my parents were staying during the Games. The people at the hotel were really nice. Each night, they would set up a buffet upstairs for some of the athletes' families they were putting up in their hotel. On this night, they left the buffet open just for us, because they knew we were coming. That was wonderful. It gave us a chance to put our feet up and reflect with everyone we loved. Of course, we all put our lumps and injuries aside to check on my mom. Even though Steven's Olympic streak was over and Mark and Diana would soon be headed for surgery, we were mostly concerned about my mom. She told us she was okay, and that the people sitting around her survived, too. We worry about our mother more than we worry about ourselves. We may be adults, but we're still her babies, and a hug from Mom is still the ultimate security blanket no matter how old you are. She doesn't have the outlet of kicking the person in front of us that we do. Every time we fought a close match, you could almost hear us thinking: Blood-pressure check on the lady in the stands. EKG for Mom.

Mark was apologizing to her, because he'd wanted her to see and hear the national anthem played in our family's honor. We all did. That was us; we knew it wasn't her thinking.

"No, baby," she said. "This is a dream for me. I feel like a queen, hearing everyone ask me about my children." Nobody talked about match details.

My dad was much calmer. He told us how proud he was of all of us, even though he didn't have to. He even convinced one of our friends who doesn't drink hard liquor to take a shot of tequila in our honor. Okay, so maybe there was one injury at the hotel.

We're still the same people, only now we have made Olympic history. We're still the same family.

We succeeded. Our dreams came true. The whole family was there. It was something we wanted for so long. It was kind of a weird time for Steven. He had a sense that people could relate to him better because he'd lost for the first time internationally in six years and because of the way he lost. He knew he did everything he could to prepare for that day. He was more human in people's eyes. He might have gained some respect from people because of the way he handled it. The lesson is this: Nothing is certain. Steven now has something to look forward to for four more years of competitions, because now that all the Lopezes have made history, we want to try to repeat history. Each of us would rather have had things go the way they did with all of us on the team together, all of us winning medals, than if any one of us had made the team by himself or herself and won another title. We will always have these moments, the memories of being able to share them with our family. Our future kids, our grandchildren will know about that.

Our cachet must have gone up a little bit in Beijing. The night after we got back from closing ceremonies, Mark didn't want to go out. We called him the old man. Our buses took us back to the Olympic Village, where we saw the NBA guys. They had won the gold medal, beating Spain in the finals earlier that morning. I don't know why I thought of this, but their table reminded me of the Last Supper. Other athletes and volunteers were taking pictures of them from the side. We waved to a couple of the guys, and Jason Kidd saw us and called us over to eat with them.

We all thought the same thing: Mark should be here. Diana called Maria, who was staying with my parents and already in her pajamas. "I'm not telling you why," Diana told her, "but you need to come out." We saw David Beckham there, and other athletes from other sports. We saw the sun come up in the morning. Joe was so exhausted from cheering for Diana that he didn't want to come out with us. She had promised him she'd go with him to the Great Wall that morning. I'm not sure how she got up in the morning, considering she didn't get to bed until after six, but she managed to meet him at his hotel at eight thirty. She was protecting her wrist a bit, and we were really hot, but it was still worth the trip.

We all got into a big bus and headed out for one of the clubs in Beijing. Kobe, LeBron, Chris Paul, Carlos Boozer, they were all there. Along the way, they picked up a cyclist and some members of our kayak team. They were all young guys, popping champagne bottles and just having a good time. Being the veteran of the team, Jason Kidd was sort of the mellow one on the bus. A security guy who usually works for Kobe came with us that night. He mentioned that Kobe always loved Martial arts and requires his guys to have a background in them. Before we reached the club, one of their guys got out of the bus and went to the owner of the club. He told the owner who was in the group and said that if they spotted anyone in the club with a camera or video recorder, the group would leave. They brought us in through a separate entrance. This was how the other half lived.

We saw the NBA guys again when we went to *The Oprah Winfrey Show* in Chicago, and we seem to have a line on tickets when some of the guys pass through Houston to play the Rockets.

Soon after we got back home, Mark underwent surgery to repair the broken bones in his left hand, and Diana had surgery to reattach a ligament to the scaphoid bone of her left wrist.

We each received a key to the city of Sugar Land. I think Steven owns the city now. We had a lot of speaking engagements and would laugh when people would ask us if we ever planned to sell our genetic code.

In October 2008 Steven and I went to Croatia to give a seminar there and help a friend with the opening of his taekwondo school. Lana actually interviewed Steven for TV. Lana, be nice, now. We did the interview at a museum dedicated to Dražen Petrović, the Croatian basketball player who played in the NBA before he died in a car accident. Lana functioned as our translator, explaining our instructions and statements in Croatian and then interpreting for fans who followed up with questions. She could have been saying anything.

I am developing a coaching certification program. In the meantime, my kids are just . . . developing. I look at Alyxandra, my ten-year-old girl, and she likes the same things as my sister. Diana likes to say, "She's turning into a mini-me."

We finally found some closure in the judging injustice that ruined Steven's last match in Beijing. Why was a rule applied that didn't exist? Why did the WTF not accept our right to hear our protest? Our federation, now working squarely on behalf of its athletes, followed up with the WTF regarding the application of its own rules. Two months after the Games, the international federation sent a letter to David Askinas, the USAT CEO, and Herb Perez, the head of the delegation for taekwondo during the Olympics.

The letter, dated October 24, 2008, read as follows:

Mr. David Askinas CEO
Mr. Herbert Perez Head of Delegation
USA Taekwondo
USA Olympic Taekwondo

Dear David, Herbert:
I am pleased with the outcome and cordial meeting that we had today, which I see as an ideal platform to further strengthen

our relations with the national taekwondo associations, as well as enhancing taekwondo and the World Taekwondo Federation.

As we had agreed, there has been positive progress made in the standard of refereeing and judging in the taekwondo competitions at the Beijing 2008 Olympic Games, as compared to previous editions of the Olympic taekwondo competitions.

Pertaining to contest No. 98: Steven LOPEZ (USA) vs. Mauro SARMIENTO (ITA) of the men's under-80kg weight category held on August 22, 2008, an unintentional judgment error occurred due in part to the application of the WTF Competition Rules.

The WTF perceives this as an ideal impetus to thoroughly review the fundamental rules that define our martial art–*cum*–Olympic sport of taekwondo.

For this reason, I look forward to the support of the USA Taekwondo in enhancing the WTF Competition Rules with the WTF.

> Sincerely yours,
> Jin Suk Yang
> Secretary General

In the world of international judging, acknowledgment of an "unintentional judgment error" is better than a cold shoulder. But that wasn't just for us; it was for everyone practicing taekwondo. It is a great, great sport, and it deserves to reap the benefits of fairness and accountability.

Last winter, among his many pieces of fan mail, Steven received one piece of mail from the parents of twins. They told Steven in the letter that they were planning to commemorate their twins' birthday by keeping a scrapbook of all the people who accomplished something significant in the year their twins were born. So they asked Steven to sign something to commemorate the birthday. It's pretty cool that parents who want to do something for the most cherished people in their lives would actually think about us. It's even better that they'd do so when celebrating their own family.

Perhaps in our minds, we're already filling our own mental scrapbooks with images of 2012, when the next Olympics will take place in London. I think Steven is on a winning streak, and he's probably taking inquiries from the British House of Commons. It looks, I think . . . yes, I think it looks like Mark has his own streak and his own hedge fund. Diana hasn't lost much either, and I believe that's her stopping off at Oxford to speak about the future of elementary education. She's filming it, too. I'm looking for fish and chips, but eating something much nastier in the name of international diplomacy. Our parents are there. The medals? Hmm, the medals are kind of foggy, kind of unpredictable. You can't always count on winning the shiniest prizes. But the people around you are clear as day. As always, we're together.

ACKNOWLEDGMENTS

Family Power best defines the strength of our family bond that makes us who we are. Our dedication to our parents can never say enough. How do you thank two people whose love, courage and honor have guided every facet of your lives, except to say that as we become parents ourselves, we can only hope to do it half as well? Our amazing journey extends from your path, and our road has been paved and smoothed by your toil. Even more than thanking you for introducing us to taekwondo, we thank you for introducing us to our dreams. We couldn't have found them without you. Many thanks to our extended family: Jean's wife, Tabetha, and their children, Alyxandra, Diego, and Andres; and Mark's wife, Dagmar Diaz Lopez. Our Olympic dream began in our living room in Sugar Land, Texas, in 1988 and it has been a long, winding and sometimes bumpy road, but also an unforgettable journey. We have shared triumphs, joys, trials and tribulations with some of our closest friends and strongest supporters. From the friends we have made while training in the garage and the support of families as we have traveled to local tournaments to the countless training partners, teammates and friends we have made over the years in our worldwide travels, every mile of our journey has brought new people into our lives, including our sponsors, reporters and sport administrators. As with any trip, the people you encounter along the way can influence the journey. For those whose influence has always been positive and helped guide us to the destination we dreamed about, you know who you are and you have a special place in our family and our hearts forever.

It means so much to our family to be able to share our story with the world. We would like to give a special thank you to Penguin Publishing with Mark Chait, Senior Editor, and Ray Garcia, Publisher of Celebra, for providing this avenue for us to put our story to paper. We sincerely appreciate our agents Cecil Bleiker and his sister Ann Bleiker of ABC Sport Management, LLC, for their diligent work on this project, as well as for always keeping our best interests in mind. When asked to select an author to work with we could think of no better person to help us write our book than Brian Cazeneuve of *Sports Illustrated*, who has been there with us all along our Olympic journeys. Brian also wishes to thank Anne Cazeneuve, his own source of family power; Terry McDonell, the managing editor at *SI*; Craig Neff, the magazine's astute Olympics editor; director of photography Steve Fine and photo editor James Colton. Here's to the memory of two great friends: Jack Falla, the wonderful writer and professor at Boston University who enriched lives in wonderful ways he may never have known; and Joe Goldstein, the ever-imaginative PR original who always made you smile even when he was making you crazy. Thanks to Melissa Segura for the invaluable research help with dates, names and results in a sport that doesn't seem to keep many of them. Finally, thank you to those whose hard work and dedication help to foster the Olympic spirit every day.